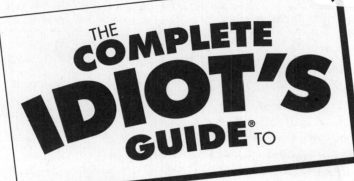

THE **COMPLETE IDIOT'S GUIDE** TO

Getting into Top Colleges

by Marna Atkin and Ian R. Leslie

ALPHA

A member of Penguin Group (USA) Inc.

Marna Atkin is honored to dedicate this book to the thousands of students she has worked with over the past 30 years and who served as her inspiration.

Ian Leslie would like to dedicate this book to his parents, Howard and Lisa Leslie, who took him on a tour of Princeton when he was in elementary school but let him find his own way.

ALPHA BOOKS

Published by the Penguin Group

Penguin Group (USA) Inc., 375 Hudson Street, New York, New York 10014, USA

Penguin Group (Canada), 90 Eglinton Avenue East, Suite 700, Toronto, Ontario M4P 2Y3, Canada (a division of Pearson Penguin Canada Inc.)

Penguin Books Ltd., 80 Strand, London WC2R 0RL, England

Penguin Ireland, 25 St. Stephen's Green, Dublin 2, Ireland (a division of Penguin Books Ltd.)

Penguin Group (Australia), 250 Camberwell Road, Camberwell, Victoria 3124, Australia (a division of Pearson Australia Group Pty. Ltd.)

Penguin Books India Pvt. Ltd., 11 Community Centre, Panchsheel Park, New Delhi—110 017, India

Penguin Group (NZ), 67 Apollo Drive, Rosedale, North Shore, Auckland 1311, New Zealand (a division of Pearson New Zealand Ltd.)

Penguin Books (South Africa) (Pty.) Ltd., 24 Sturdee Avenue, Rosebank, Johannesburg 2196, South Africa

Penguin Books Ltd., Registered Offices: 80 Strand, London WC2R 0RL, England

Copyright© 2009 by Marna Atkin

International Standard Book Number: 978-1-59257-897-9
Library of Congress Catalog Card Number: 2008941486

11 10 09   8 7 6 5 4 3 2 1

Interpretation of the printing code: The rightmost number of the first series of numbers is the year of the book's printing; the rightmost number of the second series of numbers is the number of the book's printing. For example, a printing code of 09-1 shows that the first printing occurred in 2009.

Printed in the United States of America

Publisher: *Marie Butler-Knight*
Editorial Director: *Mike Sanders*
Senior Managing Editor: *Billy Fields*
Executive Editor: *Randy Ladenheim-Gil*
Development Editor: *Jennifer Bowles*
Senior Production Editor: *Janette Lynn*
Copy Editor: *Megan Wade*

Cartoonist: *Richard King*
Cover Designer: *Rebecca Harmon*
Book Designer: *Trina Wurst*
Indexer: *Brad Herriman*
Layout: *Chad Dressler*
Proofreader: *Laura Caddell*

Contents at a Glance

Contents

Appendixes

Introduction

Applying to college today isn't the same as it was even 10 years ago. The number of high school graduates has increased exponentially, and they're applying to more and more colleges.

Consider these statistics:

◆ The annual number of high school graduates will peak at about 3 million—give or take a few hundred thousand—over the next few years.

◆ Depending on the estimate, there were anywhere from 300,000 to 500,000 more high school graduates in 2008 than there were in 1984.

◆ In 2006, more than 2 percent of college freshmen said they had applied to 11 or more schools.

So what does this mean for you? It means it's going to be even tougher to get into your first-choice school, especially if your first choice is one of the country's top four-year colleges or universities. You'll have to work even harder to set yourself apart from the pack.

I wrote this book because I know how hard it can be to undertake the process of getting into any college, let alone a college whose diploma will open up more doors than you could imagine.

High school is filled with unique challenges and life-changing experiences. Hopefully this guide will bring you a step closer to achieving success in this challenge.

Who's This Book For?

I wrote this book with three types of students in mind.

The A+ student

A lot of A+ students don't take part in the extracurricular activities that make themselves stand out. To those students, I say it's not only what you do in school that matters, but also what you do outside of school.

Harvard turned down 1,000 applicants in 2007 who had perfect scores on the math section of the SAT, according to *The New York Times*. Yale rejected a handful of applicants who had perfect scores on the SAT, and Princeton said thanks but no thanks to thousands of high school seniors who had a 4.0 GPA. That's the kind of competition you're up against.

The Straight-A "Do-It-All"

We all know the straight-A student who does it all—it might be you. You write for the school newspaper; play on the soccer team; are a member of the chemistry, biology, romance languages, and Latin clubs, and are an overall great person.

Well that's all well and good, but participating in everything is not as important or integral as becoming part of a few meaningful activities and exhibiting leadership, responsibility, and dependability. Nobody does everything well. It's just not possible or realistic. What you need to do is find your strengths and passions.

The Underachiever

There are also those who are saying to themselves, "I don't have an A or A+ average, my grades typically are Bs, but I did score a 2250 on the SAT 1. Do I have any chance at getting into a top college?"

What the 2250 on the SAT 1 shows is that you have ability and potential that, for whatever reason, has not been fully tapped. Perhaps you have some extenuating circumstances in your life that have prevented you from being as focused as you could have been. That is something you'd want to explain on a college application, and I'll show you how to do that.

How to Use This Book

This book has been divided into five parts to help you along the way. Getting into a top college is a process that should begin even before you enter high school, but once in high school there are a succession of decisions to make and challenges to take on to ensure success. This book is based on the concept of signing up for every challenge, facing it head on, and being successful at every turn. You don't have to shut out the rest of the world to gain admission into a top college, but you do have to apply yourself.

Part 1, "It's Never Too Early to Start Planning," gives you a first look at just how difficult it is to get into a top college. It's filled with information on admission rates and how to determine if you have what it takes. It also outlines the first step of working with a guidance counselor.

Part 2, "Moving Forward," is just that—a look at the basic steps you have to take to get into a top school, including which courses to take, which activities to sign up for, and an overview of College Board exams.

Part 3, "Narrowing Your Choices," outlines the steps you need to follow before you start filling out the applications. It will help you decide to which colleges you should apply and address the college tours that occur before you head to the mailbox.

Part 4, "The Application," might be the most important section and is filled with information about recommendations, essays, interviews, and how to fill out the application itself.

Part 5, "Letters Start Rolling In," discusses what to do after you've received your responses. Some will be faced with the issue of deciding between a number of acceptances; others will have to consider life after rejection.

... And There's More

In addition to the information packed into the preceding sections, I've included sidebars that will provide you with quick-hitting information about college planning.

Beware

There are pitfalls you need to be careful of when trying to get into a top college. This sidebar will offer you some warnings so you know what to look out for.

def•i•ni•tion

Just like anything else, the college planning process has its own lingo. This sidebar will help define some of the jargon for you.

Real Life

This sidebar shares the first-hand experiences of people who have been through the college application process and attended a top college. They'll tell you what they wish they had known going into the process and what they learned.

Cheat Sheet

These are tips I've collected from guidance counselors, admissions officers, and college alums. The advice ranges from simple reminders about steps along the way that you can't forget to complete, to suggestions on how to make yourself stand out.

Acknowledgments

Marna would first like to thank her parents, Mickey and Harry LeVine, for their love, encouragement, and steadfast belief in education.

I would also like to thank all the people involved with this book who were so helpful and patient throughout the process: Kimberly Lionetti at Book Ends; executive editor Randy Ladenheim-Gil; and especially my coauthor, Ian Leslie, who so beautifully and eloquently put my expertise and knowledge into words. A special thank you to Mike Panetta, former colleague and dear friend, who recommended me for this project.

Finally, to my husband and best friend Bruce … thank you for your love and support throughout my career as a guidance counselor, independent college consultant, and—most recently—author.

Ian would like to thank all the people who helped him and supported him throughout this process. Thank you to Kimberly Lionetti at Book Ends for her willingness to take a chance on a referral and putting herself out there to support a new author. To Robyn Passante, thank you for thinking of me when this project came your way and introducing me to Kimberly. Thank you to executive editor Randy Landenheim-Gil for being patient with a fellow Northerner and answering e-mail after e-mail from what became a neurotic writer. Thank you to Jennifer Bowles for making me a better writer with her edits, asking lots of questions, and being open to the answers. To Marna, thank you for the years upon years of expertise you offered and for hopping right on board with what was a new experience for both of us.

To my wonderful wife, Carolyn, whom I adore, thank you for telling me that I could do this, that I could find the time, and then believing in me. You've been able to sleep through the glow of the laptop in the middle of the night and have allowed me to step away from my fatherly duties for a spell here and there to get this book done. Your support has been nothing short of remarkable, and I don't know what I would do without your love. Writing my first book wouldn't have been the same without my best friend by my side. I love you. To Isaac and Aaron, you won't remember any of this, but I snuck out of the house during a lot of your weekend naps so that I could write. I'm sorry I wasn't there when you woke up from every nap, but I'll make it up to you.

Special Thanks to the Technical Reviewer

The Complete Idiot's Guide to Getting into Top Colleges was reviewed by an expert who double-checked the accuracy of what you'll learn here, to help us ensure that this book gives you everything you need to know about getting into a top college. Special thanks are extended to Ruth Warburg.

Trademarks

All terms mentioned in this book that are known to be or are suspected of being trademarks or service marks have been appropriately capitalized. Alpha Books and Penguin Group (USA) Inc. cannot attest to the accuracy of this information. Use of a term in this book should not be regarded as affecting the validity of any trademark or service mark.

Part 1

It's Never Too Early to Start Planning

Getting into a top college is as much about preparation as it is execution. Gaining admission into a top school is the ultimate realization of satisfying many goals in several areas. But, you can't reach those goals if you don't know what they are.

In Part 1, I talk about the top schools and, in general terms, what you'll need to accomplish over the four, five, or even six years before you even apply so you can better your chances at admission. I take you through which schools are on top and what they're looking for from top students. I also discuss how to work with your guidance counselor from the first day of high school. The race begins here.

"Ooo, I wouldn't do that. You might need him for a reference someday."

Which Schools Are on Top?

In This Chapter

- ◆ The top schools
- ◆ Making sense of rankings
- ◆ The types of students who are applying
- ◆ Getting used to the competition

What are the top four-year colleges and universities in the United States? You know all about the Ivy League schools, but don't forget about Stanford, the California Institute of Technology, Duke, the University of Chicago, and Northwestern. And those are just a few of the top universities.

When you factor in top liberal arts colleges and business programs that have acceptance rates as competitive as those at some of the Ivy League schools, there are dozens of so-called top schools out there.

Ranking Services and Resources

I knew a high school student who just flatly refused to apply to a school that was not part of the top 20 on *U.S. News & World Report*'s list of America's Best Colleges.

Like that high school student, many parents, teachers, and students consider *U.S. News & World Report*'s rankings the gospel and aren't willing to consider other ranking services or resources. At best, any ranking should be used as a gauge and shouldn't be the ultimate factor when it comes to deciding which school a student will apply to or attend.

While the lists have some differences—for example, Harvard and Princeton might be ranked No. 1 and No. 2, respectively, on one list with those rankings flipped on another—you'll find the same core group of schools in the top 15 on most lists. Use the ranking systems as a tool, but remember to take them with a grain of salt because *U.S. News & World Report* recognizes that the rankings, in part, are based on its own view of "what's important in education."

U.S. News & World Report

Typically released in August, the *U.S. News & World Report*'s annual rankings are the most frequently cited barometer of how a school ranks. The magazine uses several criteria to come up with its annual list, including freshman retention rates, test scores, peer assessments, faculty resources, student selectivity, and alumni giving.

U.S. News & World Report ranks the nation's colleges and universities under several headings, including the top national universities and liberal arts colleges, along with business and engineering programs.

The following list shows the top 10 universities on *U.S. News & World Report*'s 2008 list. The list is pretty much in line with what you'll find on other ranking services, although some might rank UCLA or Rice higher and drop Chicago or Duke from the top 10:

1. Harvard

2. Princeton

3. Yale

4. Massachusetts Institute of Technology (MIT)

4. Stanford

5. California Institute of Technology (CalTech)

5. University of Pennsylvania

6. Columbia

6. Duke

6. Chicago

Note: U.S. News & World Report's rankings do include ties, which accounts for several schools sharing the same rankings.

Beware _____

Although *U.S. News & World Report* boasts the most scientific and unbiased college ranking system, I find that many other rankings are subjective, are misleading, and produce invalid results. Sometimes factors such as the number of famous graduates are considered, which has nothing to do with the quality of education.

The Princeton Review

The Princeton Review, a national college prep firm, takes a slightly different spin with its college rankings and offers a more diverse range of categories. For example, The Princeton Review publishes an annual list of the Best Value Colleges. Several colleges on that list can also be found high on *U.S. News and World Report*'s list.

Websites

There are also websites, such as CollegeConfidential.com, that rank colleges and universities in any number of categories, including Greek life, drug scene, campus dining, and security—oh yeah, and academics.

Here is a list of some of the other college ranking services you might find useful. Again, before taking these rankings too seriously, you should take a look at which formulas they use to grade the schools:

◆ *BusinessWeek*—*BusinessWeek* ranks the top undergraduate business schools in the country.
www.businessweek.com/magazine/toc/08_10/B4074undergrad.htm

◆ The Consus Group—The Consus Group ranks everything from colleges to the performance of investment banks.
consusrankings.com/category/colleges-universities/

◆ College Ranking Service—According to the group's website, the board of the College Ranking Service is composed of Nobel Prize winners and top members of the business community.
www.rankyourcollege.com/ddmethod.html

◆ College Prowler—College Prowler boasts that it contains student-provided content, and it offers rankings based on a number of criteria. www.collegeprowler.com/find/by-ranking.aspx

Who's on Top?

Deciding whether a school is a "top" college is sort of like judging good art or deciding whether an athlete is hall-of-fame worthy: When you see it, you'll know it.

From Harvard to Yale, Duke, Stanford, Carnegie Mellon, and Vanderbilt, dozens of schools can be considered top colleges and universities. Although not all of them come with the Ivy League stamp of approval, that doesn't mean those second-tier schools won't offer just as good of an education. But like I said earlier, some people get caught up on rankings and whether they'll attend an Ivy.

When it comes down to it, you'll find that only a handful of schools have acceptance rates of about 10 percent or lower. After that, all the top schools accept students at a clip of anywhere from 12 percent to 25 percent. So, once you drop down from that upper echelon, it's really up to you to choose your school based on your educational desires and not your ego.

The Ivies

When you talk about top colleges and universities, you have to start with the Ivy League schools—Brown, Columbia, Cornell, Dartmouth, Harvard, Princeton, UPenn, and Yale.

The Ivy League schools, also known as the Ancient Eight or the Ivies, are all located in the Northeast. All the schools, with the exception of Cornell, were founded before the American Revolution. Cornell was founded in 1865. The group of schools got its "Ivy" name because of the schools' ages and the ivy that grows on the schools' walls.

Initially, the term was used to group the schools in a sports conference, but now it's better known for attracting the world's best students. Although the Ivy League isn't known for its athletic prowess, the annual Harvard-Yale football game still is regarded as one of college football's fiercest rivalries.

If you're eyeing an Ivy League school, the average acceptance rate for the class of 2012 was about 12 percent. *Admission rate* is a common term when dealing with colleges. To come up with a school's admission rate, divide the number of applicants accepted by the number of applicants. For example, if a school receives 1,000 applications and accepts 10 of them, its admission rate is 10 percent.

The following table lists the admission rates for the Ivy League classes of 2012.

School	Total Applications	Accepted	Percentage
Harvard	27,462	1,948	7
Yale	22,813	1,892	8
Princeton	21,369	1,976	9
Columbia	22,569	2,269	10
Brown	20,630	2,742	13
Dartmouth	16,536	2,190	13
UPenn	22,922	3,769	16
Cornell	30,011	6,735	20
Total	187,312	23,521	12.5

Across the board, the Ivy League schools saw their pools of applications go up for the class of 2012, while admission rates at seven of the eight schools went down. UPenn had a slight increase in its admission rate. The average acceptance rates at the Ivies dropped from 14.4 percent for the Class of 2010 to 13.6 percent for the Class of 2011, and then went down to 12.5 percent for the Class of 2012.

Why the decrease? It's really just simple math. The number of high school graduates is rising, and if you couple that with the fact that high schoolers are applying to more and more colleges, you're faced with schools considering many more applications. The number of students graduating from high school annually is at an all-time high, and while those graduates used to pick 3 colleges to apply to, several now are applying to as many as 11. When you take in more applications but you're accepting the same number of students, the acceptance rate is going to decrease.

Significant changes in financial aid policies at the Ivies have also likely contributed to the increase in applications and, in turn, the lower acceptance rates. For example, Brown—along with several other schools—has eliminated tuition for students whose families have an income of less than $60,000 per year. The school also has eliminated loans for students from families making less than $100,000. Instead of loans, which must be paid back, the school now offers scholarships instead. I dive deeper into financial aid issues in Chapter 12.

Cheat Sheet _____

Harvard leads all American universities with a $34 billion endowment and is 1 of only 76 colleges that boasts an endowment of more than $1 billion, according to an annual study released in January. Endowments are used, in part, to help offset tuition costs for students who otherwise wouldn't be able to pay for college.

The Next Tier

The Ivies, of course, generally are accepted as the nation's top colleges. But let's not forget Stanford (ranked No. 4 in *U.S. News & World Report*), MIT (also No. 4), CalTech (No. 6), and Duke University (No. 8). Those aren't Ivy League schools, but are they second tier? I don't think so.

The line between the Ivies and the tier of schools always thought to be "under" the Ivies has become almost completely blurred over the years. Over the past five years, I know of several situations when a student was accepted at an Ivy and was either wait-listed or rejected at a school typically known as the tier directly under, such as Duke, Tufts, or Emory.

Just like the Ivies, these so-called second-tier schools are seeing record numbers of applicants and are having to adjust their admissions accordingly.

About 18,700 students applied to Georgetown University for admission to the Class of 2012, surpassing the record-setting pool of applications the university received the previous year by about 2,600. Because of the record number of applications, Georgetown also set a record low in terms of acceptances, offering entry to just 3,371 students—18 percent of the applicants.

The story is the same across most of the "second tier," where schools are setting records for applications received and low acceptance rates.

Here's how other top non-Ivy schools stack up in terms of applications and acceptance rates:

School	Total Applications	Accepted	Percentage
Amherst	7,720	1,096	14
Bowdoin	6,021	1,110	18
Chicago	12,418	3,461	28
Duke	20,337	3,814	19

School	Total Applications	Accepted	Percentage
Emory	17,448	4,500	26
Notre Dame	14,506	3,548	24
NYU	37,000	8,809	24
Swarthmore	6,118	909	15
Vanderbilt	16,875	4,000	24

You can't really consider Stanford, CalTech, and MIT "second-tier" schools, either. After all, when you take a look at the top seven schools in *U.S. News & World Report*'s 2008 rankings, you have four Ivies and these three.

MIT admitted 1,554 of its 13,396 applicants for the Class of 2012. The 11.6 percent acceptance rate is a record low for the school, and the 13,396 applicants was an 8 percent increase over the previous year.

It was the same story at Stanford for the Class of 2012. The university received a record-high 25,298 applications and accepted a record-low 9.5 percent of those.

Business Schools

U.S. News & World Report most recently ranked UPenn, MIT, the University of California-Berkeley, and the University of Michigan as having the nation's top business programs. *BusinessWeek* also includes the University of Virginia, Notre Dame, Cornell, Emory, and New York University (NYU) on its list of top business programs.

Who's Applying?

Nowadays, the competition you face as a high school student applying to top colleges is unprecedented when you consider the increasing number of high school graduates along with the increasing number of schools those graduates are applying to.

By the Numbers

Let's start with the number of high school graduates. After a steady climb over the past 15 years, there now are more than 3 million high school graduates annually. You've heard of the baby boomers, right? They're the ones who were born between 1946 and the early 1960s. Well, they had kids, and many of those kids are now graduating high school.

A study conducted by the Western Interstate Commission for Higher Education states that the number of high school graduates will hover near 3.4 million before gradually decreasing in 2010–2011.

The pool of applicants is so strong that the top schools can handpick their students and create the kinds of well-rounded classes they strive for. If Harvard wants an A+ student who was the captain of the high school football team and president of the student council, chances are it will be able to find one.

Real Life

"Figures like application numbers and acceptance rates are increasingly less relevant as a metric of anything important. The question is, among those applicants in your pool who are very competitive for admission to your institution, is that number remaining consistent over time?"

—Yale Dean of Admissions Jeff Brenzel in the *Yale Daily News*

Federal statistics also back up that more and more students are not only graduating from high school, but are also taking those high school diplomas to college. According to a recent study conducted by the U.S. Bureau of Labor Statistics, about 70 percent of high school graduates from the Class of 2007 were enrolled in four-year colleges or universities in 2008. Less than half of high school graduates in the 1970s immediately enrolled in colleges or universities.

What's My Eleventh Choice?

Forget about your first- and second-choice schools; have you ever considered what your eleventh choice might be? In 2006, more than 2 percent of college freshmen said they applied to 11 or more schools. Compare that with the fewer than 2 percent of college freshmen who applied to 6 or more schools in the 1960s.

Over the last decade, the number of students who have applied to six or more schools has increased from 18 percent to 28 percent—that's an increase of more than 50 percent. And the number of students who applied to only one school dropped from 24 percent to 14 percent.

The Least You Need to Know

◆ School rankings should be used as a tool and not considered the gospel.

◆ Applications to Ivies are at an all-time high.

◆ The average Ivy League acceptance rate for the Class of 2012 was 12.5 percent.

◆ Now more students than ever are vying for college acceptances.

Getting into Top Business Schools

In This Chapter

- ◆ The top business schools
- ◆ The right school could mean big bucks
- ◆ How to shape your resumé
- ◆ Get more than just a business education

Getting into a top undergraduate business program is the same as getting into any top school—but at the same time it's different.

Just like top schools that are admitting students into regular undergraduate programs, business schools are fielding more and better applicants every year. Business schools, however, are looking for different things in their applicants than the typical undergraduate programs are—and what's at stake is big bucks.

Consider that graduates from UPenn's Wharton School of Business Class of 2007 averaged 11 job interviews and almost 3 job offers each. More than 90 percent of those graduates accepted offers from permanent employers or graduate schools. Those who did accept jobs had an average starting salary of $60,000. So, you better believe that when a probable $60,000 salary right out of college is on the line, the competition for admission to the school is going to be fierce.

How fierce? Well, of the 5,500 students who apply to Wharton out of high school every year, the college admits about 500, an acceptance rate of about 9 percent.

The Top Biz Programs

Just as with standard undergraduate programs, there are numerous rankings of undergraduate business programs. *U.S. News & World Report* and *BusinessWeek* publish the most referenced business rankings.

Both publications base their rankings on surveys of students and faculty and on important benchmarks, including the number of students who are placed in jobs and top master's of business administration programs. The rankings also consider the salaries received by the students who jump from the undergraduate programs directly into jobs.

Here's how *U.S. News & World Report* and *BusinessWeek* rank the country's top undergraduate business programs:

Rank	*U.S. News & World Report*	*BusinessWeek*
1	UPenn	UPenn
2	MIT	Virginia
3	UC Berkeley	Notre Dame
4	Michigan	Cornell
5	NYU	Emory
6	Carnegie Mellon	Michigan
7	North Carolina	Brigham Young
8	Texas	NYU
9	Virginia	MIT
10	Southern California	Texas

For years, UPenn has been home to the country's top undergraduate business program at Wharton, although many professionals believe the gap between Wharton and the other schools is closing.

Chapter 2: Getting into Top Business Schools   **15**

What's at Stake?

As I already stated, graduates from Wharton's Class of 2007 who hopped right into jobs started their professional careers with an average salary of $60,000. At Virginia, the average salary was $58,000 for the Class of 2007, an increase of more than 10 percent compared with the Class of 2006.

Graduates of *BusinessWeek*'s top 25 undergraduate business programs made an average of $54,445 right out of college in 2007, an increase of $3,000 over the year prior.

The salaries for these graduates tend to be lucrative because these top business programs have connections with the nation's top investment banking firms. Graduates of Georgetown's undergraduate business program, which *BusinessWeek* ranks as the nineteenth best in the country, were placed in investment banking jobs at a clip of 29 percent for the Class of 2007—94 graduates, compared with 63 the year prior. The *median* starting salary for those graduates was $60,000.

As we move to the future, diversity in terms of where business programs are placing students and the business sectors those schools are partnering with is growing.

"Consider these four programs that have distinguished themselves by going local: The University of Houston, in the heart of the nation's oil capital, is training the next generation of energy executives, while Florida State University offers a professional golf management program. The University of Louisville specializes in equine management. Belmont University is using its Nashville locale to help students break into the music business. For these schools, it's all about finding their competitive advantage," *BusinessWeek*'s website states.

def•i•ni•tion

The **median** is the middle of a distribution. Half of the numbers in the group are above the median and half are below.

The University of Houston launched its Bauer College of Business, which ranks 82nd on *BusinessWeek*'s list, in 2001. Since then, the school has become a pipeline for the oil industry, placing students in high-paying jobs with BP, ConocoPhillips, and Royal Dutch Shell. The school also is beginning a program on alternative energy, which is the wave of the future.

Here are the average first-year salaries for the Class of 2007 undergraduate business school students at *BusinessWeek*'s top 10 business schools:

School	Salary
UPenn	$59,948
Virginia	$55,296
Notre Dame	$53,541
Cornell	$52,045
Emory	$53,000
Michigan	$55,188
BYU	$47,458
NYU	$60,000
MIT	$60,200
Texas	$50,966

Possibly more so than with any other discipline, landing a spot in the right undergraduate business program and succeeding in that program can be your ticket to a high-paying job right out of college.

Applying to B-School

Different schools have different policies when it comes to admitting undergraduates into their business programs. Of *BusinessWeek*'s top 10 undergraduate business programs, six—Virginia, Notre Dame, Emory, Michigan, BYU, and MIT—do not admit freshmen into their programs. Instead, the students are admitted into prebusiness first-year programs. A student's academic performance in that first year often determines if she will be admitted into the business school or major.

Top undergrad business schools have different policies when it comes to transferring into a business program. Even if the school you're looking at does allow you to transfer in, you're certainly looking at an uphill battle when dealing with the transfer process.

The University of Virginia's McIntire School of Commerce factors in many things when considering transfers, including "cumulative grade point average, academic performance in prerequisites, and those courses related to business (accounting, economics, mathematics) and degree of difficulty of courses taken to date as a demonstration of the student's general ability and desire," according to the school's website. UVA typically has about 30 transfer spots open in its undergrad business program, and the number of students trying to fill those spots is ever growing. In 2008, about 300 students applied to the undergrad business school as transfers.

Policies differ even among the schools that don't offer admission to freshmen. Some allow students to enter the business program simply after successful completion of their freshman year; others require a detailed application process.

The common factor among all the top business programs is that they're looking for students who are a little bit different from the typical undergrad. The leadership component of a student's resumé is scrutinized that much more, as is work experience. So the question becomes, how best do you position yourself for entry?

Right Out of High School

As I said, only four of *BusinessWeek*'s top 10 undergraduate business programs admit students straight out of high school, including the prestigious UPenn Wharton School of Business.

Universities that allow students to immediately enter their business programs as freshmen simply ask that the applicant state that interest on his application. After that, it's up to the admissions office to decide whether the student is a good fit for that individual major or college.

Students must have a compelling reason for why they want to enter a certain program and need to be able to convince the school that they're passionate about the subject. Believe it or not, there have been students whose explanation for wanting to enter a certain program was "because I thought it would be the easiest to get into." That won't fly, and even if you're thinking that but don't share it, the college more times than not will see through the lie. Admissions officers have done this a thousand times and know what to look for.

Cheat Sheet

"Each applicant is assessed as an individual, and we evaluate high school academic performance, standardized testing, recommendations, nonscholastic achievements, leadership, and personal maturity," states UPenn's website. "The university admissions committee looks for individuals who will be future leaders. There are no fixed criteria and no cut-offs in terms of grades or test scores. Because such a high percentage of our applicant pool is qualified for admission, successful applicants are those who present the most compelling cases and distinguish themselves from other applicants."

What They're Looking For

Just because applicants to a school's business program go through the same application and admissions process as other undergraduate students doesn't mean the admissions officers aren't looking for something unique in those students.

It goes without saying that applicants to top business programs must have the best grades and test scores. The average high school GPA and test scores of freshman in a school's business program are right inline with the school's averages, so if you want to gain entry you're going to have to rise to that level.

That being said, a business school is looking for an X-factor when it comes to its business students, and if grades and tests are basically the same across the board, then a lot of that is going to have to do with extracurricular activities.

As many college admissions officers put it, they're looking for the "Big Wow!" However, that doesn't mean just being president of your high school's entrepreneurs' club.

"We saw one (applicant) who commuted an hour to school every day to get a more rigorous education, and he went home to take care of seven brothers and sisters," said Nanette Tarbouni, Director of Undergraduate Admissions at Washington University in St. Louis. "So he couldn't be on the newspaper staff. But that's still extracurricular, and to me it was a big 'wow.' We want people who can follow through."

Schools often also judge the groups and clubs that you're a part of. High school clubs are a dime a dozen, and if they haven't really accomplished anything while you've been a member of them, then what have they really accomplished for you?

> **Beware**
>
> Don't focus just on extracurricular activities that you think business schools want to see from a business student. Admissions officials with top business schools agree that high school business clubs don't mean a lot, and it's leadership and results that count. So position yourself in an activity where you'll succeed.

Instead of joining a club, you should consider starting your own small business, getting an after-school job, or taking on an internship. Those are activities that show an end product. Even if you fail with your own business, you're showing that you have initiative and aren't willing to depend on the status quo.

"Occasionally you'll see a student who has done something like start his own lawn-mowing business or trading stocks," said Tarbouni. "It separates you to do something extraordinary like that, because it speaks to your character. You're doing what you love, and you're getting results."

Admissions officers at top business colleges also advise that you consider communications skills when deciding which extracurriculars to take on.

"One big complaint we hear is a lot of people in the work force don't communicate very well," said Andrea Hershatter, Associate Dean and Director of the BBA program at Emory's Goizueta Business School. "It is particularly useful to have students who have exhibited strong communication skills (in places) like writing clubs, or oral communication like (in) debate. If you have a student who has started an organization and galvanized a cause, that shows somebody with a lot of potential."

Entrepreneurs Welcome

If there is a constant when it comes to what business programs are looking for, it's the entrepreneurial spirit.

As I've said, some students choose to go the high school club route and others pursue jobs and internships. But it's those students who are somehow able to find the time to start their own businesses—it doesn't really matter if they succeed or fail—that really catch the eye of admissions officers at business schools.

Now I'm not saying you have to become Gurbaksh Chahal, who at 16 started his first Internet advertising company in California and sold it for $40 million. But you could become Mike Gillespie, a 17-year-old Ohio high schooler who turned his single lawnmower into a lawn care business that netted him a $10,000 summer profit.

Whether you find success or failure, what's important is that you show initiative and leadership and display a willingness to try. Business schools don't want people who all are cut from the same cloth. They want leaders who are willing to try, fail, and try again.

Applying from the Inside

As I mentioned earlier in the chapter, of *BusinessWeek*'s top 10 undergrad business programs, 6 require that you spend at least a year at the university before you declare your major and are admitted into the business school. Among these schools are different policies on how they admit students into their business programs.

At Notre Dame, it's as simple as attending a career fair and deciding which area of study within the business school you want to focus on. "Students interested in a major in the College of Business decide in the spring of their sophomore year which of the five areas of interest they will pursue: Accountancy, Finance, Management (Consulting or Entrepreneurship), Management Information Systems (MIS), or Marketing," the school's website states.

> ### Real Life
>
> "We need to see that students are doing something outside of academics. We need to see a passion and a commitment to something, and we want to see students who have developed leadership skills."
>
> —Rebecca Leonard, the University of Virginia's assistant dean for undergraduate student services, said in regard to admission to the school's undergraduate business program.

The process is a bit different at the University of Virginia. There, the school considers "cumulative grade point average, academic performance in prerequisites and those courses related to business (accounting, economics, mathematics), and degree of difficulty of courses taken to date as a demonstration of the student's general ability and desire," according to the school's website. "Also, skills and personal characteristics such as leadership, communication, work experience, and time management will be considered as demonstrated through extracurricular activities and application essays."

So Virginia, because it accepts students after they've spent two years at the university, considers everything from their freshman year grades to what they're doing outside of the college classroom. All of this is included in an application to the business school and considered by the school's admission committee.

Because it's already so difficult to get into the University of Virginia, the rate of people accepted into the business program is not even as close to being as low as that of UPenn, which accepts business school applicants right out of high school.

Over a five-year period ending in 2008, Virginia accepted an average of 69 percent of the applicants for its business program—about 309 students a year. The average GPA of the students accepted over that five-year period was 3.49.

Emory University's business program also requires that applicants complete certain prerequisites and submit an essay and teacher recommendation.

MIT follows Notre Dame's protocol and allows students to declare themselves business majors after their freshman year without asking students to meet additional requirements.

> **Beware**
>
> Some undergraduate business programs require that you complete a certain num-
> ber of credits in specific courses before you're allowed to enter the business school.
> Make sure you check with the business program to see whether it has any specific
> requirements.

More than Business

Many students question whether they will be limited in their academic endeavors if
they commit to a business program, but top colleges go out of their way to ensure that
students have every opportunity to explore academics both inside and outside of the
business program.

As Wharton's website states, "it's not even that students can take courses outside of the
Wharton curriculum, it's that they have to." In fact, 43 percent of the degree requirements for Wharton are outside of the business program.

Wharton, as do many schools, also offers a dual-degree program that allows students
to graduate with degrees in business and another subject. More than 30 percent of
Wharton's students graduate with more than one degree.

"Wharton undergraduates go on to medical school, law school, and graduate school
and work for not-for-profit institutions as well as leading corporations. You will find
that a Wharton education increases your opportunities rather than limits them,"
according to the school's website.

Schools that require students to fulfill a certain number of credits outside of the business program before they're admitted into that major do so to ensure that the students
are exploring all academic possibilities. At the University of Virginia, for instance,
"students spend the first two years of undergraduate work combining liberal arts and
business prerequisite courses."

The Least You Need to Know

- Top business schools are pipelines that place graduates into top high-paying jobs.
- You need to create a "wow" factor that will separate you from other qualified
  applicants.
- Business schools look fondly on entrepreneurs, even if they've failed.
- Business school will give you the ability to explore a number of other academic
  options.

Do You Have What It Takes?

In This Chapter

- Developing and meeting academic standards
- The importance of standardized tests
- Making sure you're on pace for acceptance
- Developing a resumé

The number of students applying to top colleges is higher than it has ever been. So if you're going to take the time to go through this process, you really have to stop to ask yourself if you have what it takes.

If you're a sophomore or junior in high school, look at your grade point average (GPA) and your standardized test scores (if you've already taken the exams) to see how they match up against the students who are offered admission to top colleges. If you're not yet in high school, consider the path ahead and ask yourself whether you're prepared for the hard work.

Academic Standards

High school class rank, GPA, and standardized test scores are the basic standards colleges look at when considering admission. There are, of course, other factors that affect admission that I address later in the book, including extracurricular activities and special talents you might have. But for an initial discussion on whether you have what it takes to get into a top school, let's focus on the three basic standards.

Class Rank

Your rank in your senior class is part of the big picture when applying to a top college, but it often isn't taken at face value because all top schools typically reaverage high schools' GPAs based only on academic areas. I get deeper into the recalculation process later in this chapter.

Additionally, not all high schools rank their students, and some that do don't release that information. For example, 62 percent of Columbia's Class of 2011 was admitted from high schools that don't rank students.

A 2005 study released by the National Association for College Admission Counseling found that about 40 percent of the country's high schools didn't rank their students or didn't supply that information to colleges.

Beware

Because class rankings are based largely on GPA, and because GPAs are calculated differently from school to school, comparing your rank to someone you know at another school is like comparing apples to oranges.

The change in these schools' policies, intended to cut down on the amount of competition among students and foster academic challenges by eliminating the worry of diminishing a student's ranking, has left some college admissions officers wondering what to make of GPAs from schools that don't report rankings.

"If a kid has a B-plus record, what does that mean?" Jim Miller, Dean of Admissions at Brown, told *The New York Times* after the 2005 study was released. "If a school doesn't give any A's, it could be a very good record. You've got to position the kids in some relative environment."

But students who come from schools that don't rank their senior classes won't suffer as a result, as long as their guidance counselors provide the colleges with a good idea of what the high school is like. Because of the way Ivies analyze transcripts and dive deeper into a student's profile than the surface elements of GPA and class rank, that information (which I address later in the book) will provide admissions offices with what they need to know about you and the school you attended. So, if you've succeeded in challenging classes, your GPA will speak for itself and a missing class rank won't really matter.

All that being said, if your school does rank its students, then you want to be in the top 10 percent of your class. More than 93 percent of the Ivy League Class of 2011 that was accepted from schools that rank their students ranked within the top 10 percent of their graduating classes.

School	Percent in Top Tenth of Class
Harvard	95
Yale	97
Princeton	96
Columbia	92
Brown	92
Dartmouth	91
UPenn	96
Cornell	87

GPA

Top schools don't set a minimum GPA that they'll accept, but it's generally believed that if you don't have at least a weighted GPA of 3.0 it's likely not worth your time to apply to an Ivy League school. Across the board, at least 50 percent of the incoming freshman classes at the Ivies have a GPA of at least 3.75 unweighted. At several of the schools, that percentage approaches 90 percent.

Even outside of the Ivies, GPAs have to be very high to gain admission. More than 70 percent of the students accepted to Carnegie Mellon's Class of 2012 had a GPA of at least 3.5. At the University of Virginia, 85 percent of the students accepted to the Class of 2012 had a GPA of at least 3.75.

But the question is, how do colleges determine GPAs and on what are the annually published accepted GPA rates based?

First, you have the GPA your high school gives you. Your weighted GPA awards additional points for tougher classes, such as honors classes. But not all high schools weigh their classes the same way, and some don't weigh them at all, so here we're comparing apples and oranges.

Then, there's your GPA after it gets into the hands of the colleges you're applying to. The top colleges take your grades and analyze them thoroughly. Although there's no standard "recalculation formula," you can assume that schools initially eliminate everything but the core classes when recalculating your GPA. What's left is the so-called fundamental five: English, math, science, social science, and foreign language.

Generally, you should expect the GPA a top college uses to determine whether to accept you to be lower than the GPA included on your transcript. Those easy As you received in gym and home economics definitely won't be part of their calculations. However, if you're a straight-A student in all your classes, your recalculated GPA still will be the highest GPA possible.

But it doesn't end there. Schools even vary on how they calculate grades from those core courses. At Emory University and the University of California, for instance, admissions officers drop the plusses and minuses alongside letter grades. So, a B+ and a B- both end up being a B. Some schools, including Johns Hopkins, choose to consider grades from music and arts courses when calculating a GPA as long as the classes are *Advanced Placement (AP)*–level.

def•i•ni•tion

Advanced Placement (AP) classes are administered by the College Board and give high school students opportunities to take college-level courses. The courses are offered in 22 subjects.

Cornell and UPenn, for instance, use a holistic approach and don't subscribe to a formula when recalculating and analyzing a student's GPA. Officials from the admissions offices of those schools say there's no cut-and-dry process, and both schools look heavily at rigor of course load compared to what the high school offers.

I recently knew a student who took a rigorous course load and also took every music course that she could fit into her schedule. She received a 100 in every music course and had a graduating average of 96.6 with a 3.86 GPA. When recomputed by several colleges, each with its own system, her average was 89.7 and her GPA was 3.39.

SAT/ACT

Much has been made over the years about the perceived bias of standardized testing. But like it or not, the Scholastic Assessment Test (SAT) and American College Testing Program (ACT) are a way of life and top schools want to see you do well on at least one of them.

SAT is widely regarded as the most popular admissions exam used by colleges and universities. The first SAT exam was administered in 1901. Administered by the College

Board, the SAT 1 is a reasoning test with three sections: critical reading, mathematics, and writing. A student can receive a top score of 800 on each section, for a total score of 2,400.

The College Board also offers SAT 2 exams, which are specific to subject areas. Scores on the SAT 2, which are offered in 20 subjects and are each 1 hour long, range from 200 to 800.

The ACT was started in 1959 to compete with the SAT. It's also used as a barometer to determine how prepared high school students are for college. The ACT includes four sections: English, mathematics, reading, and science. There's also an optional writing section. A composite score is given as a total of the scores received on each section. The top composite score a student can receive is 36.

According to their respective websites, 1.5 million high schoolers in the Class of 2007 took the SAT 1 and 1.3 million took the ACT. There is some overlap in those numbers where students took both tests.

Over the years, groups have argued that standardized tests exhibit gender and other demographic bias, and because of such, some schools have shied away from requiring SAT or ACT scores for admission.

FairTest.org, a website that tracks the number of colleges that don't use the SAT 1 or ACT as deciding factors when admitting students, has compiled a list of more than 700 schools that don't make students take the exams. No Ivy League schools are on that list. MIT, CalTech, Duke, University of Chicago, and Stanford also are missing from the website's list. All the top schools require that you take either the SAT or the ACT. So, if you want to buck the trend and protest standardized testing, don't expect to gain admission to a top school.

An average of 95 percent of the Class of 2011 for all Ivies took the SAT 1. Dartmouth, at 86 percent, had the lowest rate of incoming freshman who took the SAT 1. An average of 20 percent of the Ivy League Class of 2011 took the ACT, with UPenn having the highest rate of ACT test-takers, at 30 percent.

Later in the book I get into how you should decide whether to take the SAT 1, ACT, or both.

The following table shows the 25th and 75th percentile SAT 1 and ACT scores for Ivy League freshman for the Class of 2011. The 25th and 75th percentile marks mean that 25 percent of freshman scored lower than the scores shown and 25 percent scored higher.

SAT

School	25th/75th Reading	25th/75th Math	25th/75th Writing
Harvard	700/800	700/790	700/790
Yale	700/790	690/790	690/790
Princeton	690/790	700/790	690/780
Columbia	660/760	670/780	660/750
Brown	660/760	670/760	660/760
Dartmouth	670/770	680/780	670/770
UPenn	650/750	680/770	660/750
Cornell	630/730	660/770	630/720

ACT

School	25th/75th Composite
Harvard	31/35
Yale	29/34
Princeton	30/34
Columbia	28/33
Brown	28/33
Dartmouth	28/34
UPenn	29/33
Cornell	28/32

Am I On Pace?

Determining whether you're on pace for getting into an Ivy or other top college isn't necessarily an easy task. So many factors go into acceptance that you can't solely hang your hat on a strong GPA, high school rank, or good test scores.

Several years ago I had two students apply to the same school. One's GPA, SAT scores, and rigor of courses were higher, but only the other student got into the school. In later discussions with the admissions office, I was told that it was the intangibles—one of them being that the student with the higher GPA, higher SAT scores, and tougher courses had more advantages and opportunities, while the student who was accepted, who was not as good on paper, had risen above difficult circumstances to achieve what she had.

> ### Real Life
>
> "We typically will not solely focus on GPA but will rather look at the courses a student has selected to take, the rigor, how well he or she did in the course, and how the course selection and strength align with the major/college to which he or she is applying .... We do not utilize formulas."
> —Chandra deKoven, Associate Director of Admissions, Cornell University

Aside from those types of intangibles, though, there are ways you can keep track of your standing, including trying to calculate an accurate GPA and determining your academic index (AI).

Academic Index

The Ivy League developed the academic index in the mid-1980s as a way to establish minimum academic standards for Ivy League athletes. It's a tool high schoolers can use to get a quick glimpse of where they are in terms of competing for an Ivy League seat.

A number of websites and resources is available to help you determine if you're on pace to gain entry into a top college. Of course, these websites don't take into account extracurriculars, special skills, or the rigor of your course load. Websites such as Collegeboard.com allow you to input your grades, course load, and standardized test scores; then they show you how you stack up with students who have been admitted.

The websites generally consider your GPA, standardized test scores, and class rank and should be used as a secondary tool to give you a general idea of where you stand.

The AI assigns a value to a student's GPA; class rank; and SAT 1, SAT 2, and ACT scores to come up with a score on a scale from 1 to 240. Ivy officials have established a minimum AI of 171 that all students—athletes and nonathletes—must meet to gain acceptance. Although, admissions officers typically do not use the AI except when assessing athletes.

Opinions on how admissions departments use AI outside of assessing potential athletes differ and, at times, conflict. Some former admissions officers say Ivy League schools do use the AI when considering all candidates. But admissions officers with both Cornell and UPenn say they consider AI scores only when assessing athletes, adding that the same policy goes for the other Ivies.

"Admissions decisions are driven in part by the components that make up the academic index, rather than the index itself," said Paul Sunde of the Dartmouth admissions office. "So we encourage students to focus on the strength of their academic programs, their performance in their classes and on standardized exams, and how much they are getting out of their academic experiences ...."

According to a website run by Michelle Hernandez, a former Dartmouth admissions officer turned college admissions consultant, the average AI score for an Ivy League applicant is 200. But those who are actually accepted to Ivies have AI scores closer to 211.

Finding a website you can use to calculate your AI is as simple as Googling the term "academic index." Here are a couple of websites to get you on your way:

◆ www.collegeconfidential.com/academic_index3.htm

◆ www.hernandezcollegeconsulting.com/resources/calculator.html

According to these AI calculators, a student who ranks in the top 10 percent in a class of 400 graduating seniors, scored 760 on both the math and verbal sections of the SAT 1, averaged a 720 on three SAT 2 tests, and has an AI of 214—which is about average for incoming Ivy League freshman.

That students who have strong AIs are more likely to receive acceptance to an Ivy than someone who is rejected isn't a major surprise because the AI is based on the major academic standards we discussed earlier. So, you can use AI as a simple gauge of where you stand academically. Remember, though, that your AI itself is not a key component of gaining acceptance to an Ivy.

Calculating GPA

As I stated earlier, colleges don't judge your application based on the GPA included on your transcript. Admissions officers recalculate GPAs based on a formula used by each school.

So you're not ever going to truly be able to find out what college admissions officers do with your transcript after it's in their hands. But of course you want to give yourself the best idea of where your GPA stacks up with what's generally accepted by the top schools.

The first step in recalculating your GPA is to make a list of your grades from only the classes that are part of the fundamental five: English, math, science, social science, and foreign language. Don't give extra weight to AP or honors classes, so the GPA you come up with will be unweighted based on most high schools' standards.

When you have the grades from only your core courses, follow these three steps:

Cheat Sheet

When recalculating a potential student's GPA, some schools drop the freshman-year grades. But those schools still take into account those grades when making a final decision on whether to admit a student.

1. Convert the grades your school gives to numerical values from 0 to 4. If your school gives As, Bs, and Cs, assign a 4 to an A, a 3 to a B, and so on. If your school hands out grades on a 55-to-100 scale, then complete the same conversion. In the most basic cases, a grade of 100–90 converts to a 4, a grade of 80–89 converts to a 3, a grade of 70–79 converts to a 2, and a grade of 60–69 converts to a 1. Then, add up the number of 4s, 3s, 2s, and 1s you've received.

2. Multiply each grade value by the number of classes you received that grade in. So, if you received As or grades of 90–100 in 5 classes, that would total 20 points. Do this for each grade value.

3. Add up all the grade values after step number 2, and then divide that number by the total number of courses taken.

Here's an example. A student who receives 5 As, 10 Bs, and 2 Cs would calculate her GPA by multiplying 5 × 4, 10 × 3, and 2 × 2. She would then add the product of those numbers (20 + 30 + 4) and divide that total by the number of classes taken (54/17). This student's recalculated GPA would be 3.17.

Extracurriculars

Part of being on pace to gain entry into a top college is making sure you're getting some quality extracurriculars under your belt early and often. In fact, it's a good idea to begin these activities even before high school.

Later in this book I share some guidelines to help you decide which extracurriculars are best for you and which ones help you stand out from the pack. But a general rule is to get involved in a couple of activities you're passionate about as soon as you can. You shouldn't wait until your sophomore or even your junior year of high school, and in some cases you really can start before high school. These activities will allow you to grow into a leadership position.

I once told a student that because he liked to argue every point, he might enjoy speech and debate. He joined his school's speech and debate team as a freshman, and by his senior year he was placing first in very prestigious tournaments. That's the sort of growth opportunity you should look for.

Dedicate yourself to a few activities and shy away from being partially committed to several activities. Being committed to a few activities is more fulfilling and more impressive to colleges than joining a lot of organizations just to fill a resumé.

You also want your extracurricular resumé to be well-rounded. You want to have a mix of academic and community activities that show that you're not only a good student, but also a well-rounded person. You won't be penalized for not having athletic talent, but if you are an athlete, getting involved in a team sport shows that you have the skills needed to work in a high-pressure, group atmosphere.

Am I Too Late?

From a counseling standpoint, I never want to tell a student he is too late to prepare for getting into a top college or that what he does from now on doesn't matter because he had a less-than-outstanding course grade or, worse, year. But the reality is that the top colleges have so many highly qualified students that they have the luxury of being just that selective. One poor grade, let alone a bad semester, can be enough to keep you out. Top colleges are looking for candidates who have it all, and that means students who have excelled in every course, every year.

That being said, there are exceptions to every rule, and I discuss these situations in depth later in the book. For example, some people have extenuating circumstances that have resulted in their poor grades. In addition, some people are underachievers when it comes to daily high school work but blow the lids off of their standardized tests and write stellar essays. While the process is harder for those people, you can never say never. So, if you fall into one of these categories, it's not necessarily time to throw in the towel.

The Least You Need to Know

- There's no one secret formula that colleges use to grant admission.

- You need to take either the SAT 1 or ACT, or both, to get into a top college.

- If your school maintains and shares a class rank, you should be in the top 10 percent.

- Develop a well-rounded extracurricular resumé.

Chapter 4

Working with a Guidance Counselor

In This Chapter

- ◆ Establishing common admission goals
- ◆ Compiling the right information colleges need
- ◆ Deciding whether to use a private counselor
- ◆ How to go it alone

If gaining admission to a top college is your Mt. Everest, then you should consider your high school guidance counselor your Sherpa. Your counselor will guide you throughout the process and should be someone who provides an honest opinion and becomes a key bridge between you and your school of choice. He also should be your advocate and someone who will market you and what you can offer a top college.

Unfortunately, recent studies show that there aren't nearly enough guidance counselors for the country's high school students. No one should have to go through this process alone, but the dearth of guidance counselors means some students get more help than others. Chances are if you attend a private high school, you'll get more attention than if you attend a public school.

The Counselor's Role

According to a 2007 survey by the National Association for College Admission Counseling, on average there is one guidance counselor for every 311 high school students in the United States. That ratio is much better at private schools, where there is one guidance counselor for every 234 students. But the ratio of students to counselors at some of the country's top private high schools is as good as one counselor for every 50 students.

Additionally, public school counselors told the association that they spend an average of 23 percent of their time advising students about college. Counselors at private schools, however, said they spend twice that amount of time—56 percent—on college issues and aren't required to take on issues that are bogging down public school counselors, such as keeping track of attendance records and attending to newly created anti-bullying programs. More than 50 percent of the private schools surveyed said they have at least one counselor whose only job is to advise students on college issues. Only 10 percent of public schools said they had a college-focused guidance counselor at their schools.

The role of the guidance counselor can't be understated, but regardless of how many guidance counselors there are at your school, you have to take responsibility for your college preparation and application process. It's up to you to make sure you're keeping up your student/guidance counselor relationship.

> **Real Life**
>
> "I don't remember ever meeting with a guidance counselor in high school. But I didn't have to go it alone because my father works in the high school system, and my older brother had gone through the process and was admitted to Brown University three years earlier."
>
> —Steven Tom, Cornell Class of 2001, and a product of a public high school

Getting on the Same Page

Many students coming into the ninth grade don't possess the kind of maturity necessary to set a goal and understand what it means to achieve that goal. For those who can grasp that concept, it means getting down to business on day one and mapping out a high school future that will get them into top colleges. And it's not only the students and the guidance counselors who have to be on the same page—the parents have to be part of the discussions as well. Parents often have loftier goals for their children than their children are ready or willing to accept. And sometimes, parents underestimate what their children are able to accomplish.

I once had a high schooler's mother call me early on in his freshman year to tell me that the boy would be attending nothing less than an Ivy League school after he graduated. Having no grades to go on yet, I spoke with his teachers, who described a student who was lazy, talked in class, and had to have his seat moved. Three years later, the student was lucky to be admitted to a State University of New York system college that was not even one of the top state schools. This is the perfect example of everyone not being on the same page.

Having been a high school guidance counselor for 30 years, I would tell you the time to start thinking about getting into a top college is the ninth grade. Those discussions could occur even earlier if you want to factor in whether a student would have a better chance at a top college if she attends a private high school. So, to students, I would say sit down with your guidance counselor first thing during your freshman year and get on the same page. To parents, don't wait to discuss with your children the complexities and hard work that go into getting into a top college. Students need to understand that what they do in school, both academically and personally, has a direct impact on the rest of their lives.

Expectations of Your Guidance Counselor

When you walk into a guidance counselor's office with the goal of attending an Ivy or other top college, that's a very specific outlook on where you want your high school career to take you. Your needs are not necessarily greater than those of other students, but they definitely take on a different sense of urgency.

The role of a high school guidance counselor is several fold. Basically, their duties range from working with students to create curriculums that are in line with the schools they want to attend, meeting with students to discuss college options, hosting college representatives, reviewing applications, and organizing school tours.

> **Real Life**
>
> Jeffrey Brenzel, Dean of Admissions at Yale, spelled it out pretty clearly in a 2008 article for *The New York Times* when he said a counselor's two more important roles are: "helping students understand the range of colleges to which they are reasonably likely to win acceptance and helping students understand how to present themselves effectively in an application."

Sounds simple, right? But that covers everything from a counselor working with you on class selection to ensure that you're taking the most challenging curriculum possible, to advising you on what you should wear to an interview, or whether your application essay should be about challenges in your life or how you've bettered the lives of others.

Here's how the public school guidance counselors surveyed in 2007 by the National Association for College Admission Counseling said they spent their time:

Task	Frequently	Occasionally	Infrequently	Never
Develop curriculum	33%	35%	23%	9%
Organize tours	7%	24%	35%	34%
Host college representatives	70%	22%	5%	3%
Actively represent students to admissions officers	45%	34%	17%	4%
Review/proof applications	45%	32%	20%	3%
Counsel about financial aid/ scholarships	27%	53%	19%	1%
Meet with students individually	78%	20%	2%	0%

In a perfect world, you'd want a guidance counselor who checked the frequently box on all the tasks surveyed by the National Association for College Admission Counseling. You'd also want a guidance counselor who has good relationships with the admissions officers at Ivy League schools and other top colleges and someone who has been able to place students in those schools. You'd want someone who is able to offer you as much time as you'd like. In reality, though, you have to understand that you might be one of several hundred students your counselor is working with.

It's a lot of work, and most public school counselors have a lot of students and not a lot of time. That's why some parents send their students to private guidance counselors. The number of private counselors has increased dramatically since 2004, but I'll get to that and what private guidance counselors do later in this chapter.

Forming a Relationship with Your Guidance Counselor

The best way to begin building a strong relationship between you and your guidance counselor is to go in knowing what to ask and what to expect. You very well could end up with a guidance counselor who's willing to do little more than guide you through the application and standardized testing processes. In that case, you'll have to take on a much more active role with your college preparation and application process than you would if you were dealing with someone who routinely places students at Harvard.

You also have to consider the amount of experience your guidance counselor has. Someone who spent years as an admissions officer at an Ivy—which isn't uncommon for some private school counselors—obviously knows more about the process than someone in his second year of counseling.

Scheduling a Conference

A student and his parents should ask to sit down with a school's guidance counselor to go over what's expected out of the relationship. Not all schools require guidance counselors to make individual appointments with students, let alone their parents. And while the practice is much more common at private schools, a public school counselor should be receptive to meeting with you.

It's at these conferences, which should happen as early as the first couple of months of your freshman year, that you can establish realistic goals for yourself and your counselor that will get you into the college of your choice. Your desire to attend an Ivy or other top college shouldn't be a surprise to your counselor later down the road.

Cheat Sheet

Ask your guidance counselor if you could send him an e-mail ahead of your first meeting that includes some information about yourself. This way, your counselor can start to get to know you before even sitting down with you.

When you sit down with your counselor, he should begin to advise you on the following:

- What classes you should take
- When you should take the SAT 1 or ACT
- What relationships your counselor has with top schools

You also should ask your counselor for your high school's profile, which details which classes are available at your school and other information, including the school's demographics and how many students go on to college. Getting an early look at the profile will give you a head start at seeing what colleges will see when they compare your transcript with what's available at your school.

The Guidance Counselor as an Advocate

As I said earlier, your guidance counselor needs to be your advocate in addition to your adviser.

On the adviser side, you'll discuss early-entry applications and financial aid and scholarship scenarios that might sway which colleges you apply to and eventually attend. But the advocacy side likely is more important than the adviser side in that a lot of what comes out of your counselor's role as an adviser can be found in one of any number of books, including this one.

To make your guidance counselor an effective advocate, you have to be honest with him. Trouble at home or health issues that affect your performance are things you should share with your guidance counselor, who in turn will share that information with the colleges.

There are also several not-so-obvious things a counselor should share about you and your high school with the colleges you apply to. Classes, for instance, have different names at different schools. While a science class might have a simple-sounding name at your school, it might also be the hardest course available for you to take that year. That's something your counselor needs to pass along to the admissions offices. The same goes for a teacher who simply is unwilling to give a grade better than a B+. If that's the case, your guidance counselor should explain to Harvard and Princeton why you got a B in that class. Basically, the more information your guidance counselor is armed with and shares with admissions offices, the better off you'll be.

Remember, your guidance counselor can't lie about certain aspects of your education. They can't withhold portions of your transcript or say that you would have gotten an A in a class instead of a B if the teacher was nicer to you. But what the guidance counselor can do is offer insight into your school and you as a student. The counselor can explain that one of your B+ grades came in one of the school's toughest courses, a course that traditionally nets only one A per year. You should follow up with your guidance counselor to make sure any pertinent information is being passed along to the colleges.

Gathering Information

Numerous websites are available that students can use to find out information about various colleges. Because your guidance counselor's time is limited, especially if you go to a public school, you should use these websites to vet a lot of your information before setting up a conference with your adviser. For instance, if you're averse to wearing heavy winter coats, long johns, and mittens, you might want to think about going to Stanford and not Yale.

The same thing goes for the area of study you're planning on pursuing. Give some serious thought to this on your own. Don't make your guidance counselor pull teeth and waste your limited time with him by making him question you on the basics. A guidance counselor can help you determine your strengths and weaknesses, but it's important to remember that almost 85 percent of college students change their majors. So while you want to focus on an area of study if you can, it's understood that you might change your mind.

Ultimately, this is your life. You have to make informed and educated decisions, and you need to be the captain of your own ship. So take on much of the research responsibility yourself. Find out when applications are due and what colleges require in terms of courses you need to take in high school and academic standards you need to maintain. Don't rely on your guidance counselor's knowledge alone.

Hiring Help

With admissions to top colleges more competitive than ever and the student-to-counselor ratio at public high schools growing annually, more high school students and their parents are choosing to hire private counselors or consultants. Not only are more students using privately hired counselors, but there are also more counselors out there to choose from. The Independent Education Consultants Association has seen its membership grow from 315 members in 2004 to more than 700 members in 2008. Most private counselors now stepping into the field either have retired from working in public or private high schools or were admissions officers at colleges.

Hiring a private counselor is far from a guarantee that you'll get into a top college, but in certain circumstances it can certainly help. You of course have to have the money to pony up, though.

What Private Counselors Do

Having done both jobs, I can tell you that there is a huge difference between what a high school counselor does and a private counselor does. As a private counselor, I have more time and ability to help students navigate their way through the complexities of the college search and selection system, which can be a daunting and overwhelming process.

Private counselors generally understand all aspects of the college admissions process and are able to provide insight and direction in helping to choose the right school. They have the time and knowledge to assess a student's records, goals, and objectives and can give step-by-step assistance in developing the strongest application possible.

As a private college counselor, I have the luxury of developing a comprehensive, individualized approach to ultimately finding a college that best fits a student.

But, not everyone believes in the services private consultants provide. Jeffrey Brenzel, Dean of Undergraduate Admissions at Yale, told the *Yale Daily News* that the services a consultant offers often "provide little or no advantage over what a student could gain by reading any one of a number of good books on the subject of making a strong application."

Credentials

If you decide to use a private counselor, the easiest way to find one is to open the phonebook or look on the Internet.

A Google search for "private college counselors" returns too many results to go through, but it's a start. You also can look on the Independent Educational Consultants Association's website at www.educationalconsulting.org to find a counselor who's a member of that group. Association members are required to have visited at least 100 campuses and have at least 3 years of counseling experience.

Most consulting websites list their successes. For instance, one leading consultant's website claims that it placed more than 400 students in Ivy League schools over a decade. Success stories are easy to come by on the Internet, so it's important to interview your potential consultant to make sure you're going to get the most out of the process. Ask for a consultant's references and talk to those people.

A private consultant should be:

- Someone you feel comfortable with

- Someone who will help you with the work but not do it for you

- Someone who will be straightforward and give you an honest assessment

There's also, of course, word of mouth. If you know of someone else who used a private consultant to help her gain entry into a top college, ask her who she used and what she got out of the experience. Even if you don't use the same consultant, you can ask questions that you can then turn around and use to interview your potential consultant. Ultimately, you want to find someone who fits your values and philosophical approach to college.

Beware _____

Find a private consultant whose office is located in your area. Although a lot of information can be passed via the Internet, e-mail, and over the phone, it's not nearly as effective as meeting personally and as many times as needed.

Counselor/College Relationship

Years ago, the common thought was that colleges would deal only with guidance counselors from a student's school, but that's simply not the case. Although colleges get the official grading records and other related information from the school, most of the time college admissions officers are willing to hear from a private consultant speaking on a student's behalf.

While I was transitioning from a public high school counselor to a private consultant, I asked several college admissions people if they deal with the private sector, and the resounding answer was that they are happy to talk to anyone who can provide any information, shed any light, or help and contribute in any way as an advocate for the student.

In fact, if you're looking to attend Yale and can find a private consultant who spent years working in the Yale admissions office, that certainly could be a foot in the door for you.

What It Costs

The cost of private counseling ranges based on location and the services provided. Largely, however, you'd be hard-fought to find a quality counselor who will conduct more than a one-time assessment for less than $2,500.

College counselors command a much larger fee in metropolitan areas, the suburbs, and communities around major cities such as New York and Boston. Some consultants charge a flat rate; others charge by the hour. Still others charge by the hour and designate contact hours when they're meeting with the student and noncontact hours when they're researching information. The hourly rates for the contact and noncontact hours are the same, but you need to realize that you'll be paying for time not actually spent with the counselor. You're paying for time when the counselor is off working on his own on your behalf.

One leading consulting firm's website lays out two options for services and associated fees. The first option is a one-time consultation where in addition to reviewing the student's educational and personal profile, the adviser will discuss which classes should be taken in the future, develop a schedule for standardized tests, and come up with a list of potential colleges that fit the student's profile. This service costs $800.

The second service is ongoing counseling and gives the student unlimited access to advisers. Over the period of counseling, the adviser will guide the student through her school curriculum, review grades and standardized test scores, prepare the student for her college interviews, and even help make a student's initial course selection for college. This service costs $10,500, broken up into a $8,000 retainer and a $2,500 final, senior-year payment.

Going It Alone

You don't want to have to go through the college application process alone, but unfortunately you might have to. Whether it's because of a poorly performing or overburdened public school guidance counselor or a tight budget that doesn't allow you to hire a consultant, there's a chance that the brunt of what a guidance counselor would do will fall at your feet.

That being said, going it alone really should be your last option. If you can't afford a private consultant, you should make every attempt to ensure your relationship with your school guidance counselor works out. If you don't get along with your assigned guidance counselor, see if there's another one who can take on your case.

Try to make your relationship with your guidance counselor work out. More times than not, he'll go the extra mile for you if you show a passion and willingness to go the extra mile on your end.

I worked in the public school system for 30 years, and during that time I probably worked with more than 25 counselors. Except for one or two isolated cases, everyone I worked with was knowledgeable, dedicated, caring, and hard working. Given all that, the job description and time management at public high schools simply does not allow for counselors to give the level of service and time needed to do what a private counselor does.

Cheat Sheet

If you don't like your school counselor and can't afford a private counselor, your options are limited. Some private counseling services do take on clients *pro bono*, but those cases are a fraction of a firm's usual clientele. IvyWise, a leading consulting service, takes on one pro bono case for every seven students the firm works with. To pitch yourself as a potential pro bono case, be sure to highlight your merits as a student and your dedication to getting into a top college.

The Least You Need to Know

◆ Your relationship with a guidance counselor should begin in early ninth grade.

◆ Guidance counselors are advocates in addition to advisers.

◆ Private consultants can aid the college process but also can be expensive.

◆ Whether you use a school counselor or private consultant, you're ultimately responsible for your own path.

Chapter 5

Talent Searches

In This Chapter

- ◆ Benefits of talent searches
- ◆ Which search serves which region?
- ◆ The country's top competitions
- ◆ What is expected out of a science project

Whether for students in high school or even younger, there are programs across the country designed to help academically gifted students make the most of their talents.

Although the programs for both groups—those already in high school and those in elementary or middle school—are called talent searches, they're a bit different in what they offer. The programs for students not yet in high school are aimed at students' potential and helping the students and their families figure out which academic level they're on and how they should move forward. At the high school level, it's time for that potential to turn into results, usually in the form of a math or science project.

Wherever you are in your academic career, these talent searches are useful and could be just what you need to put you over the top in the minds of college admissions officials.

Searching for the Brightest

What is a talent search like for students not yet in high school?

Just as it sounds, these programs are intended to find the brightest students and help them navigate academic careers that will keep them challenged and engaged. These talent searches usually focus on students from grades 2–8 and assess their intelligence by administering exams that are grades above what the students see in school.

No matter where you live, a talent search program is available to you. Four major talent search programs serve the country. The program you join depends on where you live. Here are a few examples:

   ◆ The Duke University Talent Identification Program (TIP) serves the Southeast and most of middle America.

   ◆ The Johns Hopkins University Center for Talented Youth (CTY) serves the Northeast and West.

   ◆ The Northwestern University Center for Talent Development serves the Midwest.

   ◆ The University of Denver Rocky Mount Talent Search serves the Rocky Mountain region.

For a full list of which states each talent search serves, see Appendix G.

Cheat Sheet _____

Most talent search programs will consider reducing or waiving their fees for students from families who can't afford the services. A decision on whether the fee will be adjusted is typically determined by whether the student qualifies for free or reduced lunch.

The four talent search programs offer similar services and are basically in line with one another. I'll explain each program in more depth as this chapter continues.

Duke TIP

The Duke program offers talent searches for fourth/fifth graders and seventh graders.

"These talent searches help gifted students and their families find out how advanced the students' abilities truly are," according to the Duke website. "Traditional testing often fails to measure the variation among many gifted students who reach the upper limits of scoring on grade-level exams. By taking advanced above-level (at least two years above a student's current grade placement) testing through Duke TIP's talent searches, gifted students and their families gain a far better understanding of where the student stands in relation to his/her gifted peers and what level of educational challenge is appropriate."

The Duke seventh grade program is the largest in the nation and has been active for almost 30 years. More than 1.5 million students have gone through the program since 1980. In the seventh grade program, students are asked to take the SAT or ACT. Duke TIP then runs an assessment of the student's test and score and advises the student on her academic abilities and the educational opportunities open to her.

Here's a sample of Duke TIP suggestions for students who score at the 75th percentile or above on a section of the SAT or ACT:

◆ Concurrent or dual enrollment. Students are enrolled in elementary school and middle school, or middle school and high school, or high school and college simultaneously.

◆ Whole grade acceleration. Students are advanced to the next grade level in all subject areas.

◆ Early entrance into college.

The Duke TIP program also comes with other perks. One is the ability to participate in scholar weekends during which students receive instruction in subjects that typically wouldn't be available to them in middle or high school.

Duke TIP students also are eligible for regional and national recognitions based on how well they scored on their SAT or ACT. The recognition and certificate showing that a student was the best of the best could be the most important part of the Duke TIP program.

Duke TIP is open to students who have scored at the 95th percentile or higher on the national norms of a grade-level standardized achievement, aptitude, mental ability, or approved state criterion-referenced test. The program costs less than $100.

Admission into Duke TIP's fourth/fifth grade program follows similar testing requirements. Instead of asking students to take the SAT or ACT, the fourth grade program focuses on the *Explore test* and on working with the students, their families, and their schools to

def•i•ni•tion

The **Explore test** was created by the ACT and is designed to assess how prepared eighth and ninth graders are for high school.

create education opportunities in their communities that will help them advance academically and keep them challenged.

Johns Hopkins CTY

The Johns Hopkins CTY talent search is a vehicle to "assess and recognize students with exceptional mathematical and/or verbal reasoning abilities." Getting its start in 1972, the Johns Hopkins talent search program really put talent searching on the map and became the standard.

There are two Johns Hopkins talent search programs. One is available to students in grades 2–6, and one is for students in grades 7 and 8. Under both programs, students take advance-level tests to see where they are academically and where they need to be challenged.

"Once testing is over, families receive a copy of test results and, later in the spring, guidance materials to help them understand what their above-grade-level test score means, and how to use this information when planning the student's education," states the program's website. "All children receive recognition certificates for their participation. High-scoring students in all grades will be invited to state awards ceremonies, as well."

The criteria for entering the Johns Hopkins program and the fees are similar to those of the Duke TIP.

Northwestern's Talent Search

Northwestern University's Midwest Academic Talent Search started in 1981 and is offered to students in grades 3–9. The Northwestern program uses the same tests as Duke and Johns Hopkins, offering the Explore test for students in grades 3–6 and the SAT or ACT for grades 6–9.

As with the other talent search programs, the assessment that's provided after the test is completed is the real benefit. "Imagine that you're measuring a roomful of kids with a yardstick. That's fine for the kids who are shorter than three feet, but for those who are taller, the yardstick is an inadequate tool," state's Northwestern's website. "The same is true for gifted kids—to measure their abilities, you need a better tool than a grade-level test, one that can measure above that 99th percentile where the yardstick ends."

The Northwestern talent search fees and admission criteria are similar to those of the other programs.

Rocky Mount

The Rocky Mountain Academic Talent
Search also serves grades 3–9 and is administered through the University of Denver.

Everything from the program's fees to its
admission requirements are in line with the
other talent search programs mentioned.
The Rocky Mountain program also offers
testing assessment, certificates of recognition,
and counseling services.

Beware

The ACT's Explore exam is
not administered as widely
as the ACT and the SAT; some
states don't administer the test at
all. This fact might require that
you travel a good distance to
take the test.

Why Talent Searches

If your in-school test scores are high enough that you qualify for one of the talent
search programs, then that's an accomplishment in itself and you should take advantage of it. Participating in a talent search doesn't cost much, and you can take the tests
anywhere they're administered. The programs themselves provide tons of opportunities and advantages that go well beyond simply adding them to your resumé.

To begin with, participating in a talent search program and scoring well on the
advanced tests could open the door for you to participate in a prestigious summer
program. All of the four sites that offer the talent search programs also have highly
touted summer programs that go well beyond assessment and expose students to areas
of study that they'd likely otherwise not have access to.

The whole experience will help you mature and give you an idea of what taking the
SAT or ACT will be like, and the more experience you have the better off you'll be.

The Contests

If the talent searches are intended to assess a student's academic abilities and potential,
the contests are when those abilities start to pay dividends. Several contests cover a
number of academic areas, but some contests are more prestigious than others.

Although winning a contest could be your ticket to a top college, just trying your hand
at a contest shows that you're willing to step out of your comfort zone and put yourself out there. You're willing to take chances, and that's what schools like to see.

The Science Talent Search

The Science Talent Search (STS) sponsored by Intel is the granddaddy of them all when it comes to academic contests and talent searches.

"The Science Talent Search is America's oldest and most prestigious science research competition for high school seniors. Since 1942, first in partnership with Westinghouse and since 1998 with Intel, the competition has provided a national stage for America's best and brightest young scientists to present original research to nationally recognized professional scientists," according to the STS website.

Every year 40 finalists are selected from a pool of thousands to attend the week-long Science Talent Institute where students present their research projects to the public and members of the National Academy of Sciences.

Not only is participation and success with STS great for your college resumé, but it's also a great way to help pay for college. More than $1 million is awarded annually to Intel STS participants and their schools. The awards range from $5,000 scholarship grants and laptop computers for all finalists to a $100,000 college scholarship as the grand prize.

> **Real Life** _____
>
> "This is how I'm going to get to college, and I've met so many people through science fairs. I have friends in Peru, Russia, and Egypt. It's been really great, and I want more people to get interested in science fairs. It doesn't change who you are, and it doesn't make you a nerd. You could be helping somebody."
>
> —Taylor Wood, a Louisiana high schooler who won an $8,000 scholarship at the 2008 Intel International Science and Engineering Fair for her work on mosquito repellants

Again, participating in the STS certainly won't hurt your chances of admission to a top college, even if you're not selected as one of the finalists. After all, only 40 finalists are selected every year, and there are many more than 40 students admitted to top schools.

Just taking on the challenge of trying to become an STS finalist and submitting your project is an accomplishment on its own. Colleges want to see that you have initiative and are willing to work toward large goals.

So what kinds of projects win awards with STS? Here's a list of the 2008 award winners.

- Shivani Sud, North Carolina—First Place: $100,000
  Shivani Sud, 17, submitted a bioinformatics and genomics project that focused on identifying stage II colon cancer patients at high risk for recurrence and the best therapeutic agents for treating their tumors.

- Graham William Wakefield Van Schaik, South Carolina—Second Place: $75,000
  Graham William Wakefield Van Schaik, 17, completed a two-year study of the long-term effects of exposure to pyrethroids, commonly found in household and agricultural pesticides.

- Brian Davis McCarthy, Oregon—Third Place: $50,000
  Brian Davis McCarthy, 18, focused his research on developing new types of solar cells. Brian synthesized extremely thin and fragile films and verified his results using scanning electron microscopy techniques.

- Katherine Rose Banks, New York—Fourth Place: $25,000
  Katherine Rose Banks, 17, submitted a mathematics paper in combinatorial geometry. A lattice polygon in the plane is a polygon each of whose vertices has integer coordinates; such points are called lattice points. Katie gave a proof of a conjecture of S. Rabinowitz that a convex lattice polygon with nine vertices cannot have exactly eight or nine interior lattice points.

- Eric Nelson Delgado, New Jersey—Fifth Place: $25,000
  Eric Nelson Delgado, 18, studied the use of novel efflux pump inhibitors (EPI) to improve the efficacy of antibiotics against multidrug-resistant bacteria. One way bacteria disable antibiotics is to use an efflux pump mechanism to expel the antibiotics from their cells.

The Siemens Foundation

The Siemens Foundation provides more than $7 million a year in support of advancement in science, technology, engineering, and math. It also sponsors the prestigious Siemens Competition in Math, Science & Technology. Competition within this contest, which began in 1998, is fierce, and it attracts almost 2,000 students in the individual and team competitions who work on more than 1,200 projects.

National finalists can win up to $100,000 in scholarships through the contest. Unlike the Intel contest, Siemens does allow for group or team entries.

So where do Siemens's national finalists come from? Here are the states that had the most national finalists from 1999–2007:

- New York (37)
- Texas (18)
- California (16)
- North Carolina (13)
- Tennessee (10)
- Michigan (8)
- Connecticut (5)
- Oregon (5)
- Illinois, Florida, Massachusetts, and Ohio (4 each)
- Hawaii, Maryland, New Jersey, Pennsylvania, and Wisconsin (3 each)
- Alabama, Alaska, Georgia, Indiana, Iowa, Kentucky, Minnesota, and Virginia (2 each)
- Kansas, Maine, Missouri, New Mexico, and Pennsylvania (1 each)

What It Takes to Win

Well, if I knew *exactly* what it took to win a national contest, then I would be a millionaire several times over. In general, though, you need a great project and you need to be creative. The projects that reach the finalist level might end up being incredibly difficult to explain to the average person, but they also are practical. For example, a 2007 Siemens finalist came up with a way to ensure that ground beef is cooked safely in commercial kitchens.

You also have to understand that participation in these contests will stretch you well beyond what you're able to accomplish at your high school. Several finalists come from public high schools that don't have significant laboratory resources. So, don't dismiss your contest chances by saying that your school doesn't have the resources for you to compete. You might have to team with a local community college or private college. That sometimes might mean driving several hours on the weekend to get your work done.

Working on a research project intended for one of these competitions is no small task and requires a significant amount of dedication from you and the people who are helping you. Here are some other things to consider when choosing and working on your contest project:

◆ **Creativity.** As cliché as it sounds, you need to think outside of the box. Many contests not only want to see a successful project, but also want to know how the student was imaginative in coming up with that project.

◆ **Explanation.** Make sure that your interpretations and conclusions are stated clearly. What you've done might make sense to you, but if you don't explain it clearly it might not be understood by others.

◆ **Presentation.** Your project might be the best work, but if it's not presented in a clear and concise manner that fact might not come through to the judges.

◆ **Practicality.** Consider how your work could be improved upon in the future and what future applications it could be applied to. The future applications aspect is critical to the project's practicality.

◆ **Teamwork.** If it is a team project, make sure you clearly define how each member of the team contributed to the overall work.

The Least You Need to Know

◆ Four major talent search programs serve the country.

◆ Talent searches give students the ability to assess where they stand academically and position themselves for prestigious summer programs.

◆ National contests are great for a student's resumé, even if his project isn't selected as a finalist.

◆ Contest prizes can be as much as $100,000 for finalists.

Chapter 6

High School Alternatives

In This Chapter

- ◆ How to stand out as a homeschooled student
- ◆ The difference between high school and homeschool diplomas
- ◆ How colleges look at public and private schools
- ◆ The pros and cons of private schools

Getting into a top college is pretty straightforward, right? Getting good grades, scoring well on your standardized tests, and being active outside of school is all it takes. But any number of variables go into the acceptance process. What if you've never set foot inside a high school? Or, what if your parents want to take you out of public school to put you in a private school? Will your chances of getting into a top college increase?

Almost all top schools will tell you that they use a holistic approach for determining who they offer acceptance to. That means they look at the whole of what you're submitting and don't break down the application and analyze all its parts separately. They want well-rounded, high-achieving students—but that's not to say applications that come in from home-schooled students or those from top private schools aren't looked at a little bit differently.

Homeschooling and attending a private school are options if your family has the time and money. Each comes with advantages and disadvantages, but neither guarantees or dooms your admittance to a top college.

Homeschooled Students

Homeschool programs aren't just for people living out on a farm, and they're not all about the mother of a family teaching several children. A homeschool instructor doesn't necessarily have to be a parent, though it frequently is. Basically, the homeschool environment enables the instructor and student to select a curriculum that plays to the student's interests and strengths and allows him to learn at his own pace.

Homeschooled students no longer are a fringe element looked down upon by those who attend traditional high schools. Estimates of the number of students in the United States being homeschooled range from 2.5 million to 4 million. Some estimate the annual rate of growth among homeschooled students between 7 percent and 15 percent.

As the number of homeschooled students has increased, schools have had to take another look at how they handle those applicants. There are few schools in the country that won't accept a homeschooled student, and the acceptance rate for homeschooled students is actually better at some top schools than that of the acceptance rate for students coming out of traditional high schools. While top colleges will give a homeschooled student a fair look, several want to see that the student has taken one or two courses in a traditional classroom setting to demonstrate that she can learn in that traditional arena.

Still, dealing with a student who is both the valedictorian and last-ranked student in his class is tricky for many top schools. But as is the story for any other student, it comes down to taking on a challenging curriculum and presenting yourself as a unique student who can't be passed up.

Curriculum

Attending high school at home really is no different from stepping into a building with 500 other students every day when it comes to applying to a top college. Schools want to see you challenge yourself just as they would a traditional student. So, that means taking top-level classes and tests, including AP courses and SAT 2 exams. Because you're not attending a traditional school admissions officers will give your application a longer look to make sure that your classes are up to par with those of your competitors.

I didn't mention International Baccalaureate (IB) classes because IB classes and degrees are not available to homeschooled students. Only students enrolled in IB World Schools can take IB classes, so that is an opportunity you miss out on by staying at home. However, it's not something you can't overcome.

Several resources for homeschool curriculums are available, and a quick search of the Internet can provide you with enough information to last you for days. Just like high schools, homeschool curriculums can have different focuses, whether it be science, math, or the arts. You should look for a curriculum that will enable you to take top-level math and science courses and will provide the same all-around course selection discussed in Chapter 7.

You have certain freedoms when learning at home, but remember that admissions officers will be that much more critical of your application than that of a traditional student. So, make sure you're taking the most difficult course load possible.

Are All Diplomas Equal?

If you follow your state's laws for homeschooling, whomever undertakes the majority of the instruction can order a diploma online, sign it, and presto, you have a high school diploma.

But the ordered and signed diplomas don't come from an accredited group. Most accredited groups have to undergo a lengthy certification process from any number of organizations, such as the National Association of Private Schools, to be recognized as accredited diploma-granting facilities. Throughout the country there are homeschool consortiums that give homeschooled students and their instructors an opportunity to be part of a homeschool community. The consortium looks out for the interests of the homeschoolers, including legislative issues, and provides opportunities to associate with accredited diploma-granting facilities.

Beware

Not all accrediting agencies are legitimate. Although colleges and universities that say they're accredited have to receive that accreditation from an agency recognized by the U.S. Department of Education of Council for Higher Education, no such oversight exists for high schools or homeschool agencies. Be sure you research the accrediting agency you're considering.

Accredited agencies also serve as umbrella groups for homeschooled students. These agencies can guide the student and instructor on which courses to take and how to get involved in athletics and other extracurricular activities.

These accredited agencies also, for lack of a better term, vouch for your diploma and are willing to say you've received a proper high school education. But not all colleges require accredited diplomas. According to a study conducted by the National Center for Home Education, about 70 percent of colleges accept parent-prepared transcripts in place of accredited diplomas, and many of the nation's top schools are included in that group.

Requirements

There's no formula homeschooled students have to abide by to ensure admission into a top school. Schools have different policies for how they judge homeschoolers and what they require of them as far as the application goes.

MIT, for instance, does not have separate requirements for homeschooled applicants. "Homeschooled applicants, like all of our applicants, are considered within their context, which includes schooling choice, family situation, geographic location, resources, opportunities, and challenges," the school's website states.

On the other hand, Notre Dame and some other schools require homeschooled applicants to submit test scores not required of candidates from traditional schools. The university uses SAT 2, AP, and IB scores for traditional applicants only if the applicant submits them because he feels they enhance an application. However, homeschoolers are required to take three SAT 2 exams—one each in history, foreign language, and science. It's important that you check with the schools you plan on applying to in order to make sure you understand what they require of homeschoolers.

Cheat Sheet

The College-Level Examination Program (CLEP) is another way for homeschooled and traditional students to show what they've learned. Administered by the College Board, the CLEP is touted as a way students can receive college credit for "what they already know." Thirty-four tests are offered under CLEP, and no classes are associated with the tests. Simply put, if you feel you know a subject well enough through your work in other classes and at a job, you can take a CLEP test. About 2,900 colleges grant credit for CLEP tests if you score high enough, but an overwhelming majority of top colleges don't. Even though many top colleges don't offer credit for CLEP, it could be a way to show additional success along with your AP grades.

Standing Out

If you're going to apply to a top college as a homeschooled student, you have to do more than applicants from traditional schools to make yourself stand out. That means participating in summer courses and extracurricular activities and contributing to your community. Just because you're not part of a traditional school doesn't mean you can't participate in the kinds of activities traditional students partake in.

MIT, for instance, doesn't have a specific mold it likes homeschoolers to fit into, but the school's website does suggest ways those students can make themselves stand out to gain acceptance.

Cheat Sheet _____

Depending on what school district you're in you may be able to participate in clubs and athletics at the traditional high school even if you're being homeschooled. Check the laws that govern your area schools to find out.

"One quality that we look for in all of our applicants is evidence of having taken initiative, showing an entrepreneurial spirit, and taking full advantage of opportunities," MIT's website states. "Many of our admitted homeschooled applicants have really shined in this area. These students truly take advantage of their less constrained educational environments to take on exciting projects, go in-depth in topics that excite them, create new opportunities for themselves and others, and more."

Cheat Sheet _____

Advice from earlier in this book that community college classes aren't necessarily worth your time doesn't apply to homeschooled students. In many instances, local colleges are your best opportunity to take challenging classes, which is a critical component of your application.

Traditional high schools aren't the only source of extracurricular activities. Homeschooled students can partake in community drama and volunteer clubs and can even play sports on local teams outside of the high school. You have to be a well-rounded student, just like one coming out of a traditional school.

Additionally, MIT suggests that you submit extra recommendations, though not more than five, to give admissions officers a clearer picture of who you are. Recommendations can come from coaches you've played for, volunteers you've worked with, or a boss that you've had.

Acceptance

The rate of acceptance and number of homeschooled students attending the nation's colleges and universities are hard to come by. But anecdotally, officials say the rate of acceptance for homeschooled students often is higher than that of traditional students. However, that increased rate often can be attributed to the much lower number of homeschooled applicants.

> **Real Life**
>
> "A lot of colleges are saying that homeschoolers are a good population to pursue. They've had positive results dealing with homeschooled students, and so they actively go out and look for them."
>
> —Hal Young, Education Vice President for North Carolinians for Home Education

Stanford is said to accept about a quarter of the less than 100 applications from homeschooled students it receives per year, and Harvard accepts about 10 homeschooled students a year out of the almost 200 who apply.

What's important to note is that all schools do accept homeschooled students. Increased test scores from that group have forced the nation's colleges to take notice. So, don't worry about getting a fair shake from the school you're applying to. Just worry about setting yourself up for success and going the extra mile in every facet of your education and community work.

Here are some general tips for finding your way through the college application process as a homeschooled student:

◆ Check the homeschool admission policies of each school you're applying to.

◆ Make sure you're aware of application deadlines. You won't have help from a guidance counselor like traditional students do, though you can consider hiring a private counselor.

◆ If you don't have a transcript, you have to provide colleges with a detailed academic record outlining the courses and tests you've taken along with any other academic work, including research projects.

◆ Know which standardized tests you have to take. Some schools require additional testing of homeschooled applicants.

◆ Show that you're prepared for college-level work through AP courses and CLEP tests and by taking courses at area colleges.

◆ Recommendations from parents aren't always allowed despite the fact that the primary teacher for many homeschoolers is a parent. Make sure you establish other relationships that will lead to recommendations.

- Be sure you find ways to engage in the same extracurricular activities that are available to traditional students.

- Consider summer programs, including COSMOS in California and those offered by other top colleges, to show how you stack up against other students.

- Choose to be interviewed by the schools you're applying to, even if the interview is optional. You want to make sure that the colleges get every opportunity to find out who you are.

Public Versus Private

A lot can be made of the advantages of going to a private school over a public one, especially for those students striving to gain admission to a top college. From smaller student-teacher ratios to the additional time guidance counselors are able to take with each student, private schools certainly have their advantages—and the numbers back it up.

A 2007 *Wall Street Journal* survey found that the 10 high schools that were best at placing graduates at Harvard, Princeton, MIT, Williams, Pomona, Swarthmore, the University of Chicago, or Johns Hopkins all were private schools. Those high schools were able to place an average of 19 percent of their graduates at those colleges.

It would be an overstatement to say that attending a private high school is your best shot at getting into your first-choice top college, though. In fact, more and more private school students are transferring to public schools because parents think their children will have just as good of a chance of gaining admission and because they'll be able to save money.

Pros and Cons

Public and private schools each come with their advantages and disadvantages. First, you have to consider the costs associated with attending a private school. Tuition for private schools can be very pricey and rival the cost of some top colleges—upwards of $30,000 a year for some boarding schools.

Just like colleges, private high schools do offer scholarships and aid, and loans are a possibility. But you have to weigh the decision of accumulating debt before you even set foot in college.

Although private schools can be pricey, some of them offer the one-on-one attention needed to help you get into a top college. In addition to smaller classes, better facilities and resources, and more time with guidance counselors, some private schools are a pipeline into the country's top colleges. Year after year those colleges come calling to recruit the private school's best students.

On the other hand, competition can be tougher at a private school, and because of the smaller classes and higher standards you'll have to do that much more to make top colleges notice you. At the average public high school, however, you'll likely have a lower ratio of students looking to apply to top colleges, which means it'll be easier to establish yourself as the cream of the crop.

Changing Schools

If your family doesn't have the time for homeschooling or the resources for private school but you're in a "failing" high school, there are some options that you can explore. Under the federal No Child Left Behind Act, students at schools that routinely don't meet federal standards can transfer to better-peforming schools.

In addition, several public school districts throughout the country have magnet schools. These schools have a specialized focus in any number of subjects such as science, technology, or art. Admittance to these schools is open to any student in the district, but you usually have to show proficiency in the subject being offered and test well enough to get into the school. Because magnet schools are public schools, they aren't looked at with the same prestige as some of the country's top private secondary schools.

The same goes for charter schools, which are publicly funded but can offer alternative programs, such as Montessori instruction. Other charter schools offer a majority of their coursework online.

Some communities have school voucher programs that allow parents to take their children out of public schools and place them in private schools with help from state-level subsidies. Vouchers are a controversial issue and aren't offered widely.

If you're in a situation where you want to get out of your public high school but can't afford a private school, research the laws in your area to see whether voucher programs are available. You also should look into magnet and charter schools that might better fit your needs.

The Least You Need to Know

♦ Homeschooled students are given fair treatment from the admissions offices of top colleges.

♦ Homeschooled students must take the toughest classes available to make themselves stand out.

♦ Private schools are the most successful high schools at feeding students into top colleges.

♦ Opportunities are available for students who want to get out of failing high schools.

Part 2

Moving Forward

Once in high school, a top student's world becomes a maze of class selections, exams, extracurricular activities, and admission tests. Making your way through that maze and making the correct decision at each turn could be the difference between admission and rejection.

In Part 2, I talk about each of these issues and how to deal with them. Each could end up resulting in an unbearable amount of stress, but they don't have to. As I discuss, if you make peace with the idea of following the toughest route and succeeding at the task in front of you, you'll be okay.

"How can I possibly get ahead if you're not offering AP Gym or AP Wood Shop?"

Chapter 7

Selecting Your Classes

In This Chapter

- ◆ Picking challenging classes
- ◆ The importance of Advanced Placement courses and the International Baccalaureate Program
- ◆ Choosing electives
- ◆ Steering clear of senioritis

Being a straight-A student won't help you get into a top school if you're taking the wrong classes, which means course selection in high school is just as important as it is in college. I'd make this chapter on course selection the first chapter of the book if I could: It's that important.

If you grasp only one concept from this chapter, it is that the country's top schools want you to challenge yourself.

I'll take that one step further by saying the most competitive schools are looking for students who have challenged themselves with a demanding curriculum and electives and, of course, have been able to succeed.

What's Required?

Your freshman and sophomore years in high school will be taken up by a lot of necessary evils. You should consider them rights of passage and get used to the fact that there are going to be a lot of classes you're not going to be able to get out of. Even if you want to study fifteenth-century English literature at Harvard, you're going to have to take a challenging—there's that key word again—and well-rounded course load that includes plenty of math and science.

The Minimum

Most high schools require that you take four years of science and three years of math to graduate. But I can't imagine anyone getting into Harvard or any top school without at least four years of math. I say *at least* because many students begin high school math in eighth grade and actually end up with five years of math, including calculus.

Here's what graduation requirements look like at New York's Bronx High School of Science, which is one of the country's elite high schools. It has produced more than 100 finalists for the Intel (formerly Westinghouse) Science Talent Search and annually places students in top colleges and universities across the country:

- Four years of English
- Three years of math
- Four years of social studies
- Four years of laboratory science
- Three years of foreign language
- One year of technical drawing or sophomore research
- Half a year of music appreciation
- Half a year of art appreciation
- Half a year of science technique
- Half a year of health
- Four years of physical education
- A senior-year science or math elective
- A senior-year fifth major

How does that jibe with what most top colleges like to see in their incoming freshman? Here's what the typical list of minimum requirements for a top college looks like:

- Four years of English
- Four years of math (usually through calculus)
- Three years of social studies
- Three years of laboratory science
- Three years of foreign language

It might seem like you won't have a lot of time to pick the classes you really want to take when having to deal with so many graduation requirements and *prerequisites*, but that's where electives, Advanced Placement (AP), International Baccalaureate (IB), and honors classes come in. But we'll get back to that in a bit.

def•i•ni•tion

Prerequisites are the classes you need to take before you're able to take top-level high school courses. Some high schools might require that you take an honors-level English class before you can take AP English.

High School Equality

Not all high schools were born equal. It's just the truth. For example, consider Basis Tucson in Arizona, which topped *Newsweek*'s 2008 list of the country's top public schools.

All of Basis's core subject courses are either AP or *honors courses*, according to the charter school's website. The school's curriculum also runs on an advanced track that allows students to enter college after three years of high school.

The question is, do admissions officers give a student from an average high school the same look as someone who goes to Basis? Colleges do understand that not all high schools have the same course offerings, but there are things students can do to bridge that gap.

Dartmouth, for one, does not have specific subject requirements for prospective students

def•i•ni•tion

Honors courses are deemed advanced-level classes by individual high schools. Unlike AP classes, they don't have a standardized test at the end of the year that gives an equal comparison of students from around the country.

but simply asks that high schoolers take the strongest course load available to them. Again, the school asks that you challenge yourself.

But if you do find yourself in a weaker performing school, other options might be available to you. See Chapter 6, where I discuss homeschooling and private school options.

The Classes

When you're faced with AP courses and the International Baccalaureate program, high school starts to look like the periodic table of elements. But AP courses and the IB program are critical components to getting into a top college. Then, you have to throw honors courses and electives into the mix. It's all enough to make an already stressed high schooler that much more on edge.

Although the classes are tough, choosing them doesn't have to be. It's just a matter of knowing where you will succeed and then applying yourself.

Honors Classes

As you select your courses every year, you need to be mindful of the various levels of courses available and select the most challenging courses offered. That means you need a lot of honors classes on your transcript.

Just as some high schools offer more AP courses than others, the same goes for honors classes. But just like AP classes, you'll need top grades to secure yourself a seat. Some schools even require recommendations to gain entrance into an honors class.

Advanced Placement Courses

You don't have to be a rocket scientist to understand what AP courses are all about—the name sort of gives it away. Run by the College Board, AP classes essentially give students an opportunity to take college-level classes at the high school level.

The majority of AP courses are offered and taken during your junior and senior years by virtue of the fact that they correspond to courses typically offered during those years. U.S. history, for instance, typically is offered in eleventh grade. Though schools don't require that you wait until your junior year to take AP classes—there are exceptions—it is the natural course of events that leads a student to take AP classes in her junior and senior years. In preparation for this, students should take every honors or advanced course available to them in their freshman and sophomore years.

Thirty-seven AP courses and exams are offered in 22 subject areas. Final exams for AP classes are graded on a scale from 1 to 5. Most top colleges give college credit for an AP class if you receive a score of 4 or better on the AP exam.

Even though not every high school offers all these classes, the following AP courses are offered by the College Board:

- Art history
- Biology
- Calculus AB
- Calculus BC
- Chemistry
- Chinese language and culture
- Comparative government and politics
- Computer science A
- Computer science AB
- Macroeconomics
- Microeconomics
- English language
- English literature
- Environmental science
- European history
- French language
- French literature
- German language
- Human geography
- Italian language and culture
- Japanese language and culture
- Latin literature
- Latin: Vergil
- Music theory
- Physics B
- Physics C
- Psychology
- Spanish language
- Spanish literature
- Statistics
- Studio art
- U.S. government and politics
- U.S. history
- World history

Taking as many of these courses as possible is a great way to set yourself apart from other applicants. I find that students who select and do well in AP courses typically exhibit the maturity and skills necessary for success in college.

Just because you score a 4 or a 5 on an AP exam doesn't mean you have to accept the college credit, though. A lot of what you run into during an AP class is the same material you'll see your first year of college. But, even if you score well on an AP exam, it can sometimes be wise to skip the college credit and take a similar class your freshman year.

For example, I had a student take AP calculus (BC) and AP chemistry in his senior year. He graduated number 6 in a class of 450 and was accepted to both the University of Michigan and Yale as a chemical engineering major. He eventually chose Yale, and although he did well on those AP exams—scoring a 4 and 5—he chose not to take the college credits that were offered him, which would have resulted in him moving to the next levels of math and chemistry.

Instead, he opted to repeat the courses because, although he had gotten a start on his college-level work, he knew how difficult the rest of his course load his freshmen year at Yale was going to be. Sixty-six freshmen started Yale as chemical engineering students that year; four years later 19 graduated as chemical engineers, and he was one of them.

If the college does allow acceleration, the student does not have to pay for the credits that he doesn't have to take because of the AP classes. So, when you factor in the cost of one year at Yale, the savings can be quite a benefit.

Universities and colleges have varying policies regarding what you can do with your AP standing. Some schools allow you to enter as a sophomore, while others allow you to use your AP credit to take a term off during your sophomore year. It's up to you to find out how your AP credits will transfer to the college you want to attend.

Some studies act as proponents or opponents of the AP program, but a majority of research finds that students who take and succeed in AP classes are better prepared for college.

So, how many AP courses should you take if you want to get into a top school? The answer is easy: As many as you can.

> ### Real Life
>
> "Studies following students into college found that students who took one or more AP exams were more likely than students who did not take any AP exams to maintain a B average, graduate with honors, and have more course work in the subject areas of their AP Exams," according to a 2007 College Board research report.

The International Baccalaureate Program

The IB program is a worldwide program designed to challenge students with an international education and rigorous assessment, with a particular focus on exposing students to different cultures.

The IB program was started by the International Baccalaureate Organization in Geneva, Switzerland, in 1968. More than 600 high schools in the United States offer the IB Diploma program. That compares with more than 14,000 schools that offer AP classes.

The program, which is run by the International Baccalaureate Organization, offers three levels of courses that are adopted by individual schools, usually as magnet programs within a school district:

♦ A Primary Years program for ages 3–12

♦ A Middle Years program for ages 11–16

♦ A Diploma program instituted in high schools for ages 16–19

The number of high schools that offer the IB Diploma program worldwide increased from 1,115 in 2003 to 1,623 in 2007. Although IB is gaining in prominence across the country, it still isn't as well known as the AP program.

If you do opt for IB over AP, you should go all in and make sure you're on track to receive an IB diploma, instead of just an IB certificate. The IB diploma is a two-year program that includes classes in six groups: language, second language, individuals and societies, experimental sciences, mathematics and computer sciences, and the arts. Students typically are required to take higher-level exams in three of the six groups, and the diploma track culminates with a 40,000-word theory of knowledge essay.

Cheat Sheet

A student who chooses to receive an IB certificate instead of a diploma can take IB courses in her area of academic strength. The student will receive a certificate for each course successfully completed but will not be eligible for the IB diploma.

Remember how I told you to challenge yourself, though? In this case, that means going after the IB diploma and following through with the essay. It's a lot of work that not everyone is up to. But if you are up to it, it'll make your transcript stand out.

I recently had two seniors who enrolled in the IB program during their junior years, and both had planned on pursuing IB diplomas. One of the students still was part of the diploma process when she sent out her college applications, but she had decided to drop out of the diploma track by the time the admission interviews rolled around. During her interviews, both of her top schools were disappointed that she no longer was a diploma candidate, and both asked why she dropped down to the certificate program.

Admission into an IB program varies by school. Some high schools have no prerequisites or admission criteria for enrollment into an IB program, but others do require that you show proficiency in honors and other advanced-level courses.

AP Versus IB

Incoming freshman with an eye on a top college often ask which course load they should pursue, AP or IB.

There's really no hard-and-fast rule when it comes to picking one of them over another, and it's something that has been debated for years. The easy answer is that top colleges want to see one of the two on a student's transcript.

A 2004 article in *The Washington Post* profiled a "bitter debate" over AP and IB between parents, students, and faculty at two high schools. "In 1999, for instance, a committee of teachers, parents, and students at Woodson (Va.) voted 15 to 10 to reject a planned IB program because it meant losing AP," the article states.

But both the school that embraced AP and the one that went with IB had high participation and success rates and were able to place students at top schools. So where does that leave us?

Although founded in 1968, the IB program still is a relatively new phenomenon. But it is catching on with all universities and colleges.

Here's what Cornell's admission website has to say about the IB program: "Cornell is a leader among American Universities in enrolling undergraduate students who have earned the International Baccalaureate. Cornell regards the IB program as a rigorous advanced program of study .... Cornell may award credit and advanced standing for your IB Higher Level Exam test results."

The biggest difference between AP and IB is that IB is a whole embedded program, whereas AP classes are challenging and rigorous individual courses. IB leaves little room for creativity in terms of course selection. Seniors typically are allowed to take one elective, while eleventh graders don't have room for any electives. All the IB courses are laid out for students and fit like a puzzle.

Most top colleges award college credit for outstanding IB and AP test scores, although those standards are getting tougher all the time. Most top colleges traditionally have awarded credit for a score of 4 or better on the AP exams, but some now require the maximum 5 score.

Also, you can pursue an IB diploma and still take AP exams in certain subjects. Many AP and IB classes are co-seated, which means IB program students are in the same classes with students who aren't in the program but who plan to take the AP test in the course. The IB program students can choose to take the AP test for the class, but the students who are not in the IB program can only take the AP test and won't receive any credit toward IB.

Some schools do have both IB programs and AP classes. Albany High School in New York, for instance, offers 17 Advanced Placement classes and the International Baccalaureate diploma program.

Cheat Sheet

Look at what's available in your community if your school doesn't offer AP or IB programs. Consider internships and classes at an area college. But be careful because, although college classes can be interesting and challenging, they're somewhat subjective and not as prestigious as AP and IB.

Dual-Enrollment

Dual-enrollment is when a high school student is also taking classes at a local community college or university that go toward both college credit and a high school diploma.

Although the dual-enrollment trend has picked up over the past 10 years, more top colleges, including Princeton, now are deciding not to award college credit for so-called dual-enrollment classes.

Beware

Georgetown University advises students who are enrolled in joint high school/college programs to apply as first-year students and not to expect college credit for more than four courses. Participation in dual-enrollment programs will not "significantly shorten the length of a degree program at Georgetown," according to the university's website. Several other colleges are instituting the same policy.

Your Electives

Not all high schools have the same course offerings, but whenever possible, electives should reflect your passions and interests. For example, I tell students interested in majoring in English to pursue electives such as journalism, creative writing, playwriting, humanities, and public speaking.

Here are some basic tips to keep in mind when choosing electives:

◆ Not all high schools have the same standards for how many English, math, history, and science courses you need to take to graduate. So use your electives to make sure you take at least four solid classes in each of those subjects. For example, you can take a literature course to fulfill a fourth year of English.

◆ Use electives to show off your foreign language skills. If you can take more than two foreign languages without hurting your GPA, you should.

◆ Think about your career. It's wise to take classes that could help you with the profession you choose, and those classes also can help you earn a place in a particularly competitive college major, including business and engineering programs.

◆ If you have a hole in your schedule to fill, by all means try to fill it with an AP class.

Real Life

"Colleges first and foremost look for the core curriculum, but they also like to see the breadth and depth in the high school experience."
—Marybeth Kravets, an educational consultant and author, told to the College Board.

Slacking Off

Somehow, somewhere a myth was started that senior year was a time for taking an academic easy road. Guess again! The most competitive schools are looking for you to avail yourself of every academic opportunity your high school provides, and that goes for all four years.

Because a vast majority of students applying to Ivy League schools are qualified candidates, admissions officers look at those senior grades for two things:

◆ Senior classes should be as difficult as the classes you took during your freshman through junior years.

◆ Your grades should be consistent or better than what you already have presented on your transcript.

Senior year is a great time to take all the AP courses you previously didn't have the prerequisites or time in the day for. In all cases, except if you've been accepted in an early decision program, college admissions officers will scrutinize your senior mid-year grades.

Even if you were accepted early, colleges have mechanisms in place to keep track of your senior grades. If those grades start slipping, you can expect a letter in the mail asking for an explanation, or worse, taking your offer away.

You've worked hard for three years to get to this point, do you really want to throw it away now? Recognize the changes your senior year will bring and meet them head on. You'll be busy getting ready for social events and college, but remember that maintaining your grades needs to be the most important thing.

Here are some tips the College Board offers for fending off senioritis:

- Maintain a challenging course load that will force you to open the books. Continue to schedule AP classes you might be able to turn into college credits.

- Continue your involvement with athletic teams and other community and extracurricular activities. The responsibilities you take on will force you to stay focused.

- If you're interested in a certain subject you want to pursue further, challenge yourself by taking a class in that subject at a local college.

The Least You Need to Know

- Take as many AP and honors classes as you can.

- If you start on the IB diploma path, see it through.

- Earning credits from dual-enrollment is losing popularity.

- Slacking off your senior year could cause your application to be denied or your early acceptance to be revoked.

Chapter 8

Extracurriculars

In This Chapter

◆ Doing what you like

◆ What top colleges look for

◆ Limiting your scope

◆ How not to overextend yourself

As I've said, it takes more than straight As and stellar standardized test scores to gain admission to a top college. You also have to have a strong resumé outside of the classroom. For some, that means joining an athletic team or the chess club. For others, it means volunteering at a local hospital or with Habitat for Humanity.

Top schools are turning down students with the country's best grades, and they're handpicking students that they feel will create a diverse atmosphere on their campuses. So you have to make yourself stand out with a resumé that shows an admissions officer what you'll bring to campus life.

There's no formula top schools abide by when it comes to deciding which high school students have stronger extracurricular portfolios than others. What's important is that you pick activities you feel passionate about and that resonate with you for reasons other than your desire to get into a top college. In short: Do what feels natural.

What They Look For

Extracurricular activities play a very important role in your college application. While grades and your GPA show college admissions officers what kind of student you are, extracurricular activities show the college what kind of person you are.

def•i•ni•tion

> **Extracurricular activities** are the activities that you take part in outside of the classroom. They could be academic based or take place on the athletic field. Extracurriculars often are referred to as *ECAs* by college admissions officers.

Admissions officers are able to tell very quickly if you've taken on an activity simply to put it on your application or if it's something you gave your all to—something you truly care about it. A lengthy commitment to an activity and taking on responsibility within a club or group shows that you're dedicated to that extracurricular. Colleges measure extracurriculars in different ways, but they're basically looking to see that you've grown and matured over your four years of high school, taken on a leadership role, and given back to your community.

Depth Versus Breadth

It's hard to balance the depth of your extracurricular activities against the number of activities you take on. Many admissions officers will tell you that they want to see you take on at least three to five activities and dedicate yourself to those activities. So, how do you do that?

The best way to show a school what you've contributed to a group or an organization is to get a letter of reference from that group's advisor. A letter highlighting your accomplishments within a group will give extra weight to an item on your resumé that on its own simply says you were a member of a group.

Long-term commitment to a group or an activity also will show that you became a member not only to strengthen your resumé, but also to work toward a goal. Simply put, if you wait until your senior year to partake in several extracurricular activities, then you've waited too long.

Leadership

Leadership is the $100,000 word when it comes to extracurricular activities. Top colleges, especially Ivy League schools, like to believe that they're breeding the leaders of tomorrow. So if you're showing leadership at the high school level, you've got a jump on what they're hoping to mold you into.

So, what does it take to become a high school leader? It doesn't necessarily mean you have to be president of the student council or captain of the football team. It could be that you took on the planning duties for a community activity or large-scale fund-raiser and led a group of several hundred students toward achieving one goal. Maybe you lead an area chapter of Habitat for Humanity or are the lead chef at an area soup kitchen. Leadership comes in many forms.

In addition, many statewide leadership programs enable high school students to learn what it takes to become a leader. For instance, the University of Virginia's Sorensen Institute for Political Leadership runs a High School Leaders Program that teaches students about public service and the political process. You should contact your school's guidance counselor to find out which leadership programs are available in your state.

There is no question that a person who is active, mature, confident, knowledgeable, respected, and hard working will emerge as a leader over the course of his high school career. Just remember that leadership, however, isn't born overnight, and you will become a leader if you continue to apply yourself to an activity and have passion for that activity.

Community Work

College admissions officers aren't expecting you to change the world over your four years of high school, but they are looking for you to have an impact in your community. Often, schools will weigh your extracurricular activities based on how the activities you selected impacted the school you went to and the community around it.

For instance, someone who served on a committee to revitalize a neighborhood park across the street from her high school might be considered in a better light than someone who was president of the Romance Languages Club. While there's nothing wrong with being a member of interesting clubs, you have to look at the bigger picture. As I said, schools want to see that your activities move the meter a little bit, and the Romance Languages Club just doesn't measure up to community outreach programs.

The Possibilities

Some high schools have more extracurricular activities than others. Not all high schools field National Science Bowl and handball teams. Still, there are some basic groups that extracurricular activities fall into: government, debate, entrepreneurship, community service, and athletics.

A majority of the nation's high schools have activities in most if not all of these categories. So the trick is simply finding the ones that you'll enjoy and succeed in.

Cheat Sheet _____

If your school doesn't have an activity or a club you're interested in, consider starting one yourself. If your school isn't willing to back your effort, consider partnering with a local community college, private high school, or business.

Government

An active role in your school's student government is a great way to take on a leadership role and show that you're ready for the responsibility of attending a top college. But colleges don't care that you were simply president of your high school class; they want to see what you did with that position.

If you indeed plan to pursue an active role in student government, go into it with an idea of what you'll do once elected. It's not enough to promise new basketballs for gym class and better sodas in the vending machine. Consider taking on large community projects and fundraisers. Look for a need in the community and get your school to rally around that need. A top college will be impressed with how you were able to bring a large group together to focus on a specific goal.

Debate

If you're opinionated and well-spoken, your school's debate team might be right up your alley. Admissions counselors look favorably at applicants who have debate club listed on their high school resumés. That's because debaters tend to have excellent speaking and critical thinking skills.

Cheat Sheet _____

The National Forensic League's website, www.nflonline.org, is a great site for students interested in debate.

Although Ivy schools don't offer scholarships specifically aimed at debaters, several schools in the tier just below the Ivies do offer such scholarships, including Emory University and the University of Southern California.

Entrepreneurship

Entrepreneurship in high school certainly can add a shine to your college application, especially if you're looking to enter the business program of a top school. Not all high schools have entrepreneurship programs, but several universities offer regional training. The University at Buffalo School of Management, for instance, recently partnered with the Meszaros International Center of Entrepreneurship to create a 19-week program that teaches high school students about ethical entrepreneurship and business operations.

Whether you work in a class or club to develop a business plan or you intern with a local company, any business experience you can get while in high school will be beneficial for your application.

Students who show a proclivity for entrepreneurship could end up the owners of a profitable startup tech firm, and in turn could donate money back to their university after graduation. That makes entrepreneurial spirits very likely candidates for admission. A study released by the Ewing Marion Kauffman Foundation and researchers from Duke and Harvard universities found that tech startups in 2005 averaged sales revenue of $5.7 million. But tech startups with founders with advanced Ivy League degrees averaged $6.7 million in revenue, according to the study.

If you're considering a future in entrepreneurship, it's essential that you look into becoming a member of DECA/Delta Epsilon Chi, an international association of high school and college students who are studying marketing, management, and entrepreneurship. Visit DECA's website at www.deca.org to find out more.

 Beware

Don't wait until your junior or senior year to take on extracurricular activities. Extracurricular activities should begin your freshman year of high school, if not earlier.

Community Service

A common theme throughout this chapter is that colleges want to see you impact the world around you, and there's no better way to do that than through community service. The trick is to think broadly when it comes to community service projects. The more you take on and the more people you lead, the better your application will look.

Let me backtrack for a second and say that the primary reason you should take on community service is to better your community. If you're active simply to better your career, your lack of enthusiasm will eventually become evident and you won't benefit much from your effort. That being said, think big picture when it comes to the projects you take on. Tutoring children after school is great, but is there a school that doesn't have a tutoring program that needs one? Can you start and staff that program?

One of the best ways to come up with a community service project is to sit down and think about where there is a void in your community. Then, consider how you can fill that void and how you can get other people to help. If money is an issue, again, consider partnering with your school, a neighboring community college, or an area business.

Also remember that you don't have to take an expensive trip to another continent to get good community service experience. Many communities have several service opportunities, including literacy groups, hospitals, nursing homes, and blood drive groups, not to mention Habitat for Humanity, 15-love (a tennis program for inner-city children), and other youth sports organizations that enable you to improve the quality of life right in your backyard.

> **Real Life**
>
> Lukas Zyblut was accepted by seven Ivy League schools. On his resumé was the following: co-captain of the school's United Nations Team, founder of its debate team, president of its mock trial team, editor of the school newspaper, and member of the soccer team.

Almost as important as the community service you perform is making sure that activity is clearly explained on your college application. If your service is in a broad area, try to be as specific as you can when explaining to a college what it is you did. If you organized a soup kitchen, explain that you gathered volunteers, shopped for food, and identified a group of people in need.

Athletics

I'm not talking about athletes who are recruited to play sports at top colleges in this section. Rather, I'm talking about athletes who play multiple years of high school sports but don't intend to pursue their athletic careers in college.

Playing sports is another way to show a college your dedication and leadership. Whether you're the team captain or the last player on the bench, you're showing colleges different but equally important aspects of your personality. As a team captain you're obviously showing an admissions counselor that you can lead a group of people.

But if you're not the best at your sport and don't get a lot of playing time but choose to stick with it, that shows you have the maturity to honor a commitment.

Years ago I had a student who wanted to join a sports team. Her aunt told her to join the tennis team—even though she'd never held a tennis racket—because she'd meet nice people. On the day of tryouts she had no idea what she was doing, but she muddled through enthusiastically and the coach was impressed enough that he made her a substitute player on the junior varsity team. Well, she stuck with it, and after four years of practicing and playing she ended up being the team's No. 1 player and captain during her senior year. What's the moral? Schools love to see the kind of passion, determination, and follow-through that this student exhibited.

Work Experience

Work experience is just another way to show a college you have a diverse personality and resumé. Colleges, of course, aren't expecting you to hold a 40-hour–per-week job. Instead, they want to see that you're able to juggle the responsibility of a job along with what you're taking on at school. Working as a high school senior isn't a rarity, though, and has become the norm. According to a University of Washington study, more than half of high school seniors surveyed—56 percent—said they were working during the spring of their final year of high school.

Work can take the place of an extracurricular activity, especially if you pick a job that is in line with what you hope to study in college or one that is community focused. For instance, you could consider working at an area hospital, nursing home, parks department, homeless shelter, or after-school program. Additionally, taking on a job doesn't mean you won't have an opportunity to take on a leadership role.

It's important that if you do choose to work, you explain in your application what you learned from your time as an employee and how you were able to lead a group of people and problem-solve.

While some people choose to work during high school, others have no choice other than to get a job to help support their families. Often those students have to work more than 20 hours per week, leaving little time for other extracurricular activities. If you have excellent grades, admissions officers won't necessarily hold your lack of extracurriculars against you. But, you have to share your situation with your guidance counselor who will advise you on how to explain your situation to the admissions offices. The burden you bear of having to help support your family also could be an excellent subject for your admissions essay.

Summer Experiences

Some high school students have the ability to choose between spending their summer flipping burgers, attending a prestigious Ivy League summer program, working as an intern, or traveling overseas.

The experiences that come with attending Columbia's Barcelona Experience or traveling to help rebuild an area of the world devastated by a natural disaster, of course, would look incredible on an applicant's resumé. Unfortunately, however, the average high schooler can't afford to travel halfway across the world or pay for a summer program at Columbia or Harvard.

The cost of summer programs and admissions officers' tendencies to take a longer look at students whose applications include these activities recently was criticized in a *Boston Globe* article. "If colleges consider the sorts of summer experiences that only some people can afford to pay for, then they are effectively privileging the already privileged," Richard Kahlenberg, senior fellow with the Century Foundation, told the *Globe*.

Bill Fitzsimmons, Dean of Admissions and Financial Aid at Harvard University, said high-priced internships can be "wonderful experiences," but "in and of themselves, they will not give a student an advantage in the admissions process because the playing field is not level. The substantial majority of high school students cannot afford to do these things."

The fact of the matter is, however, that if you have the means, you should look to challenge yourself over the summer. Many summer programs are as competitive to get into as top colleges, requiring a review of your transcript and standardized test scores. So if you are admitted, it'll give you a good idea of where you stand in relation to your peers.

Ivy Summers

Several prestigious summer programs are available across the country that will look much better on your resumé than a summer working at McDonald's. Take Columbia University, for instance, where you can spend the summer taking any number of courses ranging from constitutional law to biomedical engineering. Columbia also offers a program in Barcelona, Spain.

Like the Columbia summer school program, similar programs at Cornell, Harvard, and Brown review your academic record when deciding whether you'll be allowed to attend. Not all the programs require interviews before admission, although Columbia's does.

Cheat Sheet

If you can't afford to attend an expensive summer school program, there are more affordable opportunities you can pursue. Several states run governor's schools that are supported by state and federal dollars and require a much lower out-of-pocket contribution than the Ivy programs.

Although Ivy League summer programs definitely have their benefits in that they give high school students a foot in the door with an Ivy and expose them to rigorous class work, they are expensive, which means they're available only to those who can afford them. Columbia's New York City program costs more than $6,000, and the school's Barcelona program costs more than $11,000. However, some scholarships are available. Check out Appendix F for further information on these programs.

Internships

Internships aren't solely for college students, and they can open a world of work experience that will make your college resumé stand out. If you really want to go for the gusto, you can look for exotic internships overseas taking on humanitarian work or cataloging exotic plants. But internships also can be as simple as running errands at a local newspaper or public radio station, or working as an office clerk at a local company. The thing with internships is that they give you real-life experience in the working world, and if you succeed, you should be able to garner a strong recommendation out of them. A bonus is that some summer internships are paid positions, so you're killing two birds with one stone.

There are several places you can go to find a list of available internships. The Internet obviously is the easiest place to start looking:

- ◆ **The Internship Search Engine**
  www.internshipprograms.com
  This website offers a clearinghouse of internship opportunities throughout the United States.

- ◆ **Intern Abroad**
  www.internabroad.com
  This website shows internship opportunities overseas.

- ◆ **Idealist**
  www.idealist.org
  This website allows users to search for internships with groups that fit Idealist's philosophy on bettering the world and helping people.

- ◆ **International Volunteers Programs Association**
  www.volunteerinternational.org
  This website showcases volunteer and intern opportunities abroad. The opportunities are aimed at fostering cross-cultural understanding.

There are also books you can check out, including *Peterson's Internships* and *The Best 109 Internships*, which, combined, list hundreds of opportunities.

If you don't find what you're looking for in a book or online, you always can go to the businesses, newspapers, and radio stations in your community. If those groups don't have established intern programs, do some research and go out there to pitch yourself as some free, hardworking summer help. There aren't a lot of businesses that will turn down that offer.

Overextending Yourself

There's always a fear that in their frantic pursuit of admission to a top college, students will overexert themselves and burn out. The fear is a realistic one, and students need to consider their health and sleeping patterns when getting involved in too many activities.

The downside of spreading yourself too thin also could impact your college application, not just your health. While colleges want to see a well-rounded application, they also want to see you give 100 percent of yourself to each of the extracurricular activities you choose. No matter how you slice it, being committed to a few activities is far more fulfilling and impressive to colleges than joining a lot of organizations just to fill a resumé.

Your Health

Overexertion is nothing to laugh at and could result in serious health issues. You might say there's no downside to being an overachiever, but consider these possible side effects of overexertion listed by the College Board:

- **Loss of focus or passion.** "Overachievers are often spread quite thin. With only so many hours in the day and so much energy and effort to give, you have to divide your attention among a number of endeavors if you overschedule your time. Consequently, you are likely to lose sight of what you truly like and to get less enjoyment from the things you do."

- **Poor physical health.** "The workload and time constraints of the typical overachiever leave relatively little time for sleep. In fact, sleep deprivation is common among overscheduled students, with many of them sleeping less than six hours per night. Excessively busy kids tend to suffer from poor eating habits, as well."

◆ **Poor mental health.** "The American Academy of Child and Adolescent Psychiatry states that 'school demands and frustrations' and 'taking on too many activities or having too high expectations' are the leading causes of teenage stress."

◆ **Unhealthy self-image.** "Overachievers often base their feelings of self-worth on their accomplishments. The more they do, and the more they do well, the better they feel about themselves. Reliance on external validation, though, can be extremely harmful."

So how do you achieve balance while creating a resumé that will impress the top colleges? The College Board has some good tips when it comes that, too:

◆ **Do what you like.** "Rank your commitments according to how much you enjoy each one. Weed out the activities from which you gain little or no pleasure. Instead, create a schedule of activities that reflects your true interests and passions, and don't be afraid to cut something out or to say no."

◆ **Schedule time to relax.** "If you never have a minute to rest or have fun, you are doing too much. Take a look at your calendar and carve out specific times to ease off your usually hectic pace."

◆ **Take care of yourself, inside and out.** "Make sure that you eat healthy foods and that you get a sufficient amount of sleep each night. Also, remember that exercise is a necessary ingredient for both a strong body and a strong mind. And when you're feeling overwhelmed or stressed, take a break."

Active to a Fault

As I said before, if you overextend yourself without fully committing to any one given thing, you run the risk of a top college passing on your application. Participating in everything is not as important or integral as becoming a part of a few meaningful activities and exhibiting leadership and responsibility.

According to the College Board, "The majority of colleges indicate that they are looking for well-rounded students. Essentially, they prefer applicants who achieve balance among their academic pursuits, their extracurricular activities, and their personal lives. When admissions officers look at resumés, they are attempting to assess leadership, commitment, and integrity. If you're an overachiever, beware. More is not necessarily better."

The Least You Need to Know

- ◆ Commitment means success.

- ◆ More isn't necessarily better.

- ◆ Seek leadership opportunities.

- ◆ Overextending yourself can lead to poor health.

Chapter 9

Admission Tests

In This Chapter

- Differences between the SAT 1 (reasoning) and the ACT and SAT 2 subject tests
- What's on the tests
- How many times you should take the tests
- Getting yourself ready

On the list of items that factor into getting accepted into a top college, your standardized test scores certainly rank at or near the top. In Chapter 3, I mentioned how, over the years, it has become trendy to protest standardized tests such as the ACT and the SAT, with some people claiming that they are biased toward the wealthy. Still, despite those protests, the tests are a reality you have to deal with if you're going to be admitted into a top college.

An overwhelming majority of the country's top colleges require that you take either the ACT or the SAT 1. And just because a school doesn't require that you take one or the other doesn't mean you get away scot-free. Connecticut College, which is considered one of the country's more competitive liberal arts colleges with an admissions rate of 35 percent, requires that applicants submit SAT 2 subject tests along with Advanced Placement (AP) or International Baccalaureate (IB) exams if they don't take the SAT 1 or the ACT.

So, now that you've faced up to the reality of having to take one or more of the tests, which one(s) should you take? Well, a lot of that depends on the individual. Everything from whether you're male or female to your ability to sit still for more than three hours factors into the decision. And like I said, it's not a decision you should take lightly. But remember, although SAT and ACT scores are important, they're intended to supplement the student's record and are only one of many considered factors.

The Differences Between the Tests

Back in Chapter 3, I gave overviews of the ACT, the SAT 1 and SAT 2 exams, and their histories. This chapter focuses on the tangible differences between the SAT exams and the ACT.

Since its inception, the ACT has been the main test of choice for high schools in the Midwest while the SAT has been the dominant exam along the coasts. But that has changed over the past decade and the ACT has seen exponential growth to the point that a record 1.4 million high school graduates—43 percent of the country's graduates—took the ACT. In fact, from 2002 through 2007 the number of students taking the ACT on the East Coast increased by 66 percent and the number of students taking it on the West Coast increased by 46 percent, according to the ACT website.

Some of the increase in test-takers is due to five states now requiring that students take the ACT as juniors. But in addition to that, areas of the country that traditionally have been solid SAT states also are moving on to the ACT. Officials said ACT growth also has been seen in the Northeast, where students are taking both tests to try to better their college applications.

Cheat Sheet _____

Over the years arguments have been made that gender should help a student determine whether to take the SAT or ACT. Some believe that the way the ACT and SAT 1 tests are structured sets up female students to score better on the ACT and male students to score better on the SAT 1. The argument is that female students are more likely to fit the description of an overachiever who is thought to do better on the ACT. The male students, however, are thought to be better suited to use their analytical brains to score well on the SAT 1. But studies of SAT 1 and ACT results shows there's really little difference between how each gender scores.

Students shouldn't just blindly watch the trends and take the tests based on what's popular at the time, though. There are differences between the tests that could translate into you doing better on one than the other. When it comes down to it, most colleges give a fair look at both SAT and ACT scores but take a stronger look at the higher of the two scores. That's not to say that you should submit a great SAT 1 score and a weak ACT score just to show that you were willing to take both tests. If your score on one test clearly outweighs that of the other exam, then just submit the better results. Thus, it's critical that you figure out which one best fits your test-taking style.

Real Life

"Since it's a choice you can make, it has the feeling of being a significant choice, fraught with implication, but I don't think it does matter. Either is fine with us, and we don't have a feeling that either favors students with any particular profile."

—Marlyn McGrath-Lewis, Director of Admissions at Harvard University, talking to *The New York Times* about the choosing between the SAT 1 and ACT

The Formats of the ACT and SAT 1

The structures of the ACT and SAT 1 vary from the number of sections each test includes to the topics covered and the time allotted for each test.

Here's a basic breakdown of how the tests differ:

	ACT	SAT 1
Times administered per year	6	7
Sections on test	English, math, science, and reading	Critical reading, math, and writing
Level of math	Up to trigonometry	Goes up to algebra and geometry
Essay	Optional	Mandatory
Length	2 hours, 55 minutes*	3 hours, 45 minutes
Scoring	No penalty for wrong answers	Penalty for wrong answers

Add an additional 30 minutes if you write the optional essay.

It's important to consider the differences in formats when deciding which test to take. For example, the ACT is about an hour shorter than the SAT 1 if you don't take the optional essay. So if you struggle with maintaining your focus and can't sit still for almost three hours, the ACT might be the test for you.

In 2005, the College Board added a mandatory essay section to the SAT 1. So besides a shorter exam time with the ACT, you also could avoid what might be a weakness for you in an essay. You know you'll have to write an essay on your application, so you might want to avoid writing one on your standardized test if that's not your strength.

Keep in mind that most, though not all, top schools do want you to take the writing portion of the ACT. Schools that don't require the essay might say it's "recommended." Princeton, for instance, recommends that applicants submitting ACT scores take the writing portion of the test. Cornell requires the essay portion, as do Brown, Columbia, Harvard, Yale, UPenn, Dartmouth, Stanford, NYU, and MIT. Check with the admissions offices of the schools to which you intend to apply to find out whether they require the ACT writing section.

Additionally, you have to consider the kind of test-taker you are. Are you someone who is sure of your knowledge, or lack of, when taking tests? Or, are you ambivalent and often unsure of your answers? The reason that matters is because the SAT 1 deducts points for wrong answers, which means you really shouldn't guess. A key to taking the SAT 1 is knowing what you don't know. The ACT, however, does not penalize for wrong answers. So, if there are 10 questions that you're completely clueless on with the ACT and you take a shot in the dark on all 10, the odds are in your favor of getting at least one of them right.

What the ACT and SAT 1 Test

The ACT and SAT 1 not only have different formats, but they also essentially test different things. The SAT is considered more of an aptitude exam that tests reasoning, verbal abilities, and critical thinking. The ACT, however, is considered more of a curriculum exam that tests what you've learned throughout your four years of high school.

It's those differences that lead some in the counseling industry to suggest that coasters—students who are bored in the classroom and get by on little studying and their natural smarts—do better on the SAT 1 because it calls on them to use the reasoning skills that don't kick in when they're staring at a text book. So-called overachievers, or the bookworms who aren't naturally gifted but get by on hard work and grit, are thought to have more success on the ACT because its goal is to test overall knowledge and what you've learned throughout your high school career.

The overachiever/coaster issue is something that can be debated, but what can't be debated is that what's included on the ACT is different from what's on the SAT 1. For instance, the ACT includes a science section that the SAT 1 does not. This section could cast a light on your strengths or weaknesses in that subject. Remember that it's your *composite score* on the ACT that schools look at. So you might think that if you do well on the English, math, and reading sections—basically the equivalent of the SAT 1—and you bomb on the science section, the science score won't be held against you. But that's not the case. The science score factors into your composite score, and the composite score determines where applicants rank.

The ACT's math section also goes up to trigonometry, whereas the SAT 1 does not. When the College Board released its newly formatted SAT 1 in 2005, it was said to have included a tougher math section, although most still believe the ACT's math section is more difficult.

def•i•ni•tion

Your ACT **composite score** is the average of the scores you receive on the test's four sections: English, math, science, and reading.

The Princeton Review has estimated the following equivalents on SAT/ACT scoring based on data from the class of 2010:

ACT Score	SAT 1 Score
36	2400
35	2340
34	2260
33	2190
32	2130
31	2040
30	1980
29	1920
28	1860
27	1820
26	1760
25	1700
24	1650
23	1590

continues

continued

ACT Score	SAT 1 Score
22	1530
21	1500
20	1410
19	1350
18	1290
17	1210
16	1140
15	1060
14	1000
13	900
12	780
11	750

Real Life

"Girls tend to fit pretty well into the group of high achievers, who get good grades and do well in school, who also do well on the ACT. I sometimes give the advice that if you were to flip a coin, just go with the SAT if you're a boy and the ACT if you're a girl, in part for that reason."

—John Katzman, chief executive of the Princeton Review, told *The New York Times*

SAT 2

In all the talk about the ACT and SAT 1, don't forget about the SAT 2, or SAT subject tests, which some counselors say are just as important as the SAT 1 and ACT. Top schools have different policies regarding the subject tests, but most of the top schools require that you submit scores for at least two of them. Check with the schools to which you plan to apply to check their subject test policies.

The SAT subject tests are given the same day as the SAT 1, though you can't take them the same day that you take the SAT 1. Each test is an hour long, and you can take up to three in a day. Twenty SAT subject tests are given in five general categories: English, literature, math, science, and foreign language.

Most of the tips for preparing for the ACT and SAT 1 that are included later in this chapter also apply to the SAT subject tests. The most important thing is that you know the specific format of the subject test you're taking, along with what's allowed and not allowed. For example, you need to bring a CD player to the foreign language listening subject tests, but the CD player has to meet the College Board's criteria and, for example, not include a recording device. You also should remember to bring extra batteries.

Try, Try Again

If at first you don't succeed, try, try again, right? Well that's a great motto in certain aspects of your life, but it wasn't always the case when it came to the SAT 1. For years a major deciding factor for students who needed to decide between taking the SAT and the ACT was that you can choose which ACT scores schools get to see regardless of how many times you take the test. The same wasn't always true for the SAT. If you sent an SAT score report to a school, they'd see all the tests you took.

The College Board decided that, starting in 2009, students would be able to decide which SAT 1 scores their prospective colleges saw. I'll get more into that in a bit.

Despite the change, the question of how many times someone should take the SAT and ACT still lingers. One factor to consider is cost. Not everyone has the means to pay for multiple tests multiple times. In 2008–2009, taking the ACT without the essay section costs $31. If you added the essay section, the cost to take the ACT was $46. The cost of taking the ACT includes sending score reports to up to four colleges. By comparison, the cost of taking the SAT 1 was $45 in 2008–2009. That also includes sending scores to up to four colleges. So if you take each test two times, you're looking at close to $200 in testing fees.

Another factor is burnout. You simply don't want to get to the point where you're constantly studying for and stressing over a standardized test. It's simply not good for your health. Also, studies show that there is rarely any gain in scores after a second time, unless there were extenuating circumstances such as illness on a test date.

Reporting Changes

Whether it was done to "reduce student stress," as was publicized by the College Board, or to compete with the ACT, the board recently decided to allow students to send scores from individual SAT 1 and SAT 2 exams to colleges and universities instead of having to send a full report that includes the results of each time a student takes the test. Scores cannot be broken up by section (math and English), though. For example, if someone scores 2300 on the SAT 1 in a February sitting and then scores 2100 in a later sitting, he can choose only to send the better score.

It's also important to note that the SAT's new score-reporting feature is optional, so if you don't choose which score you want sent to a college all your scores will be sent. Students can send any or all scores to a college on a single report—it does not cost more to send one, multiple, or all test scores.

Along the same line, it's important that you arrange for the correct scores to be sent to the colleges to which you apply. Because you can't decide which sections of the SAT or ACT a college sees, this mostly applies to which SAT 2 subject tests you need to send. Some schools use the SAT 2 results to determine where you'll be placed for English or math classes. Check with the school's admissions office to see which SAT 2 tests it uses to determine freshman placement.

When and What to Report

Scoring well on your standardized tests doesn't do you much good if you don't submit the correct scores or fail to report them in time. It's up to you, not the College Board or ACT, to make sure your scores get to the schools you're applying to in time.

There's no uniform test score due date for top schools. Princeton, for instance, wants to receive ACT and SAT 1 scores by March 1, while Yale wants them by February 1 and Stanford wants them by January 1. College due dates for the scores should help you determine when you should take the tests. Most students take the SAT and/or ACT during the spring of their junior years and then again in the fall of their senior years. So if you plan on applying to Princeton, which requires standardized test scores by March 1, you don't want to take the SAT 1 exam on March 14.

It usually takes about three weeks after a test is administered for SAT 1, SAT 2, and ACT results to be available online. So, give yourself a cushion just in case a computer crashes or tests are lost. (Stranger things have happened.) But even once available, it can take an additional three weeks for scores to reach a school; even a rush score can take a week.

How Many Times?

Now that you know you can decide which scores a college sees, how many times should you take the SAT or ACT? Taking the exams twice is the norm, and there's really no reason to take them more than that. If you don't score high enough to get into your top choice after the second time, chances are you're not going to see vast improvement the third or fourth time. However, there is a possibility that you're not scoring well because you're not a good test-taker and are suffering from anxiety every time you take the SAT or ACT. If that's the case, establish a program for yourself that will get you over the hump. I get more into test preparation later in this chapter.

Some counselors advise that you take the standardized tests at least twice, but there's really no reason to take a test a second time unless your score doesn't match up with what you need to get into a top school or you were sick or unfocused and feel you can score much better the second time. The thing is, it's probably not worth taking the test a second time to boost your score of 2300 by a handful of points. At that point, admissions officers are going to decide on your application based on things other than your SAT score. Those few points between 2300 and 2400 likely won't be the determining factor. So, if you did well on your first test, consider letting it ride.

If you're thinking about taking the SAT or ACT a fourth time—don't. Unless you're trying to hit a certain mark to qualify as a student athlete (schools often have a minimum mark you have to meet in order to be a student athlete), there's really no point sitting for the exams four times.

> **Beware**
>
> Don't treat your first crack at the SAT or ACT as a practice test. Go in prepared and ready to succeed. There's no reason you should plan to take the tests a second and third time. Remember that you might not be able to take the SAT 1 or ACT a second time before your early-decision application is due.

Preparation

You should set two alarm clocks, get a good night's rest, eat a good breakfast, and have your two No. 2 pencils sharpened to get ready for your exam. That's still good advice when it comes to preparing for standardized tests. But there's a lot more that goes into the prepping for standardized tests than a good night's rest and a good meal.

A ton of resources are available to help you get ready. At the very least, students should review old SAT tests to know what to expect on test day. Be sure to review and repeat SAT questions and take practice tests. In addition, test prep services and individual counselors can help you get ready for standardized tests. Both College Board and ACT offer prep questions on line for free or a minimal fee.

Preparation is doubly important for people who tend to suffer from anxiety on test day. Establishing a system that will make you feel comfortable on test day is as important as knowing what'll be on the test because if you're not comfortable and can't focus, you've already failed.

Prep Programs

Certainly, to have that edge for the most competitive colleges, a test prep program of some kind can be beneficial. A number of programs can help, including Kaplan, Princeton Review, and Abelson. However, I've found that students get the best results from a private tutor.

Some things a test prep program or tutor can do for you that preparing on your own won't include:

- They offer the most current test-taking strategies.
- They focus on a student's specific needs.
- They use practice diagnostic tests.
- They keep parents involved in the process.

Both Princeton Review and Kaplan offer group, private, and online tutoring options for SAT and ACT prep, and each makes its own claims of success. Princeton Review claims that 90 percent of the students who use its courses get into their first-choice school. Kaplan guarantees that if its class doesn't raise your test scores you can get your money back. Princeton Review also has a money-back guarantee.

One thing you definitely get out of a prep service that you won't get from studying by yourself is someone to grade your essay and point out places where improvement is needed. Although you might not think that's worth the price of the course, doing well on that essay could mean the difference between a thick envelope from Harvard and a thin one.

Each test prep service offers its own special formula for how it will help you increase your standardized test scores. For Kaplan, it's the "SmartPoints" system. Under that system the company assigns a value to each skill and then creates a study plan that gets the most out of your strengths and focuses them on the skills that are worth the most points.

It's best to check the websites of the test prep program that you're considering to see which one you think would work best for you. Programs are helpful, but they are also expensive. Both Princeton Review and Kaplan's group courses cost at least $1,000. The prices go up for small group classes and individual tutoring. Most testing services also offer programs for the SAT subject tests.

Practice Tests

You don't need to sign up for a prep program to take practice tests. Several books and websites can provide you with all the practice tests you need. Because the SAT 1 and ACT each follows a standard format and the questions are similar from test to test, practice tests give you the best opportunity to figure out what you know and—more importantly—what you don't know.

As I said earlier, the SAT 1, unlike the ACT, penalizes you for wrong answers. So if you're taking the SAT 1, pay attention to the questions that give you a hard time during the practice testing so you learn which types of questions you shouldn't guess on.

The website www.testprepreview.com is just one of many great sources on the Internet for practice tests. Simply do an Internet search for practice SAT or ACT exams. Be sure that you're taking a post-2005 SAT 1 exam that includes the tougher math section and essay.

When you take a practice test, set up an environment that's as close to test day as you can. Don't sit at your desk with a sandwich and a can of Coke if you don't plan on bringing some caffeine into the real test with you. Also, make sure you're timing yourself and taking the proper breaks between sections. If at all possible, try to take a practice test all in one sitting, just as you would the real thing.

Cheat Sheet

Don't wait until you start prepping for the SAT or ACT to make the dictionary your friend. Possibly the toughest part of studying for standardized tests is cramming to increase your vocabulary. So, start expanding your vocabulary any way you can beginning your freshman year, if not earlier.

Practice tests also give you a chance to get over your testing anxiety if that's something you suffer from. One of the best ways to deal with anxiety is to establish a sequence of events leading up to the practice test that you can repeat when you take the real test. You know you're going to take the SAT or ACT on a Saturday morning, so take all your practice tests on Saturday mornings. On the mornings of your practice tests, wake up, go through your normal routine, and eat one of your favorite breakfasts—just as long as it doesn't make you too full or give you an upset stomach. Put on your favorite shirt—the same shirt you'll wear on test day—and listen to some music that will relax you. Now, go and take your practice test.

Follow these same steps for all your practice tests and then again on test day, and you should be able to create a comforting atmosphere that will keep your nerves at bay.

Another good way to calm your nerves is to steal a page from athletes who deal with anxiety. Athletes use a visualization technique during which they picture themselves running a race or playing a basketball game and let the event play out in their heads. They visualize their success before they ever set foot on the track or the court. In your case, you should spend time leading up to the test visualizing yourself in the classroom and imagining how you'll go about answering each question in a calm manner.

Of course, if these techniques do not work for you and your anxiety is too much to cope with on your own, you should consider seeing a professional.

PSAT

Another way to prepare for the SAT 1 is to take the Preliminary Scholastic Aptitude Test (PSAT). You take the PSAT in October of your junior year as a way to help you prepare for the SAT 1 and to qualify you for the National Merit Scholarship Corporation's scholarship programs.

Students also have the option of taking the PSAT during their sophomore year. Most California kids now take it freshman and sophomore year as well. Taking it your sophomore year gives you an opportunity to receive earlier feedback on the academic skills you'll need to work on for college. The PSAT includes questions that are similar to those on the SAT 1, so taking the PSAT as many times as you can is just another way to get more practice.

The PSAT isn't simply a practice test, though. Its role in determining who's a National Merit Scholar is important as you consider applying to a top college. All juniors who take the PSAT automatically have their scores sent to the National Merit Scholarship Corporation, which is a nonprofit group that has run this academic competition since 1955. The corporation uses PSAT scores to initially determine who should be included in the National Merit Scholar search process. After you're selected for consideration, your advancement through the selection process is based on a number of factors, including your SAT 1 scores and high school transcript.

Eventually, a pool of more than 1.3 million students who take the PSAT is trimmed down to 8,200 students who will each receive a $2,500 scholarship. Many finalists actually do not get scholarships, but it certainly enhances an application. Other students who do not become finalists could receive certificates or commendations recognizing their academic abilities.

Needless to say, being one of 8,200 people who's able to become a National Merit Scholar out of a pool of 1.3 million people looks great on your college application. In fact, most testing services also offer PSAT prep programs, which shows you just how important the test can be.

The Least You Need to Know

- ◆ The ACT and SAT 1 are widely accepted at colleges across the country.
- ◆ Study the formats of each test to determine which best fits you.
- ◆ Test prep programs can help you get a leg up on your competition.
- ◆ Good PSAT scores qualify you for the prestigious National Merit Scholarship program.

Part **3**

Narrowing Your Choices

Now you know what you have to do to get into a top college, but how will you decide to which schools you want to apply? And just as important, how do you know if you can afford to attend? Additionally, did you know that where you live in relation to a school could impact whether you're accepted?

In Part 3, I go into everything you should consider when applying to a school. From college tours to the financial aid policies at each school, there are several things to consider before submitting your application.

"Can I buy a rear window sticker even if I don't get accepted?"

Chapter 10

The Intangibles

In This Chapter

- ◆ How race affects admission
- ◆ How to embrace your disabilities
- ◆ The advantages of where you live
- ◆ Keeping it clean on the Internet

Sure, everyone knows grades, standardized test scores, and extracurricular activities are crucial components of being accepted to a top college. But what about the intangibles such as race, ethnicity, where you live, or whether you have a family member who went to the school? Yes, when dealing with a pool of applicants that's so close in terms of grades and test scores, all those items can matter in the end.

That's not to say that just because your grandfather went to Yale you're going to get in despite a B average and a 1600 on the SAT 1, because it's not going to happen. But if you're up against another applicant and you have very similar transcripts, test scores, and resumés, any little thing could become the deciding factor.

So, don't skip that extra Advanced Placement (AP) class just because you get to check a box that says your father went to the school to which you're applying. Although the intangibles can help, they don't make up for a lack of hard work.

The Obvious

When it comes to the intangibles, there are some obvious ones that schools are going to look at if your application is teetering between acceptance and denial. In some cases, these intangibles could move your application over to the accepted pile.

Some of the obvious intangibles are basic, such as whether your mother or father attended the school to which you're applying. Others, such as race, are a little more complex and controversial. How you handle the intangibles is up to you. Do you want to get in based solely on your merits—or partly based on your skin color or where your parents went to school? That's your decision.

The intangibles that set you apart from your peers could be your hook for getting into a top college. Because Ivy League schools are turning down straight-A students and people with perfect SAT 1 scores, you need a hook to set yourself apart, and one of these obvious intangibles might be just that.

Legacies

If your mom or dad went to the college you're applying to, then you're considered a *legacy.* If your mom, dad, grandfather, and grandmother all went to the school, well that's just plain lucky.

def•i•ni•tion

A **legacy** is someone who has at least one parent who attended the school she's applying to. Some schools extend legacies up to grandparents.

In a 2008 *ABC News* report, several of the nation's top colleges were unwilling to release their admissions rates for legacy applicants. The schools that did report their rates only confirmed what everyone already knew: If you're a legacy, you have a significantly better chance at getting into a top school.

Princeton's average rate of acceptance for the class of 2012 was 9 percent, but for legacy applications that rate soared to 40 percent. Officials at Dartmouth, which had an admissions rate of 13 percent for the Class of 2012, said admission among legacies generally is about two times higher than the general admission rate. And, officials at Bowdoin said its legacy admissions rate generally is about 40 percent while its overall admission rate was 18 percent for the Class of 2012.

So why do legacies get the special treatment? It's because their parents and grandparents tend to be donors who might stop sending checks if their relatives aren't accepted. According to a study released by the Council for Aid to Education, alumni contributed almost $8.3 billion to their schools in 2007, making up more than a quarter of all the charitable donations handed over to the nation's colleges.

The legacy policy isn't without controversy. Many attempts have been made to bring an end to preferential treatment for legacies. Even President George W. Bush—a legacy at Yale—spoke out against the policy in 2004. "I think it ought to be based upon merit," he said of the college admissions process.

It's not just a money issue—the legacy controversy also crosses into race. Although top colleges are trying to diversify their student bodies, if legacies who tend to be the children of rich white families continue to get preferential treatment, that diversification will occur at a much slower pace, college admissions experts say.

All that said, in most cases you still need the grades to give your status as a legacy a chance to deliver. Several years ago I had a student apply to the University of Michigan. Her grandmother, mother, and sister all had attended and all remained active alumni. When she was denied admission, I immediately called the school just to be sure that they realized she was a legacy. Yes, they had definitely realized it and taken it into consideration, but they could not justify the acceptance.

Race

After working in a public, urban high school for 30 years, I can tell you—whether this is spoken aloud or not—race is a major factor for college admissions. All colleges, especially the top colleges, are looking for qualified, under-represented minorities. Typically, these are students who have succeeded in spite of insurmountable odds and a deck stacked against them throughout their lives. They were able to achieve success in spite of these odds, not because of any advantages they had in their lives.

Voters in Michigan and California in recent years have approved constitutional amendments banning public colleges from considering race as a factor for admission. The immediate fallout from that decision was a decrease in minority enrollment at public colleges in California and then Michigan. But private universities are not affected by the amendments and are still able to bring in racially diverse students that the public universities cannot.

I recently had a very talented, bright, and hard-working black student accepted to Amherst College with an almost full scholarship. She was in the much lower ranges of what is a typical acceptance to Amherst, but it's easy to see why they would want to take this student, despite her lower test scores. She was someone from a single-parent home who had demonstrated, in spite of incredible obstacles, that she could succeed.

Real Life

"With respect to achieving diversity at the most competitive schools, I think the key is always to evaluate students as individuals, in light of whatever opportunities and challenges that have been presented. Race and socioeconomic class are relevant aspects of an applicant's context, and to the extent we do a good job overall of weighing context, we will sustain a diverse undergraduate body with exceptional talent and promise."

—Jeff Brenzel, Dean of Admissions at Yale

That being said, that doesn't mean a white student from a single-family home can't exhibit the same ability to overcome struggles and achieve despite his circumstances. It's silly to think that schools don't consider race when it comes to these situations, though. Although schools say they don't have a specific profile for the type of student they'll admit or the class they're trying to build, race does play an important role.

Over a 16-year period from 1992 through 2007, the average acceptance rate of black applicants at Ivy League schools has increased by 27 percent, according to numbers collected by *The Journal of Blacks in Higher Education*. Harvard led the way with an increase of 45 percent. Blacks made up about 6 percent of Harvard's Class of 1996, and now black students routinely make up about 11 percent of Harvard's classes. Brown was the only Ivy that saw no increase in its black acceptance rates over the 16-year period, and its classes were made up by about 6 percent of black students.

Here's how all the Ivies stacked up in the study by *The Journal of Blacks in Higher Education:*

School	Percent Increase of Black Students
Harvard	45
Cornell	40
UPenn	40
Princeton	32
Dartmouth	28
Yale	15
Columbia	14
Brown	0

Accepting black students is only part of the process of diversifying a school's student body. The yield, or number of accepted students who end up enrolling, also has to increase among black students to increase diversification.

Real Life _____

According to *The Journal of Blacks in Higher Education*, 16 of the country's top colleges saw increases in the number of black students who entered as freshmen from 2006 to 2007. The University of California Los Angeles led the way with a 115 percent increase in its yield of black students. University of Virginia had a 38 percent increase, and Johns Hopkins, Carnegie Mellon, and Columbia all saw increases of more than 20 percent.

Over recent years several of the top colleges had seen significant increases in the number of black students entering as freshmen, while others, including many Ivies, were seeing their numbers go down. The decrease in black attendance led to substantial changes to how some of those schools help students pay for a college education. See Chapter 12 for more on how top colleges have changed their financial aid systems.

The push to diversify the student bodies isn't without controversy, even among those who are being helped. Another study by *The Journal of Blacks in Higher Education* claims that the black students being helped by race sensitivity in admissions offices aren't necessarily the children of parents and grandparents who suffered from generations of American discrimination during the Jim Crow era. According to the 2007 study, 41 percent of all black students at Ivy League schools had at least one foreign-born parent. That number was almost twice the national average for black students at all colleges and universities.

"Clearly, the historical goals of affirmative action to help black students who were descendants of slaves and who had undergone generations of economic hardship during the Jim Crow era are no longer the driving force behind racial diversity efforts at selective American colleges and universities," the study states.

Regarding Hispanic students, the question arises of what *Hispanic* actually means. On his website, private college counselor Mark Montgomery discusses a question raised by a student whose parents were born in Spain. She wanted to know whether it would be okay to check the Hispanic box on her college application.

"This student is asking the question precisely because she understands that to claim to be a 'minority' is, in a sense, to claim that she is somehow underprivileged," Montgomery says. "Or that she is a victim of discrimination. She knows, in her heart of hearts, that her Spanish surname is the only thing she has in common with a girl with a similar last name who grew up in Queens of a single mother who cleans hotel rooms for a living."

It's a moral dilemma that each person needs to work out for himself: whether to benefit from a minority heritage even though you've not been subject to the trials of other minorities.

On the Asian side of the issue, Asian-Americans no longer are considered underrepresented minorities at top colleges and universities. Across the country, Asians make up anywhere from 10 percent to 40 percent of a top college's student body.

Disabilities

The disabilities that make you who you are also might help you get into the college of your choice. As I said earlier, you need a hook to get your college application on the yes pile. Everyone at Harvard or Yale is going to be at the top of their classes in high school and have near perfect standardized test scores, but doing that while overcoming a disability—whether it be physical or mental—is something that definitely can make your application stand out.

For some, the hook might be a physical disability; for others it might be a learning disability she overcame. Although you might feel uncomfortable using your disability to help get you into college, realize that it's just another part of the process. If you were diagnosed with a mental or physical disability, you should mention it on your college application and consider using it as the subject of your admissions essay. In fact, according to one estimate, the percentage of college freshmen in the United States with a learning disability has more than doubled from 15 percent in 1985 to 32 percent in 2008.

> **Cheat Sheet**
>
> If given the opportunity, include a photograph of yourself with your college application. The photograph will give admissions officers someone to identify with and provide a face for your name.

In addition to mentioning your disability on your application and in your essay, take the following steps to ensure your disability doesn't slow your college application process or set you back when it comes to standardized tests:

◆ Start early on your college application, and be sure you give yourself enough time.

◆ Mention your disability, but don't make it the focus of your entire application. Schools are under no obligation to give you a longer look because of your disability, so make sure you highlight all your other strengths.

◆ Find out which programs are available to assist you with your disability. For instance, you might be allowed to take extra time for the SAT or ACT. Find out early in high school if this is true. The process to get extra time or accommodations is hefty and must be done through the school.

Talent

Do you juggle? You know, like balls and pins—not your classes and extracurricular activities. Do you paint, take photographs, or mold clay? Talent could play an important role in making you stand out from other applicants. I'm not telling you to send the admissions office the macaroni self-portrait you made, but if you have real talent you should mention it somewhere in your application or essay.

I have had extremely talented students in the past who sent a few art slides to their schools of choice even though they weren't applying as art majors.

When I talk about talent, though, I'm sort of joking about the juggling thing. Don't submit a video of yourself juggling five tennis balls. Now, if you're the No. 1 ranked juggler in the country (I guess there's gotta be a juggler ranking out there somewhere!), then sure, make mention of that on your application and include a video.

Cheat Sheet

The general rule of when to focus a portion of your admissions process on a talent is when it's something that really sets you apart—something you've been recognized for. If you've won regional or statewide art contests, definitely send a sample of your work. If you're an excellent local athlete who doesn't have the desire to play in college, submit tapes of yourself at a track meet or playing in a basketball game and be sure you include references to any records you might have set.

When considering the talents to mention, always consider the most important question: What makes you stand out from the pack?

Not So Obvious

Things like family history, race, and talent are pretty obvious intangibles when it comes to applying to a top school, right? There are also a couple of important intangibles that aren't so obvious.

For starters, where you live could help your chances of getting into a top school. Just as with the racial makeup of a college class, schools also want to diversify where that college class comes from. If you're from an underrepresented section of the country, you might have a better chance of gaining entry than someone from New York City or Boston.

Where You Live

Top colleges take geography into consideration because they want their classes to have as many states and countries represented as possible. What colleges won't tell you is that sometimes someone applying from a remote place is given a little more leeway on test scores and grades than someone applying from a big city.

The largest percentage of applicants to the Ivy League schools, as well as most of the top schools, come from New York State public schools, and more than 85 percent of those students fall into the range of what is acceptable by those colleges. It only stands to reason that if you are applying from states less represented in the application pool, standards will not be quite as stringent.

Many years ago I had a top sophomore student relocate with her family from New York to Iowa in the middle of her sophomore year. As a freshman and sophomore, she had taken the most challenging and difficult courses and had taken the SAT 2 in biology after her freshman year and received a 680. Clearly, she would have been a viable candidate for the top schools but would have looked the same as most of the other applicants.

After her move to Iowa, this student was accepted to Harvard, Princeton, Yale, Columbia, Cornell, and the University of Chicago. In one of her letters to me, she said that moving was a double-edged sword because on one hand it was difficult to leave her family and friends, but on the other, she knew that had she stayed in New York she never would have gotten into all those schools.

Whether colleges admit it or not, geography certainly plays a role in acceptance.

The Internet

If you post something on the Internet, you're putting it out there for all the world—and admissions officers—to see. Do schools check the blogs and MySpace profiles of 100 percent of their applicants? No, that would be next to impossible. But they run students' names through Internet searches on occasion, and you have to ask yourself whether you'd want a college admissions officer to see what might come up if she searched your name.

The Internet no longer is the wave of the future; it's the present, and colleges are catching on. An official with MIT's admissions office said he has accounts on all of the major community websites, including Friendster, Facebook, and MySpace.

In an article published by the National Association for College Admission Counseling, Ben Jones, Communications Director for the MIT Office of Admissions, said the websites are used to communicate with applicants to help them, not hurt them.

"I don't 'research' applicants online using their pages in these communities—although other schools do, from what I read in the news. My interactions with applicants and current MIT students are initiated by them—not by me," he said.

The most important thing to take from Mr. Jones is that some schools do look up pages on these online communities, and what you have on there, including pictures of you partying or off-color posts about your boyfriend or girlfriend, could be a strike against you.

Beware

If you're going to include an e-mail address in your college application, make sure it's something respectful. Don't make your e-mail address partyguy4ever@ e-mailplace.com. Use something basic, such as an arrangement of your initials. Another thing to consider is that you don't want an address that uses 0 (zero) versus O (the letter O), underscores, or l/I versus L/I if possible. You want to avoid any chance of error.

Jeannine Lalonde, Assistant Dean of Admission at the University of Virginia, said there were two reasons she started talking to high school students on these community websites. The first reason, she said, was to show students that they shouldn't be afraid of admissions officers. The other reason was to make students understand that their sites could be seen by college staffers and that they should stop and think before posting questionable photographs or writings.

All that being said, the Internet doesn't have to be a scary place where you're trying to hide things from college admissions officers. If you have a website or blog where you have a lot of in-depth writing or a collection of photographs, you should consider including that information on your college application.

When considering what to include on your personal, MySpace, or Facebook site, ask yourself this simple question: Is this something I'd want my parents or grandparents to see?

The Least You Need to Know

◆ Top schools are looking to diversify their classes based on race and where students are from.

◆ Find a hook to make your application stand out from the others.

◆ If you're a legacy, you likely have a leg up on your peers.

◆ Anything you put on the Internet could be seen by admissions officers.

Chapter 11

The College Tours

In This Chapter

- ◆ Where to tour
- ◆ What to look for
- ◆ Collecting your thoughts
- ◆ Trusting your initial reactions

What better way to decide which schools you want to apply to than to visit them and get a firsthand look at campus life and what you'll be diving into. You really should visit as many schools as possible—or at least your three or four finalists. Sometimes geography, time constraints, financial issues, or other logistics make it difficult to visit every school you're considering, but I ask students if they would buy a pair of sneakers without trying them on. The same goes for colleges.

Choosing a college is the most important decision you're going to make in your first 18 years, and maybe in your life. And although setting up visits at 10 schools in different locations around the country might seem overwhelming, you'll regret not visiting a school if you end up choosing it and then disliking it after you get to the campus.

To assist you in your pursuit to visit all the schools you're applying to, consider making regional trips covering four schools in two days.

Try not to visit more than two schools per day if possible. Visiting more than two schools will overload you with information, and you'll forget what you liked or didn't like about each campus.

Why Visit?

Everyone knows the Ivies, along with schools like MIT, Stanford, and Duke, are the country's top colleges. So if deciding which school to go to were as easy as just picking a top college, then you'd apply to the schools, post the ones that accepted you on a dart board, and let fate have its way. But there's a lot more that goes into selecting the right school, and a lot of what you need to know can be found out during a college tour—and not from a college's website or brochure.

For instance, a tour gives you the opportunity to:

◆ Talk to active students

◆ Taste the cafeteria food

◆ Get a feel for the campus

◆ Get a sense of the demographic makeup

Most importantly, while on a campus you can ask yourself the critical question, "Can I picture myself here?" If the answer is no, obviously you've done yourself a service by checking out the school before deciding to attend.

Preparation

Touring a college campus is a bit more complex than loading the family into the car and driving cross-country. There is some planning that must go into it.

First of all, you need to contact the school to find out when tours are offered and whether you have to schedule one. You'd hate to drive hundreds of miles only to find out that your tour will consist of you and a guide book. Calling ahead of time and letting the admissions office know you're coming also could set you up for an informal interview where someone from the college will get a first look at who you are. I'll explain later in this chapter how this interview is different from the interview you'll likely have after you send in your application.

> **Real Life** _____
>
> "Research, research, research. Through the school's website and/or a college tour, learn as much as possible about the school's academic and cultural atmosphere. Knowledge about the university will prepare the applicant to sit down and successfully complete the application. A passion for a school will tend to come out naturally if the student has really done his or her homework."
>
> —Rachel Korn, a former Ivy League admissions officer and editor of *How to Survive Getting into College*

You also want to do some research on the school before you get there. Find out everything you can so you know what questions to ask. Arriving well armed with a knowledge of the school also will help you avoid any missteps, like asking about a major that the school doesn't offer.

Pack your tour bag with a map of the campus so you don't get lost for four hours looking for the student union, a camera, and a paper and pen so you can take notes.

Finally, make a list of your college priorities before you arrive. That is, list the things that are most important to you. This way, if your tour guide doesn't mention those things throughout your time on campus, you can be sure to follow up with him later. Don't get home only to realize you forgot to ask a question about something that's important to you.

When to Go

The best time to go on a college tour is when you should be in class yourself. Monday through Thursday, when a college campus is in full tilt, is the ideal time to visit. Because the college year typically begins in the late summer before high school classes do, you might be able to avoid missing any class yourself. But teachers and guidance counselors generally are willing to accommodate your need to visit colleges; it simply comes with the territory.

Here are some other when-to-visit tips suggested by the College Board:

◆ High school holidays that fall on a Monday, when most colleges are in session, are an ideal time to visit.

◆ Late summer before your senior year and through that winter generally are the best times to visit college campuses.

◆ Juniors who are considering early action and students who play fall sports should consider spring visits.

So you know when to go, but what about when not to go? It seems simplistic, but don't visit a college when it's not in session. So don't go during major holiday periods such as Thanksgiving and Christmas. Also, college campuses might look beautiful in the middle of the summer, but if there aren't students there, a visit really does you little good. Also, avoid going during exams and on weekends.

On Campus

Now that you're on campus, it's not time to be shy. Get that deer in the headlights look off your face and assert yourself by meeting with admissions officers and asking questions of students on campus. You'll never get another opportunity to make a first impression with the admissions officer, and you'll never get a better opportunity to get answers from students who truly know about the school.

Your time on campus should consist of everything from eating in the cafeteria to checking out the library and dorms. You want to get a real feel for the area and what it's like to be a student there. Most importantly, you're going to want to remember what you liked and didn't like about the school. I'll give you some tips on how to do that later in this chapter.

Hi, My Name Is ...

The interview you have during a campus visit likely will be a little more informal than the one you could have after you've submitted your application. You'll likely have what's called an *on-campus informational interview*. Unlike evaluative interviews, informational college interviews are, at least in theory, not about deciding whether you're a good fit for the school. Instead, colleges set up informational interviews to add a personal touch to the admissions process and to answer any questions you might have as an applicant.

Informational interviews could be with an admissions officer, but they could also be with a student employee or volunteer. Read Chapter 17 to find out how to prepare for and present yourself during an interview.

> **Beware**
>
> In any informational interview, and particularly one with an admissions officer, you should realize that the interviewer might take some notes about your session and share that information with the committee—despite the fact that you were promised only an "informational" interview.

What to Ask

Yes, if you're on a college tour you have to be that annoying person who stops students and asks them a bunch of questions about what it's like to attend that college. Don't worry, though, they'll feel special because you asked them and will want to show off in front of their friends. Seriously, though, the most honest answers you'll get to your questions about a school will come from the students already at the school. Admissions counselors have a goal of trying to lure you to the school, especially if you're a top student who likely will gain admission to more than one Ivy. But students have no agenda and will tell you the truth.

So, if you take a tour on a nice day, stop someone while walking on campus and politely ask whether you can talk to him for a couple of minutes. If it's raining, head to the cafeteria or student union.

Here's a list of questions to take with you on your college tour for just this occasion:

 ◆ What do you like about the college?

 ◆ What don't you like about the college?

 ◆ If you had to do it all over, would you attend this school?

 ◆ How is the food?

 ◆ What is a typical weekend like?

 ◆ What percentage of students partake in Greek life?

 ◆ Is Greek life a strong influence?

 ◆ Does social life take place on campus or off?

 ◆ Will a student who doesn't drink be happy?

 ◆ Can people of different ethnic, racial, and cultural backgrounds be comfortable here?

 ◆ What is it like here for gay and alternative students?

 ◆ Do you feel safe here?

 ◆ Are people proud to be here?

 ◆ Do you feel that you are getting a good education here?

 ◆ Are you generally taught by professors or teaching assistants (TAs)?

 ◆ How large are the class sizes of introductory courses?

- What are the strong, popular majors?

- What are the weak majors?

- Is it a cutthroat atmosphere, or are students willing to work together and help one another?

- Do many people spend their junior years abroad?

- Where are some of the places that students are doing internships?

- How hard is it to get into courses, especially as a freshman?

- Where else did you apply?

Cheat Sheet

Schedule half a day for yourself at each school you visit. Half a day should give you enough time to tour the school, speak with students, and meet with an admissions officer or their designee.

What Else to Do

The basics of visiting a college are what I've already mentioned: taking a tour, eating in the cafeteria, setting up an interview, and talking to students and professors. But there are a lot of other small things you can do to enhance your experience and get your foot in the door.

For starters, pick up any piece of campus literature you can get your hands on, including the school's student newspaper. You'll get to look this stuff over after you've left campus, and it'll help you come up with questions about issues you might not have thought about. Also, visit the school's financial aid office and try to sit down with a financial aid officer. In addition to getting an idea about what financial aid and scholarships options are out there for you, it's also a good opportunity to build up a rapport with someone in the office just as you would with someone in the admissions office. This relationship and name recognition could help you with your financial aid in the future. It's always better to be able to ask for someone by name instead of simply asking for "someone who can help me."

Others things you can do on campus are:

- Get business cards and names of people you meet for future contacts

- Attend a class that interests you

◆ Check out bulletin boards to see what's going on around campus

◆ Shop in the school's bookstore

◆ Ask people what they do on the weekends

◆ See a dorm that wasn't on the tour

◆ Drive around the community outside of campus

Virtual Tours

So what happens if you just don't have the time or money to visit every school on your list? Well, lucky for you a number of websites offer great resources and almost make you feel like you're on campus.

One such site is www.campustours.com, which includes slideshows and panoramic views of several areas on hundreds of college campuses. The site's panoramic function actually allows you to zoom in and out and change the angle of what you're looking at, making you feel like you're actually in the room.

The website also includes basic information such as available courses and tuition costs. Simply do an Internet search on *virtual college tours* to come up with a list of options. And, don't forget to check out each college's own website. Those sites will have a wealth of information if you're not able to get to campus.

But it doesn't stop there—virtual college fairs are starting to become a popular trend. In 2008, a group called College Week Live hosted a virtual two-day college fair held completely online. People who participated were able to be part of online interviews with admissions officers and chat with current students. Plus, lectures about the college application process were held in virtual meeting halls. Although none of the several dozen colleges that have partnered with College Week Live are Ivy League schools, it seems that this technology is the wave of the future and soon will be standard for all schools.

def•i•ni•tion

A **virtual college tour** enables you to view a school's campus on the Internet without setting foot outside your house. Several websites provide detailed photographs and videos, giving you a sense of what a college is like.

The Assessment

As important as visiting a college is, being able to remember what you saw after you left is imperative. Good notes not only will help you decide which school you want to attend, but could also help you get into that college. Sometimes college applications ask why you chose to apply to that school and/or why you chose to apply to a particular program. Good notes will help you distinguish one school from another, sometimes months after you have visited. With specific, clear, detailed notes, your answers to the application questions will be well thought out, comprehensive, and specific to the question.

Additionally, good notes will help you make lists of pros and cons about each school. And those lists ultimately can help you decide where you want to go.

Worksheets

The easiest way to take notes about a school is to arrive with a worksheet you can fill out throughout the tour or immediately after. You can find several worksheets on the Internet, but here are some of the basics that should be included on your worksheet:

- Name of college
- Date visited
- Name of tour guide
- Name of interviewer and impressions
- Name of professors you met and impressions
- Strength of possible majors
- Overall strengths
- Why you would apply
- Weaknesses/drawbacks
- Overall impression of school

The best time to fill out the worksheet if you can't do it while on the tour is immediately after, when you're in the car or back in the hotel room. This way everything you've seen and heard still will be fresh in your mind. Don't get all the way home and not be able to remember which school had the nicer dorm room or better food.

Gut Feelings

When it comes down to it, the decision you make about which college to attend will be a gut feeling. Sure, you need to utilize all the tools in this chapter to make that gut decision as educated a decision as possible. But it's up to you to determine how you think you'll feel on a certain campus and whether you can see yourself spending four years there.

If you're a top student who has a chance at gaining admission to several top schools, you know you're going to get a great education one way or another. But if you're not happy on campus, you're jeopardizing your future because if you're unhappy you might not work as hard.

So, do yourself the benefit of collecting as much information as you can, and ask for help from your parents, peers, and counselors. But remember—it's up to you to decide.

The Least You Need to Know

- Tour as many schools as you can.
- Try to set up interviews.
- Ask as many questions as you can.
- Take good notes and bring a camera.

12

Can I Afford It?

In This Chapter

◆ What it costs

◆ Changes to financial aid and scholarship policies

◆ Ways to pay

◆ How to research scholarships

There's no surprise here: A college education is expensive and is getting more so each year. And it's even more expensive when you're eyeing an Ivy or other top college. Consider these figures: The annual average college cost for a private, four-year college was $23,712 for the 2007–2008 school year. That was up 6.3 percent compared with the year before. Compare that with the annual average cost of a public four-year school, which was $6,185 for the 2007–2008 school year. That, too, was up 6.6 percent compared with the year prior.

The average cost of tuition at an Ivy for the 2008–2009 school year was $36,760. Over four years, not including likely increases, that's more than $147,000 in tuition and fees alone. That's not including room and board, books, and other costs that come up, like a Saturday night pizza. If you factor in room and board, your four-year total jumps up to more than $200,000.

Most people can't afford to plunk down about a quarter of a million dollars on a college education. But there are other options, including financial aid and scholarships. I also discuss later in this chapter how, after years of criticism, Ivy League schools are trying to open their doors to more students who otherwise wouldn't be able to afford an Ivy education. While an Ivy education still might not be available to all who want it, it's certainly becoming more accessible.

What's It Pay For?

There are what colleges call *billable* and *nonbillable costs*, but as I said in the opening of this chapter, the biggest ticket item you'll pay for falls under the heading of tuition and fees. Fees include things like a college healthcare plan and the cost of providing you with an identification card.

def•i•ni•tion

College costs are broken down into two main categories: billable and nonbillable. **Billable costs** refer to tuition, room and board, health fees, and student fees. **Nonbillable costs** refer to the cost of books as well as personal and travel expenses.

After tuition and fees, there's your room and board, which is your dorm and meal plan. Then there are your books, which typically cost about $1,500 per year at an Ivy League school.

Here's the tuition, fees, and room and board breakdowns for the Ivy League schools along with Stanford and MIT for the 2008–2009 school year.

Columbia

Tuition and fees:	$39,326
Room and board:	$9,980
Total:	$49,306

UPenn

Tuition and fees:	$37,526
Room and board:	$10,622
Total:	$48,148

Dartmouth

Tuition and fees:	$37,250
Room and board:	$10,930
Total:	$48,180

Brown

Tuition and fees:	$37,718
Room and board:	$10,022
Total:	$47,740

Cornell

Tuition and fees:	$36,504
Room and board:	$11,690
Total:	$48,194

Harvard

Tuition and fees:	$36,173
Room and board:	$11,042
Total:	$47,215

Yale

Tuition and fees:	$35,300
Room and board:	$10,700
Total:	$46,000

Princeton

Tuition and fees:	$34,290
Room and board:	$11,405
Total:	$45,695

MIT

Tuition and fees:	$36,390
Room and board:	$10,860
Total:	$47,250

Stanford

Tuition and fees:	$36,030
Room and board:	$11,182
Total:	$47,212

When considering what it'll cost you to attend an Ivy League school, you can't stop at the basics of tuition, fees, room and board, and books. You also have to consider that Saturday night pizza and the cost of getting to and from school over the holidays.

There are dozens of miscellaneous costs—or nonbillable costs—that schools don't tell you about. But it's up to you to determine whether you'll need a car for college and whether you can afford that car as well as the insurance for it. Additionally, even though you might be eligible for financial help with the tuition and room and board costs—or billable costs—you aren't going to receive help from the school for that pizza or car insurance. So as important as it is to determine whether a school is the right academic fit for you, you also have to determine whether it's the right financial fit. Perhaps you have to ask yourself if you'll feel out of place or embarrassed if you can't afford that ski trip over winter break that everyone else is going on.

Ways to Pay

There are several ways to pay for an Ivy education, including school-based scholarships, private scholarships, federal aid, and private loans. As I mentioned earlier, more than ever before, top schools are looking to open their doors to students who typically wouldn't be able to afford it. A majority of the Ivies and other top schools recently rewrote their rules for how they discount tuition for low- and middle-class families.

You need to consider several factors when deciding how you'll finance your college education, and it's a tough road to navigate. But the important thing is to not get sticker shock when you see how much it'll cost and to realize that you might end up paying less at an Ivy because of their deep financial pockets than you would at a non-Ivy private school.

Getting Help

Before I address the various ways you can pay for college, it's important to know that you don't have to make these decisions alone. Just as independently hired advisers can walk you through the application process, there also are people who can help you figure out how you'll pay for college. It might seem silly to think that, if you don't expect to be able to pay for college, you'd pay someone to consider your options. But the money you spend on a financial adviser could end up saving you money on your tuition. More importantly, the financial adviser can see to it that you indeed are able to afford tuition at a top college.

Beware

Be weary of any financial aid consultant who promises to "get you all the money you need to pay for college." Consultants can't make those guarantees.

A financial aid consultant has no interest in the school you pick and doesn't try to sway you toward one lending institution over another. Instead, the consultant's goal is to help your family receive the best financial aid possible. Typically, college aid planners are financial consultants as well as accountants and experts in tax law.

The process of hiring a financial aid consultant should be similar to what you go through when you hire a private admissions counselor. You should ask for references and check with peers who also have used financial counselors.

You can use the following websites to check out a financial aid consultant:

◆ www.studentaid.ed.gov/students/publications/lsa/index.html

◆ www.bbb.com

School-Based Aid

Ivy League schools for years have been criticized for their inability to open their doors to low- and middle-income students. According to *The New York Times*, 27 of the 30 top-ranked American colleges saw a decline in the percentage of low-income students between 2004 and 2006. Low-income students typically are qualified as students who are eligible for Pell Grants—a federal, low-income loan program based on several factors, including income, the number of people in the household, and the state in which you live.

"In a society that claims to believe in equal opportunity, our top universities should lead by example," a *Times* opinions writer said of the trend.

The criticism also came from inside the Ivies. In 2004, Lawrence Summers, then president of Harvard, noted that three-fourths of the students at selective colleges come from the top income quartile and only 9 percent come from the bottom two quartiles. Summers then announced a new initiative that would make the cost of attending Harvard free for students who come from families with incomes of less than $40,000.

And that was just the beginning. Since late 2007, a majority of the top colleges have recalculated how they distribute financial aid for low- and middle-income students. Here are some of the most recent tweaks that have been made:

◆ In December 2007, Harvard capped family contributions at 10 percent of income for families that earn up to $180,000 per year. In 2006, the school extended its free-ride program to families that make up to $60,000 per year. Families that make between $60,000 and $120,000 contribute to tuition based on a sliding scale.

◆ In January 2008, Yale announced it would eliminate 50 percent of tuition for students from families that make up to $200,000 per year. Yale is free for families that make up to $60,000 per year.

◆ In January 2008, Dartmouth announced free tuition for students who come from families that make up to $75,000 per year.

◆ In February 2008, Brown eliminated tuition for students from families making up to $60,000 per year.

◆ In March 2008, Columbia announced free rides for students who come from families that make up to $60,000 per year. The same month, MIT announced free rides for families that make up to $75,000 per year.

According to Princeton's website, families whose yearly income is less than $53,000 per year will have a "majority" of their costs covered through a combination of grants and student earnings. The average grant awarded by the school for the Class of 2011 was $43,900.

Cornell and UPenn don't have cutoffs or a set structure for how they provide aid but determine their packages based on a number of factors. Visit each school's website to see how it comes up with its aid packages.

Other top schools around the country are following the path being laid by the Ivies. In February 2008, Stanford announced that it would eliminate tuition for students who come from families with annual incomes of less than $100,000. The university also pays for most of the room and board for students from families that make less than $60,000 per year. CalTech also announced in late 2007 that it would replace loans with grants for its neediest students.

Private schools finance their aid through the returns of their endowment programs, and as far as endowments go, the Ivies are rolling in cash. Close to 100 colleges, including all the Ivies, have endowments of more than $1 billion. Harvard led the way in 2008 with an endowment of more than $34 billion; Yale followed with $22.5 billion. Not only are these endowments huge, but they're growing. Harvard's 2008 total was up 20 percent over 2007, and Yale's pool had grown by 25 percent.

Federal Aid

All students applying for financial aid must complete the Free Application for Federal Student Aid (FAFSA). Students should fill out the form online or on paper as soon as possible after January 1 of their senior year. This might mean students and parents will need to prepare their taxes earlier than usual. Each potential college's website should be visited to determine all the appropriate deadlines.

The FAFSA data is processed by the Central Processing System (CPS), and the federal need-analysis formula is applied. The information on the FAFSA form is used to calculate the student's expected family contribution (EFC). The EFC is, in accordance with the federal formula, how much the family should be responsible for or capable of paying. This amount is not necessarily what the family will pay. The EFC—sometimes in conjunction with something called the College Scholarship Service (CSS) profile—is used as a point of reference for determining how much institutional aid, in addition to federal and state aid, a student may receive.

> **Cheat Sheet** _____
>
> In addition to the FAFSA, many private colleges and universities require that the college scholarship service (CSS) profile be completed. The profile is used by schools that need additional information above what the FAFSA supplies to award institutional need-based or merit-based aid. The website provides a list of schools that require the CSS profile. You can visit it at apps.collegeboard.com/cbsearch_ss/welcome.jsp.

Federal Student Aid is the office you'll deal with when it comes to federal financial aid. Just as its name states, it administers federal financial aid support. The agency, which is an office of the U.S. Department of Education, oversees $391 billion in outstanding loans; annually processes about 14 million FAFSAs; and in 2005–2006 handed out $78 billion in new aid to almost 10 million post-secondary students and their families, according to the office's website.

Here are the basics of the federal financial aid process:

◆ The student fills out the FAFSA.

◆ A need analysis is conducted.

◆ A Student Aid Report (SAR) is generated by the federal government and mailed to the family. An Institutional Student Information Record (ISIR) is sent to the colleges.

◆ After the student has been accepted and all the necessary financial forms have been filed, the college sends an award letter notifying the student of the financial package being awarded. The package consists of the total cost of attendance (tuition, books, supplies, room, board, transportation, and miscellaneous) at that school and then a breakdown of the various financial aid being offered to assist in covering those billable and nonbillable costs.

The maximum amount of federal and state aid available often is insufficient to offset demonstrated need. It is the decision of the college to determine how much of the deficit will be made up with its own money.

Some of the federal programs that aid is handed out under include the Pell Grant; the federal supplemental opportunity grant (FSEOG), which does not have to be repaid but is not offered at all schools; and federal work-study (FWS), which provides part-time jobs with the money raised going directly to tuition.

Real Life

"Do not accept your first aid package offer if you believe it will not be enough for you to enable your access to the college. Colleges compete for good students and are willing to sit down and listen. If you have 'special' circumstances, such as excessive medical expenses, which are not reflected in the base needs analysis, this needs to be shared and documented. Make it known that this is very important to you. Most schools and financial aid officers respect this and will do whatever they can to help you with access."

—Howard Leslie, Dean of Student Financial Services at New York's Monroe College and Second Vice President of the New York State Financial Aid Administrators Association

The loans that are going to be part of your financial aid package—federal direct student loan programs and federal family education loan program—are fairly low interest if they are subsidized and don't have to be repaid until after graduation.

Subsidized loans always are awarded on the basis of financial need. The federal government essentially is subsidizing the interest on the loan by paying back the interest until you can begin payment, which typically isn't until after you've graduated. An unsubsidized loan, if you qualify for one, has the interest charged from the time it is disbursed until it is paid back in full. Unsubsidized loans are awarded to students who do not demonstrate financial need.

Private Lending

In years past you couldn't swing a stick without hitting a private lender. But those days are long gone, and the pool of private lenders and loans is drying up. According to *The Wall Street Journal*, about 10 percent of the 9 million college borrowers in the United States seek private loans. But in 2008, lenders such as Bank of America, Citigroup, and Wachovia stopped or curtailed private lending. The change came as private investors stayed away from investing in the securities these banks use to raise capital for the loans.

And those banks that still are providing loans have set much stricter credit standards. Students who don't have co-signers for their loans don't have the credit history to build up a strong credit score and are being left out in the cold. Mark Kantrowitz, publisher of Finaid.org, projected that the policy change would leave as many as 200,000 students ineligible for private loans for the 2008–2009 school year.

But even if you could take out a private loan, would you want to? Variable rates of private loans range from 6 percent to 16 percent and could include fees as high as 11.5 percent. Federally backed Stafford Loans, however, carried a maximum fixed interest rate of 6.8 percent in 2008. PLUS Loans, which are for parents, charged 8.5 percent.

The difference between Stafford Loans and PLUS Loans is that Stafford Loans limit borrowing to $3,500 for the freshman year, $4,500 for the sophomore year, and $5,500 annually thereafter. PLUS Loans, however, allow parents to borrow up to the full cost of attendance.

So if you qualify, the most cost-effective bet is to try to secure a federally backed loan.

Scholarships

In addition to school-based and federal aid, scholarships are another way to help pay for college.

Some scholarships are based on whether you're left-handed and have red hair. Other scholarships are based on your interests and the field you plan to study. Still other scholarships are merit-based and require that you maintain a certain grade point average.

Your high school could be a great source for scholarship information. Many private agencies and corporations, including Coca-Cola and Tylenol, advertise their scholarships through local high schools. Also, your guidance office or college center can be a great resource for local and state scholarships. Various credit unions, engineering firms, architectural firms, and banks offer local scholarships.

Many colleges have their own scholarships. Some of those are based solely on what's on your application, whereas others require a separate application. Always check a college's literature and website for scholarship specifics.

Cheat Sheet

You'd be surprised how many obscure scholarships are out there that are based on your last name, hair color, or what your father does for a living. Don't sell yourself short when it comes to potential scholarships. Try to think about anything that makes you unique—there might be a scholarship out there for you that rewards that uniqueness.

The Least You Need to Know

◆ Top colleges are doing more to open their doors to low- and middle-income students.

◆ Financial advisers can help you through the financial aid process.

◆ Federal help is available, although it likely won't cover the whole cost of college.

◆ Try to stay away from high-interest private loans.

Part 4

The Application

If you've done everything you can to help yourself gain admission into a top school, then the application is your place to let all that shine. From the essay to the recommendations and the interview, you have several opportunities to show a school who you are and what you can bring to the table.

In Part 4, I discuss the most effective way to get your message across—and that message is that you're the best fit for that school. I also discuss the advantages and disadvantages of applying to college early and how the rules of that process have changed.

"I don't care how fast you can make the delivery, it's too presumptuous to submit your application by hand.
And don't hold it so tightly—you're getting it all crinkled."

Chapter 13

Applying Early

In This Chapter

◆ The differences between early entry programs

◆ Types of early entry programs that are binding

◆ Early decision vs. early action

◆ The schools that have dropped early decision programs

A little more than 8 percent of the high schoolers who applied to Yale for the Class of 2012 were accepted. But more than 18 percent of students who applied early action to Yale received a thick envelope instead of a thin one. It's not hard to understand that an 18 percent chance of getting into the school of your choice is better than an 8 percent one.

Across the board, acceptance rates are higher for students applying to top schools during the early cycle than they are for those who go through the regular cycle. The percentage of students who were accepted early to Yale was 10 percentage points higher than the rate accepted during regular admission for the Class of 2007. The 10 percentage point disparity at Yale actually was one of the slimmer disparities for the class of 2012 when compared to other top schools.

Just like every other step toward gaining admission into the school of your choice, you need to pay close attention to each school's admissions guidelines, deadlines, and protocols. Some early-admission programs are binding. Others aren't but don't allow you to apply to more than one school early.

The early application process can be confusing because there are so many types of early programs that schools use, including the following:

♦ Early decision   A school with an early decision *(ED)* application policy allows a prospective student to apply to the school early but doesn't allow the student to apply to other schools until the regular admission process. Acceptance from an early decision school typically is binding.

♦ Early action   A school with this type of application policy allows prospective students to apply early to as many schools as they want. Acceptance to an early action school isn't binding.

♦ Single-choice early action   Under single-choice early action, the university provides an admissions decision by December 15 but the admitted student has until May 1 to decide whether he will accept the admission.

def•i•ni•tion

Many schools use the acronym **ED** when discussing their early decision programs. Schools that offer a second round of early decision also use the term *ED II.*

Some schools even offer a second round of early admission applications. It's critical that you understand the process from the beginning so you're not stuck in a situation you wish you could get out of.

Almost all early application programs have three acceptance options. You can be accepted, be rejected and not allowed to reapply, or have a decision on your application deferred until the regular application deadline. At most schools, though, a deferment usually turns into a rejection.

Early Decision

If you know with absolute certainty which school you want to attend, don't need your senior year grades to strengthen your GPA and make your application look better, and are able to deal with the stress of preparing your college application over a shorter period of time, then an early decision application could be your ticket into college.

Early decision is the ultimate "put-your-money-where-your-mouth-is" application, and it usually has to be submitted during the early fall of your senior year. Early decision programs are binding, which means that if you're accepted, you'll be expected to attend that school. I discuss the binding nature of early decision applications a bit more later in the chapter.

People who apply early decision have a better chance to get into a top school than through the regular application process. Whether you want to use early decision as a strategy is up to you, but you have to decide whether you have the time, grades, and stomach to handle the stress and rigor that come with an early decision application.

Beware _____

If you plan to apply to a college through an early admissions program, you have to schedule your standardized testing dates accordingly. In most cases, you should plan on taking the SAT 1 no later than November of your senior year and the ACT no later than October.

Upsides and Downsides of Applying Early

The obvious upside of applying early decision is that statistics show that early decision applicants have an overwhelmingly better chance of getting into a top school. Cornell accepted 1,142 students for the Class of 2012 through the early decision program—a 36 percent acceptance rate. By comparison, the school accepted 18 percent of the students who applied through the regular admission process. In essence, the probability of getting into Cornell's Class of 2012 was doubled if you applied early decision.

The same disparity in acceptance rates is applicable for all the nation's top schools, although the gap between early decision and regular decision is wider at some schools than others. At Johns Hopkins, for instance, the school usually accepts early decision applicants at a clip of about 50 percent, while about 25 percent of the regular decision applicants are accepted.

Cheat Sheet _____

Acceptance rates tend to be better for the early decision round of applications because the resumés of the students are stronger and schools know that the acceptance is binding, which means they have an opportunity to hand pick the types of students they want at their universities.

Top colleges like to be able to handpick the students who will make up their classes, and early decision enables them to do just that. Because early decision is binding, top colleges know if a student is offered admission he is required to accept it or else he will lose a significant deposit. So, the schools are able to pick the types of students they want without worrying that the students will turn them down and opt for another top school.

So, even though your chance of getting into a top school is better if you apply early decision, this form of an early application also favors the college more than any of the other policies because of its binding nature.

What It Takes

Applying early decision means you have to have all your application material in order and perfected well before the people who apply regular entry. This means that while other seniors are focusing on their early-year grades, you'll be working on your application, writing your essay, and tracking down letters of recommendation.

The rate of acceptance through early decision is higher than regular decision, but don't assume you're going to be accepted. This means you can't let your senior year grades suffer just because you're trying to get your application done. You have to be able to both study and complete your application. Know that most schools will want to see your first-quarter grades of senior year.

Here's an outline of how your junior and senior years have to shake out for you to get your early decision application completed in time:

◆ January–May of junior year:

Take the SAT and/or ACT.

Go on college tours.

◆ May–June of junior year:

Finish up any required SAT 2 exams.

◆ September–October of senior year:

Collect recommendations.

Complete application.

File application.

Take October SAT/ACT if necessary for regular application cycle.

◆ November of senior year:

Work on regular decision applications.

File any necessary financial aid forms.

As Cornell's website explains, several schools use the early decision process as a reward for students who decide that a certain school is their top choice and show no desire to attend any other school.

Just because you apply early decision and express a desire to attend that school above any other doesn't mean you're going to get in with a B average and subpar standardized test scores, though. It's hard to track how the grades and scores of students accepted early decision stack up against those who are accepted through the regular process. Although you might have a little more flexibility through early decision—you're typically competing against several thousand fewer students when applying early—the grades and scores required won't be that much different.

Real Life

"Because enthusiasm for Cornell is considered a plus, early decision applicants stand a better chance of gaining admission."

—Cornell University's website

It's Binding

As I mentioned earlier, early decision programs are binding. If you're accepted early decision at Cornell, you'll find out by mid-December. After you receive your acceptance, you're required to submit your deposit by early January. If you later decide that you don't want to attend Cornell, you'll lose that deposit.

Under early decision, you can't apply to other schools early decision. You have to pick just one. The system is based on the honor system, and if you don't abide by it your guidance counselor will. Your early decision application obviously has to be accompanied by your transcript, and your guidance counselor will send out an early decision transcript to only one school.

Beware

If by some chance your guidance counselor is overworked and you think you might be able to trick him into sending an early decision transcript to more than one school—don't. If you get caught, every school you've applied to early will reject you. It's a small world, and word of your dishonesty might even harm you during the regular admission cycle.

The major issue for students applying early decision is that they have to commit to a school before they are able to compare financial aid packages with other schools.

The inability to get a good look at what a financial aid package would look like has excluded many middle- and lower-class students from the early decision process over the years, though the new financial aid policies at most schools are changing that some.

If you accept a binding, early decision acceptance and your financial aid package doesn't work out, you won't always lose your deposit. In some cases the early decision commitment can be broken if the financial aid offered just isn't enough. It is difficult to break the contract, and there is a lot of red tape, but it's not unprecedented.

Changes at the Top

Facing criticism that early decision programs are aimed at the country's financial elite, several top colleges have decided to amend their early entry programs or abolish them all together. The criticism of the early admission programs came from what I mentioned earlier about an applicant's inability to compare financial aid offers if she applies early decision.

Harvard, Princeton, and the University of Virginia are the most notable colleges to end their early decision programs. Harvard announced its decision in 2006—it said the early decision process had become too stressful for students and was robbing them of their high school experience. But, the real criticism surrounding early decision programs is that they tend to favor the nation's wealthy.

Real Life

"This probably will not impact Harvard's ability to enroll their most desired students. It would be a very different matter if this bold move was taken by schools that sit just outside the Ivy League. We see early decision as a still important opportunity for students to express their strongest desire to be a member of our community."
—Karen Giannino, Colgate University's senior associate dean of admission, said of Harvard abandoning the early application process

Because binding early decision programs require that you attend that school if accepted, students are unable to compare financial aid from different schools. This typically leads to lower- and middle-class students forgoing the early decision application process and instead opting for a school that offers nonbinding early application options, such as MIT, Yale, and the University of Chicago, or waiting for the regular decision deadline. Nonbinding early applicants still are accepted at a higher rate than traditional applicants but have the ability to compare financial aid packages.

Some schools say they have no plans to drop the early-decision process, calling it an admissions tool that for decades has been effective in allowing them to recruit and accept the most talented students.

The Fallout

Some top schools recently have seen their largest pools of early applicants because other top schools have decided to do away with their early decision programs.

According to the *Daily Princetonian*, Yale received a record 4,888 early applications for the Class of 2012, a 36 percent increase from the Class of 2011. Columbia and Brown saw early applications go up by 6 percent, and Dartmouth's and Duke's early applicant pools went up by 9 percent and 5 percent, respectively. MIT, Georgetown, and the University of Chicago saw even higher increases of 13 percent, 31 percent, and 42 percent, respectively.

The increase in early applications at these schools can be directly attributed to Princeton and Harvard dropping their early decision programs. The result of the increased early applications is that although there are still much higher admission rates for early applications than for regular applications, the admission rates for the early round actually decreased at some of the top schools. For example, Yale accepted 20 percent of the students who applied early for the Class of 2011, but that number decreased to 18 percent for the Class of 2012.

With early applicants migrating elsewhere, Princeton officials said they weren't worried that by dropping the early application process they'd be losing the cream of the crop.

> **Real Life**
>
> "We literally had 10,000 students in our pool last year of almost 19,000 students who were qualified to be here, at the highest level. So what if some of them decide to go early somewhere else? We will still have thousands more from which to choose."
>
> —Princeton Dean of Admission Janet Rapelye in 2007

Other Early Admission Options

Although some schools have abandoned the early decision process, others have embraced less controversial approaches.

Under the early action program offered by many schools, students are able to apply early to only one school. Unlike early decision schools, though, students have until May to decide whether they'll accept their admission and their decision isn't binding.

The May date is key because it gives students more time to consider their financial aid options.

Still, some schools perceive even that program to be disadvantageous and too stressful, so those schools use an early application process that isn't binding and allows students to apply to other schools early.

The opinions about which program works best are almost as many as the number of colleges that exist. Again, it's really up to you to decide which works best for you.

Restrictive but Not Binding

Stanford calls it "restrictive early action," and Yale calls it "single-choice early action." Whatever they call it, both programs are basically the same.

Under restrictive early action, the university provides an admissions decision by December 15, but the admitted student has until May 1 to decide whether she'll accept the admission. May 1 is the same deadline for responding to schools you've applied to during the regular admissions process.

"Because a student's financial aid offer is often a critical factor in making a final college choice, Stanford's Restrictive Early Action program provides time for families to consider financial aid awards from multiple schools before making a final commitment to enroll," the school's website explains.

An overwhelming majority of schools that offer restrictive early action do not allow you to apply early to other colleges. But just like early decision, schools that offer restrictive early action or single-choice early action allow you to apply to other schools during the regular admissions cycle.

School	Early Admission Program
Yale	Single-choice early action
Harvard	N/A*
Cornell	Early decision
Princeton	N/A*
UPenn	Early decision
Dartmouth	Early decision
Columbia	Early decision
Brown	Early decision

School	Early Admission Program
MIT	Early action
Stanford	Restrictive early action
U of Chicago	Early action

Harvard and Princeton have gotten rid of their early application programs.

Early Action

Early action favors the students more than any of the other application processes. Just like early decision, schools that offer early action programs tend to accept students at a much higher rate through the early application process than they do the regular cycle. But unlike early decision, early action programs aren't binding and students have until May 1 to make their decision.

Also in the students' favor is that they can apply early action to as many schools as they want. Even though this plan clearly benefits the students, some would argue that because the commitment isn't there and because a student could apply to as many schools that have early action as he wants, colleges tend not to look at the student with the same seriousness of purpose that they look at an early decision candidate.

While the early action process might not give as critical a look at grades as early decision does, it's still used by several top schools that believe it enables them to give students of lesser financial means the ability to apply early and afford a top education.

> ### Real Life
>
> "We carefully reviewed our early action program in light of our fundamental commitment to making a University of Chicago education accessible to talented students, regardless of family financial resources. In many respects, our program, in contrast to early decision programs at other institutions, allows us to admit more students of limited means, while enabling those students to be sure they are getting the best possible financial aid packages."
>
> —Kenneth Warren, Deputy Provost for Minority Affairs and Research at the University of Chicago

Program	Binding	Can Apply Early to Other Colleges	Allowed to Apply to Other Colleges Regular Admission
Early decision	Yes	No	Yes
Early action	No	Yes	Yes
Single-choice early action	No	No	Yes

Round 2

Several schools, such as Rensselaer Polytechnic Institute, Emory, Union College, and Wesleyan, offer two rounds of early decision admissions.

For schools that do have a second early decision round, the rules for the second round usually are the same as they are for the first early decision applicants. You can apply to only one school early decision, and it's binding.

So, why do schools have two rounds of early decision applicants? The intended purpose of the second early decision round was to give schools more time to recruit students from geographically targeted locations and minorities who might not have had the opportunity to work with a guidance counselor. But several schools have done away with their second round of early decision after finding it ineffective. Stanford got rid of its second early decision round in 1998—only two years after it began—because the university realized more minority students were being admitted during the first early decision round than through regular admission.

Rolling Admission

Although not applicable to most of the country's traditionally top schools, several colleges and universities throughout the country offer rolling admission.

Under rolling admission, the admissions office reviews the applications as received and renders a decision when all application information is complete. The admissions process is "rolling," but most schools do have preferred deadlines, such as Nov. 15. Other schools only review applications over a four- to six-month period and don't truly keep admission rolling throughout the entire year.

Advantages to rolling admission are that you have more time to prepare your application and take your standardized tests, limiting the amount of stress you'll feel. But just because you have more time to apply doesn't mean you should use all that time. If schools award admission, financial aid, and housing assignments on a first-come first-serve basis, you don't want to be one of the last people to apply. You want to get applications in early to rolling admissions schools because many of the West Coast/Arizona/Colorado schools basically stop admitting kids, no matter how qualified, once they fill their classes.

You might consider using a school that utilizes rolling admission as a backup in case you don't get into the schools at the top of your list. Most top schools don't use rolling deadlines, though some of the smaller top liberal arts colleges do. Penn State is probably the highest-ranking large university that uses the rolling deadline.

Spring Admission

How would you like to take the first six months after high school to travel, work, or take on some community service?

Several schools—mostly liberal arts schools—now offer spring admission, affording students the opportunity to explore different opportunities after high school and take a break from studies for a couple of months.

Middlebury College, which is a top 5 liberal arts college according to *U.S. News & World Report*'s rankings, has offered February admission to students since the 1970s, and the February entries make up about a quarter of the school's freshman class.

"The reason we started it, originally, was the revenues, but, boy, I think we'd do it anyway," Kathy Lindsey, Associate Director of Admissions at Middlebury, told *The New York Times*. "It enables us to take more great kids. Of course, you can only do this if you have a deep enough applicant pool that there are more kids you want than you can accommodate. We look for a particular personality profile for kids we bring in in February."

> **Real Life**
>
> "Students electing to enroll in January use the fall semester to pursue a wide range of interests; some elect to take courses at other colleges, some work, travel, volunteer, or use the opportunity to 'take a break' from their educational journey."
>
> —Rensselaer Polytechnic Institute's website

Some schools allow you to mention on your application that you prefer a spring start date; then, how you use the time before you head to college is up to you.

The idea of starting college six months after everyone else sounds great on its face, but some people say they have a hard time settling into the college campus late and aren't able to join activities midway through the school year. That's something you'll want to think about if you're offered a midyear admission.

The Least You Need to Know

◆ Apply early decision only if you're positive you want to go to that school.

◆ Check each school's early application policies and deadlines to ensure you're on track.

◆ Several top schools now allow you to apply early without entering into binding contracts.

◆ Rolling admission can be helpful, but don't wait until the last minute.

Chapter

14

The Application

In This Chapter

- ◆ Getting organized
- ◆ The advantages of filing online
- ◆ How to deal with deadlines
- ◆ How to check on your application

Welcome to where the rubber meets the road. If everything leading up to this chapter was the pregame and walkthrough, then this is when you suit up, put on the pads, and play for real. The college application is where all your hard work starts to pay off. It's time to show the top schools who you are and why they should offer you admission.

The college application also can be where your dream falls short. A misspelled word or a typo could doom you, and an online application filed with the e-mail address party4life@e-mailplace.com can leave you contemplating whether to attend your fifth or sixth choice.

Trying to get into a top college is every bit as much as a game as it seems, and the college application is just another venue for the competition. So, it's important that you know the rules and play by them.

The college application as a whole typically is broken up into eight sections:

◆ The application form

◆ The fee

◆ The essay

◆ Letters of recommendation

◆ High school transcript

◆ Standardized test scores

◆ Audition or portfolio, when applicable

◆ Interview, when applicable

For the purpose of this chapter, I will discuss the application as a whole and the forms you have to complete. Other areas, such as the essay and recommendations, are covered in depth in later chapters.

Paper, Paper Everywhere

College applications can be as diverse as the colleges themselves. Some applications are longer than others and ask more of you. Some require that you answer the essay questions they provide, while others allow you to utilize something called the Common Application.

Cheat Sheet

If possible, try to submit all of your application material online, while keeping hard copies for your records. Using online services is neater and more time efficient for both the applicant and the college.

You also have choices for how you submit your application: online or via snail mail. More and more, students are submitting their college applications online and colleges are requesting that it be done like that.

These differences come with advantages, disadvantages, and pitfalls you must avoid.

Get Organized

Whether you're using an independent counselor, working with your high school counselor, or navigating the system alone, there are several items that you need to bring together in a timely manner to complete a successful college application.

The task of applying to college is too daunting to do all at once. First, decide which colleges you're going to apply to and find out what each college requires for its application. Consider buying a dry-erase board and setting it up in your room. On the board, write down the name of each college you're going to apply to; then under that list each item that each college requires for its application. As you complete each item, put a checkmark next to it or cross it out.

You can also start a Word document as early as possible with a simple resumé of honors/awards, extracurricular activities, community service, and work experience.

The following is a sample college application checklist provided by the College Board. It not only includes what needs to be accomplished, but also leaves room for deadlines and intermittent steps.

Application Item	College 1	College 2	College 3
Request info/ application			
Regular application deadline			
Early application deadline			
Request high school transcript be sent			
Request midyear grade reports be sent			
Take SAT			
Take ACT			
Take SAT Subject Tests (SAT2)			
Release SAT Subject Test scores			
Send SAT scores			
Send ACT scores			
Send AP grades			

continues

continued

Application Item	College 1	College 2	College 3
Request recommendations			
Send thank-you notes for recommendations			
Write essays			
Proof essays for spelling and grammar			
Have two people read essays			
Interview at college			
Send thank-you notes to interviewers			
Send and track application			
Make copies of all application materials			
Apply online			
Include application fee			
Sign application			
Confirm receipt of application materials			
Send supplemental material, if necessary			

Several websites can help you learn what colleges want in their applications, but those websites might be outdated. It's always best to get application information from the school itself.

Be sure to consider the timeline and give yourself enough time to get the application completed and in the mail in time. I get into the whole timeline thing a little bit later in this chapter.

The Musts

It seems silly to say, but the most important thing you have to do when filling out these applications is to read the directions. You'll kick yourself if you jeopardize your opportunity to get into the school of your choice because you failed to answer a simple question, submit the proper paperwork, or complete the correct number of essays.

Besides reading the directions, there are several things to watch out for when submitting your application:

- Don't misspell anything. Few applications have spell check, so whenever possible, write it first in a Microsoft Word document, spell check it, and then upload the file or cut and paste it. Always have someone else check your application for typos/mistakes.

- If you apply online, make sure it goes through—print the document so you have a time-stamped application.

- Sign and date where asked.

- Write legibly.

- Use a grown-up e-mail address.

- Check your e-mail for queries from the schools.

- Don't let mom and dad do your work.

Most of these musts are pretty self-explanatory. As I said earlier in the chapter, a misspelled word can doom your application so be sure you spell check it over and over, and then have someone else proof it for you. Now, proofing doesn't mean having someone else do the work—don't let mom and dad fill out the application for you. College admissions officers can tell if the handwriting or writing style changes in the middle of an application.

Cheat Sheet

It's important that your handwriting is legible. You don't want an admissions officer having to spend time deciphering your chicken scratch. If you decide to submit a paper application, consider running it through a laser printer instead of handwriting the answers.

Filing Online

Paper applications are so 1990. Welcome to the Internet age when all the top colleges not only offer online applications, but actually prefer that you file online. More than

90 percent of schools offer online applications, and a recent study showed that more than 50 percent of high school students who apply to college filed their paperwork online.

Everyone wins when you file online. The college benefits by having everything in an easy-to-catalog electronic form. When your application is filed online, it's less likely that a school will lose a portion of what you've submitted.

Students also benefit by filing online because no postage is involved and they don't have to worry about whether the school has received their application. After you file online, you immediately get a confirmation e-mail sent to you or are taken to a confirmation page.

I'm not saying that you're more likely to get into a top school if you file online, but the online process just makes things easier on everyone involved. If all things are equal between you and another student who filed a paper application, filing online could give you the slightest of edges you need—stranger things have happened.

There are a couple of issues to watch out for when filing online. First, don't wait until the last minute just because cyberspace enables you to submit your application from your home in Mississippi to Rice University in Houston, Texas, in a nanosecond. Waiting until the last minute still means you're rushing, and rushing heightens the likelihood that you'll make a silly mistake on the application. Also, you don't want to take the chance that your application gets lost in cyberspace and you don't receive that confirmation e-mail. What if all you see after you hit send is that dreaded pinwheel spinning on and on? Basically, it's just not a good idea to wait until 11:59 P.M. on the day before the deadline to file your application.

Beware

Traffic on college application servers increases markedly over the last 48 hours before applications are due, and it can sometimes be difficult to get online to submit your paperwork.

Speaking of the confirmation e-mail and page, you should print that as soon as you receive it. This is your receipt that proves you've filed your application online. You also should save copies of everything you've filed online, either to a CD or memory stick. This way, if a school has a computer glitch you have everything backed up for it.

Here's the most important thing to remember when filing your application online: This isn't an e-mail to your best friend or a text message to your girlfriend. Don't abbreviate words and, again, don't include an e-mail address that makes you look immature. These rules apply to any electronic correspondence you have with the school to which you're applying. You sometimes have to abbreviate some words to fit it into the site's character limit, but try to be certain that your message is clear. If you get an e-mail after you've applied asking for another recommendation because you submitted only two of the three required, don't respond with, "OMG, I can't believe I forgot to include that. My guidance counselor is going to kill me. lol :-)" If you want to be taken seriously, act seriously and stay away from texting lingo.

The last thing you have to remember when filing electronically is to routinely check the e-mail account you include in your application. You might not include your primary e-mail account because your name on that is something like mulletmanmike. So, remember to check the e-mail account you include in case you're asked to submit any additional information or any of your information is lost.

Real Life

"Electronic communication is characterized by both speed and informality. It seems very ephemeral, but a college application is not an ephemeral document. Thinking of it that way can hurt your chances of admission."

—Ted O'Neill, Dean of College Admissions at the University of Chicago

Fast Apps

You might have heard about some of your friends receiving applications in the mail with some of their personal information already filled out along with an offer to waive the essay requirement and application fee. These sorts of applications are called *fast apps* or *snap apps* because they're so easy to fill out.

Schools that use the so-called fast apps typically are B schools looking for A students. They're trying to attract successful students from targeted areas of the country by offering an easy application process. On the other hand, if the school interests you, don't just ignore it because you and your friends all got one. For example, Tulane currently uses a fast app because they're rebuilding from Hurricane Katrina. Top schools never struggle to find a great pool of students to pick their classes from, so they don't typically utilize the fast app.

The Common Application

If you're applying to more than a handful of schools—and even if you're not—the *Common Application* might be something you want to consider. Many schools, such as Tufts, now use only the Common Application.

The Common Application membership association began in 1975 as a way to standardize the college application process for high school seniors. During its first year, only 15 private colleges agreed to use the Common Application. In 2008, 347 colleges and universities, including most of the country's top schools, accepted the Common Application.

def•i•ni•tion

The **Common Application** is a college application accepted by more than 300 schools and created to even the playing field among students. Most top schools require students to fill out a supplement in addition to the Common Application.

In 2008, Columbia was the only Ivy League school not to accept the Common Application. In addition to the seven Ivies, Bowdoin, Boston College, the University of Chicago, Rensselaer Polytechnic Institute, Rice, Stanford, and dozens of other top schools accepted the Common Application.

The first question students have when introduced to the Common Application is "Do colleges give it the same weight as their own applications?" According to all reports, the answer is yes. Common Application schools also belong to the National Association for College Admissions Counseling, which requires that they not discriminate against applicants based on the particular form an applicant uses. Although that might be a difficult thing to enforce, most colleges advertise on their websites that they accept the Common Application. You wouldn't think they'd do that if they didn't want you to use it. In fact, the only applications Harvard offers on its website are the Common Application and the Universal College Application, which is a similar program but is used by far fewer schools. Harvard does have a supplement application, but the main paperwork is the Common Application and isn't unique to Harvard.

In addition to you not having to fill out the same information repeatedly, another benefit of the Common Application is that you sometimes don't have to answer the zany essay questions some colleges ask. The Common Application comes with its own essay questions, which typically are pretty vanilla and include subjects such as writing about someone who has influenced you the most. But several colleges, including most of the top colleges, do require that you submit supplemental information if you use the Common Application. Often that supplemental information includes writing an essay using one of the college's topics.

Both the Common Application and the Universal College Application can be submitted through the mail or online, but few schools want it through the mail.

Snail Mail

Although almost all schools give you the option of submitting your application online, some students still want to submit it in the traditional snail mail way. Maybe it's similar to those people who refuse to read a newspaper online and want to feel the newspaper in their hands. Some students would rather fill out an application with a pen and give it that real "personal" feel.

Most of the rules that apply to online applications also apply to written applications, but you need to be aware of a few important differences. For instance, when you apply online, confirmation of your application being received comes within seconds. When you file through the mail, you're dealing with real people and real circumstances that could lead to your application not making it there on time or being lost. You also have to consider that when mailing in your application, some schools want you to mail things in at different times. When applying online, though, you might be able to submit everything at once. Again, it all comes down to what you're most comfortable with, but just be sure that you check in with the schools to which you're applying to ensure that you're following their most recent rules and deadlines.

Timeline

Each school has different deadlines for its applications. Not only do applications have to be filed at different times, but the separate sections of the application might also have to be filed at different times.

For instance, Georgetown asks applying students to complete a personal data form as soon as possible. The personal data form includes basic information such as where you live, your parent or guardian's name and address, and whether you're applying regular decision or early. Georgetown, which does not accept the Common Application, then has you submit a secondary form along with a secondary school report and teacher's report by November 1, if you're applying early action, or January 10, if you're applying regular decision.

The University of Chicago, however, has no early personal data form for you to fill out and asks that you complete the school's application or the Common Application and submit that along with your secondary school report, teachers' evaluations, and test scores. The school allows you to send all that information at once or as it's available to you.

Most top schools also have you submit a midyear grade report by February 1.

To have all these things prepared in time, you must establish a schedule for yourself. The schedule might change a little depending on the school and whether it offers rolling admission, but here's a general schedule you should stick to:

- May of junior year: Take SAT 1 or SAT 2.

- June: Take SAT 1, SAT 2, or ACT.

- July: The year's Common Application will be available; many rolling admission schools release in early July as well.

- July-September senior year: All applications are available online.

- September: Meet with your guidance counselor and go over the application protocol. Begin filling out applications and give teachers their recommendation forms.

- October: Take SAT 1, SAT 2, or ACT.

- November: Take SAT 1, SAT 2, or ACT. Early application deadlines typically are the first or second week of November. First-quarter grades will be sent to all the schools you apply to early.

- December: Continue working on applications. You will receive your early application decisions.

- January: All other applications are due.

- March–April: Decision notifications are received from most schools.

- May: Submit your acceptance deposit by the deadline.

Separate or at Once?

Many students ask whether they should submit their application information as they collect it or all at once. Again, this largely depends on the school to which you're applying. Some schools ask that you send things all at once; others want things in parts. As I mentioned, Georgetown asks that you submit a very basic personal form before sending any other application information.

Other schools actually have you print labels and ask you to submit each part of the application separately with a different label on the envelope. Still other schools really don't care one way or the other.

Again, the most important thing is that you research the school and find out whether it has a specific preference. If a school asks that you send each part of the application to the school in a separate envelope with a separate label, as Harvard does, then you should do it that way. Part of getting into a top school is being able to make yourself stand out from the crowd, but you don't want to accomplish that by not following the rules and upsetting an admissions officer.

Beware _____

> With ample planning time, there is no reason a student should submit his application on the day of the deadline. A missed deadline is a missed opportunity. If you wait until the deadline and something is missing, you will not have met that deadline. This could mean the difference between meeting a rolling admissions priority deadline, an early action deadline, a financial aid deadline (which can result in the loss of thousands of dollars), or any other number of other possibilities.

If you're given the option of submitting everything at once or piecemeal, the safe bet is to submit it all together. That will lessen the chance of a portion of your application getting lost in an office or by the post office.

Application Status

First, be sure your application gets to the schools to which you apply. If you send your application snail mail, make sure you have some proof that it was mailed by the deadline. That means you should pay a little extra and send it certified mail or return receipt.

Gone are the days of sending a little postcard with your application that the school would then send back to you after it received your application. E-mail is the new postcard. Most schools will set up an admissions account for you after your application is received and then e-mail you with your username and password. Through this account, you are usually able to check on the status of your application and see which materials the school has received and what's still missing. This is where having a mature e-mail address and checking that e-mail account comes into play. I can't stress enough that if an admissions officer has to send an e-mail to ILOVEBRADPITT@ e-mailland.com, things are starting off on the wrong foot.

Just like every other step of this process, schools have different rules about whether you should contact them if you have questions about your pending application. Stanford's website makes it quite clear that the school doesn't want applicants calling the admissions office with questions about their applications. "Due to the large volume of applications our office receives, we are unable to respond to inquiries regarding the status of any application," the site states.

Other schools will allow you to check the status of your application only by using the school's website. Still other schools set aside certain times of the day when the admissions office is available to field calls about applications. At Duke, for instance, the admissions office takes calls about whether your application is complete from 3 P.M. to 5 P.M.

Missing Information

Admissions offices typically will send you an e-mail to let you know if anything is missing from your application. But some schools are stricter about missing information than others. I have seen this go different ways. Sometimes, if something is missing a phone call to the admissions office can make all the difference in the world. I had a student apply early action to a very competitive school, and she received a letter one week after the deadline indicating that the school had not yet received her application payment. In checking, she realized in fact that she had not send the payment. That particular school was very understanding; she made a credit card payment over the phone and all was well. She was not penalized, and in fact did get admitted early action.

Not all schools are so accommodating, though. I had another situation in which a student applied to a school that has a very strict early response admissions policy. All application materials must be received in the admissions office by October 31. At this school, that deadline does indeed mean received and not postmarked. If an application is not fully received by October 31, it automatically defaults to rolling admissions, no ifs, ands, or buts.

In this particular case, missing a deadline could be detrimental to your acceptance at that school because after October 31, admission gets more competitive as spaces fill up.

It's important that you find out whether the deadlines for the schools you're applying to refer to when the applications are actually received or when they're postmarked.

The Least You Need to Know

◆ Make sure you send everything that's expected with your application.

◆ Don't fool around with deadlines. They're called *deadlines* for a reason.

◆ Filing online is more efficient and allows you to immediately confirm that your application has been received.

◆ The Common Application allows you to avoid having to rewrite or type the same information repeatedly.

Chapter 15

Getting Recommendations

In This Chapter

◆ The importance of recommendations

◆ Picking your recommenders

◆ Providing all the necessary information

◆ How to follow up with your recommenders

Letters of recommendation are an important part of your college application because they give admissions officials another opportunity to see who you are as a person—instead of just a grade, GPA, or test score. The best possible recommendation comes from someone who knows you well and has seen you grow, mature, and succeed during your high school career.

Not everyone has close relationships with teachers, advisors, coaches, and bosses, though, so you might have to make do with what you have. Average recommendations likely won't lead to your acceptance or rejection on their own. However, a stellar recommendation—or a terrible one—could end up being the tie breaker between you and another applicant. Try to be perceptive enough to ask for a recommendation from someone you're confident will give you a good one, and if you're not sure then ask whether he or she can give you a good one. I'll get into the specific recommendation request process later in the chapter.

Why Recommendations?

Recommendations enable admissions officers to get a peek at who you are both inside and outside of the classroom. So much of the college application process is based on grades, test scores, and extracurricular activities. When admissions officers consider those factors, they really don't need to know who you are or what kind of person you are; they truly can just substitute your name for a number. But recommendations, along with interviews and the essay you write, give the colleges an opportunity to better get to know you, the person—not just you, the transcript.

The National Association for College Admission Counseling in 2006 reported that a majority of colleges and universities rank counselor and teacher recommendations fourth in order of importance—after grades, test scores, and written essays. Although recommendations are not the most important thing, everything you are judged on makes a difference.

Most admissions officials will tell you that recommendations are a bigger factor for students who are:

- Candidates for a merit scholarship

- Borderline admissible

- In a tight competition for a seat in a selective college

Recommendations also carry more weight depending on which high school they're coming from. Colleges tend to give more credence to recommendations that come from the schools that are pipelines for top students. Also, a recommendation from someone who frequently has written recommendations for students who have been accepted to the same top college carries greater weight than one from a teacher who is writing to that college for the first time.

Recommendations usually come from teachers, but colleges often allow you to pick someone you've worked with in the community to also write a recommendation for you. Later in this chapter, I discuss who you should ask for recommendations—both in the school and outside of it.

> **Real Life**
>
> "Teacher recommendations are a valuable opportunity to give an admissions committee a deeper glimpse into your potential to contribute and succeed on their campus. A strong recommendation letter can support and even uplift your entire application, while a lukewarm one is an opportunity lost. In the worst-case scenario, damning words from a teacher can raise just enough doubt in an admissions committee's mind to get your application tossed into the 'deny' pile."
>
> —Carolyn Lawrence, a California-based independent college counselor

Here's What's Recommended

Just like every other portion of the college application process, you need to know what each school expects from you before you move ahead. You're probably tired of hearing me say that by now! After you find out what the forms look like, how many recommendations you'll need, and when they're due, you can decide who to ask.

Almost as important as whom you ask to write your recommendation is what you provide that person with. Don't bank on the person knowing everything she needs to know about you; be sure to provide meaningful background information that will help with writing the recommendation.

All in all, several details go into securing a good recommendation. It's more than simply putting a piece of paper in front of your teacher and asking her to complete it by a certain date. If you want a good recommendation, you have to do some work on your end, too.

What Recommendations Look Like

It sounds silly, but letters of recommendation for college applications aren't actually letters—they're really more like forms.

Schools that use the Common Application, which I discussed in Chapter 14, use one of two forms: either the recommendation form that's included in the College Application or a supplement application that includes a unique recommendation form.

Schools that don't use the Common Application obviously will use their own recommendation forms. Be sure you know whether the school you're applying to has a unique form that needs to be filled out.

Most recommendation forms have the recommender state his relationship to the student and then ask that person to rank the student in a number of categories, including academic achievement, maturity, motivation, reaction to setbacks, and independence. The Common Application includes 16 categories for the recommender to rank the student in and offers rankings from "below average" to "one of the top few encountered in my career." The form also includes a "no basis" box for each category that the recommender can check if the category isn't applicable in terms of his relationship with the student.

The forms also ask the recommender to write a little about the student's strengths and weaknesses and give examples for each. The Common Application includes a section that asks the recommender to write "whatever you think is important about this student, including a description of academic and personal characteristics, as demonstrated in your classroom."

Cheat Sheet

Although I said letters of recommendation are actually forms and not letters, there is an opportunity for your recommender to attach a letter. Most colleges allow the person writing the recommendation to attach a previously written letter if it answers the questions asked on the form. There's nothing wrong with your recommender attaching that letter, but be sure you mention to him that the letter must answer all the questions asked on the form.

Schools that don't use the Common Application's teacher recommendation have similar recommendation forms. For instance, Princeton's recommendation form also includes a section that asks the recommender to rank the student on her academic achievement, extracurricular/community contributions, and character and personal qualities; it also asks for an overall ranking.

The Princeton recommendation differs from the Common Application in that it asks several more detailed follow-up questions, including asking the recommender to write about how the student stands out and any special circumstances that would help the college "better understand and appreciate" the student's academic and extracurricular performance.

As you can see, the Common Application and Princeton's recommendation differ in their specificity. While the Common Application asks the recommender to write about "whatever you think is important," the Princeton form asks for specific details and doesn't leave it up to the recommender's discretion.

Who Writes Recommendations?

Most colleges ask for three recommendations: two from teachers and one from your guidance counselor. As I've said time and time again, it's critical that you read the application instructions when deciding who will write your recommendations.

An overwhelming number of colleges ask students to get their teacher recommendations from instructors in two different academic subjects. That doesn't mean a seventeenth-century literature teacher and an eighteenth-century literature teacher. Academic subjects are considered English, math, science, social studies, and foreign language. So if one of your recommendations comes from an English teacher, the other has to come from a teacher in science, math, social studies, or foreign language.

Typically, you should ask for a recommendation from someone who taught you during your sophomore or junior year. It shouldn't be someone who worked with you for just a couple of weeks your senior year or someone who taught you during your freshman year and hasn't been your instructor again.

The best-case scenario is to ask a teacher who has taught you multiple times over the years in different classes in the same academic area. It also would be great if one of those classes were an honors, IB, or AP class. The benefit of having someone who has taught you multiple times write your recommendation is that he'll be able to vouch for your growth and maturity as a student. If the class he taught you was one of the tougher classes you've taken, he'll be able to write about how you handled pressure and a heavy workload.

In addition to your two teacher recommendations and your guidance counselor recommendation, some colleges will allow you to submit a recommendation from someone who has worked with you through a sport or an extracurricular activity, or in the community. If given the option, you should take advantage of this additional recommendation and ask someone who can show a unique side of you that your teachers and guidance counselor can't. Again, pick someone who can detail your maturity, passion, and work ethic.

Many students ask if they should submit more recommendations than is asked of them. If you have three teachers who you know will write glowing recommendations for you, then you could consider submitting an extra recommendation, but there's no guarantee that it will be read. For those students who want to send two, three, four, or even five extra recommendations: don't! Admissions officers won't read them, and you'll run the risk of annoying them because you didn't follow their instructions.

An important question to ask yourself is "Will this teacher write me a good recommendation?" Recommendations are sent directly from the teacher to the school to which you're applying, so you'll never get your hands on it. How do you know if the teacher is going to write a good report about you? The best way to find out is to ask. When approaching teachers about recommendations, simply ask if they will write a positive assessment of who you are. If they say that they honestly can't, then politely tell them that you will go in another direction and that you appreciate their honesty. Don't assume that someone is going to write a positive recommendation for you—always ask.

When Should I Ask?

You should let your teachers know at the end of your junior year that you hope to receive college recommendations from them. In the fall teachers are inundated with requests for recommendations, but if you give them a heads up before the end of your junior year, they'll be more likely to get your recommendation done first and dedicate the most time to it.

Most teacher recommendation forms are not available until the summer of your senior year, so actually giving the teacher a form may not be possible until then. Recommendations typically aren't due until early fall, particularly for early decision or early action.

Beware _____

It's always better to get your recommendation request and information to your teacher or guidance counselor earlier than later. A good recommendation takes at least a couple of weeks to write, and if you don't give your recommender enough time, you run the risk of receiving a sloppy, poorly thought-out recommendation. You also don't want to risk annoying your recommender because you gave her so little notice.

Often I tell students to provide their recommenders with a table that lists the schools they're writing the recommendations for and when the recommendations are due. This way the recommender doesn't have to hunt down information when the writing is done.

Providing Important Information

You need to provide your recommenders with enough information to make the letters the best that they can be. This includes your resumé, transcripts, a cover letter, and a copy of your admissions essay.

◆ **A cover letter.** In this letter you formally ask for the recommendation and list the schools for which the recommendation will be used. Although you'll provide a separate worksheet with the deadline for each recommendation, you can repeat that information in the cover letter. You also should include any other requirements that the recommender should be aware of, including information the college wants to see from the recommender. The cover letter is a useful place to tell the recommender why you picked her to write the recommendation. This will give the person an idea of what you hope to get out of the recommendation. For example, if you state that you chose this teacher because of how you've seen your critical writing skills grow in his class, then the instructor will know what strengths you'd like him to focus on in the letter.

◆ **Your resumé.** Including your resumé gives the recommender an opportunity to find out more about who you are both inside the classroom and out. The resumé also will remind the recommender of information that he might already know, but could overlook.

◆ **Your application essay.** Including a copy of the essay you will send to the college gives the recommender a glimpse of who you think you are and how you see yourself.

◆ **An unofficial transcript.** Although your recommender knows how you've performed in her class, she might not know that you've been pulling in great grades across the board.

◆ **Envelopes and stamps.** If a recommendation needs to be mailed instead of submitted electronically, be sure you include the proper envelopes and postage.

The College Board's website also features a *self-assessment* that students can fill out and give to their recommenders. The self-assessment especially could be helpful for teachers who don't have a great relationship with the student they're being asked to recommend. For a copy of the self-assessment go to the College Board website and search for the recommendation tips section.

Questions included on the College Board's self-assessment are as follows:

def•i•ni•tion

A **self-assessment** is when you answer questions about yourself that will provide your recommender with a better understanding of who you are as a person and a student. You can find various self-assessments on the Internet.

- List your school activities and talk about the one that was most important to you.

- What books have had the greatest impact on you?

- What kind of learner are you?

- List your three most distinguishing or most admirable qualities.

- What do you hope to accomplish in college and after?

Although all this information will help your recommender write a comprehensive piece, be sure that you remind the teacher or guidance counselor that she shouldn't simply regurgitate your biography. Your recommenders have the opportunity to be specific about ways that they've seen you succeed in the classroom and in life, and those examples shouldn't be omitted to make room for a listing of your athletic accomplishments—the admissions office will be able to see that information for itself when it looks over your resumé.

Following Up

It's okay to check in with your recommenders to ensure that they have all the information they need and that the recommendations have gotten out on time.

The college application process is one of the most important processes you'll ever be part of, and your recommender realizes that. He won't feel like you're hounding him if you check in a couple of times. After all, if the recommendation is late, it's your responsibility, not his.

You also want to show your appreciation for your recommenders and should follow up with thank-you notes. In fact, a subtle way to remind a recommender of an upcoming deadline is to send him the thank-you note about a week before the recommendation is due. You never know when you're going to have to call on this person again, so it's important that you leave him with a good feeling about you.

Guidance Counselor Recommendations

Recommendations from a guidance counselor, which are required by almost every top school, are a little bit trickier than teacher recommendations because of the variability of the student/guidance counselor relationship.

Often, a student doesn't really get to know her guidance counselor until her junior year, and the relationship sometimes isn't a deep one because of the counselor's workload. It's in these situations that providing your recommender with as much information as possible becomes especially critical. Additionally, a guidance counselor is able to write a recommendation that is a bit broader than what your teachers can write. While your teacher's recommendation will focus on your work in the classroom, a guidance counselor's recommendation can cover your entire high school career and how you've grown from a freshman to a senior.

In order to make sure that your counselor writes a comprehensive recommendation, you need to follow all the steps previously listed. Additionally, try to make time to get to know your guidance counselor better—after all, the better he knows you, the better the recommendation will be. So, see if you can schedule monthly or twice-monthly meetings with your counselor so you can simply update him on what you're doing inside and outside of school.

If you or your counselor can't make time for regular meetings, ask if you can send an e-mail every now and then providing him with updates on what you're up to. Your counselor might not take the time to always read the e-mail, but he likely won't tell you not to send it.

Tips for the Recommender

Making recommendations to your recommender is tricky. You don't want to insult the person you've asked to help get you into college, but there are times when you realize she might need a little guidance.

This doesn't mean you're going to tell the recommender what to write about you. You, of course, aren't going to say, "Well, I think you should write that I'm the best student ever and that you wish you had a classroom full of students like me." Instead, the kind of advice I'm talking about is tips on how to structure the recommendation.

Here are tips for teachers and guidance counselors provided by the College Board. Be sure to offer this advice only if asked, though:

- Start with an image for the reader that the body of your recommendation develops.

- When possible, include anecdotal information.

Cheat Sheet

Don't assume that the best recommendations will come from English teachers. Plenty of English teachers out there are great writers of fiction but struggle when it comes to writing about a real person. Plenty of great recommendations have come from teachers in all subjects.

♦ Provide an overview of the student, including academic, extracurricular, and volunteer activities.

♦ Show not only that a student has succeeded in high school, but also how she has stood out.

♦ Explain why you think a student is a good match for a college. This is especially important for early decision and borderline applicants.

♦ Discuss the student's personal life if it is relevant to her academic record.

♦ Conclude with a paragraph that conveys the strength of your endorsement.

The Least You Need to Know

♦ Recommendations are most important for students vying for merit-based scholarships and those who are in tight competition with another applicant.

♦ Read all the recommendation requirements and convey them to the recommender. This includes making sure you know what form the recommender needs to fill out.

♦ The more information you provide your recommender with, the better your recommendation will be.

♦ Relationships with guidance counselors sometimes are harder to establish than with teachers. Try to work out a system that allows you to get information to your counselor on a regular basis.

16

The Essay

In This Chapter

◆ What to write about

◆ Questions you'll be asked

◆ Tips for great writing

◆ Proof, proof, and proof again

If you had a penny for every tip someone gave you about how to write your college admission essay, you'd probably be rich enough to skip college.

But college essays aren't a joking matter. They're actually quite important and possibly the best way a college gets to truly see who you are as a person. Interviews (which I discuss in Chapter 17) are important, but they often are conducted by alumni and big donors to the school who don't carry the weight of an admissions officer.

Your goal is to get the admissions officers to identify with you as he reads your essay. Write an essay that changes you from a number—application No. 1,628—to a person.

The Subject

In his book *On Writing the College Application Essay: The Key to Acceptance at the College of Your Choice*, Harry Bauld notes some clichès that should send you running for the garbage can if they show up in the first paragraph of your college essay:

♦ Don't write about your summer camping trip, or any other trip for that matter, and how you had to adjust.

♦ An overview of your "favorite things" is not what admissions officers want to read about.

♦ Your essay isn't a beauty pageant, so stay away from world hunger and trying to save everyone.

♦ Your athletic accomplishments and how being the team captain turned you into a leader is the same story that hundreds of other students have to tell.

♦ Stay away from the autobiography. This should be just a little bit about who you are: a piece of the pie, not the whole pie.

♦ Not every story has to lead to you being successful in some fashion. If your essay ends with, "I ultimately came out on top," you may want to stay away from that topic.

♦ Death is not something to belittle, but we all lose friends and family members, so your story better be unique if you're going to go there.

Different colleges ask for different things in their essays. Some leave the subject up to you, but others give you a specific question to answer. Each format holds certain pitfalls to avoid and certain things you want to make sure you achieve. If a college provides a prompt, you must answer the prompt!

Who Are You?

The most common question asked by colleges is "Who are you?" or "Tell us about yourself."

Because these questions are so general, students often have a hard time picking one thing to write about and get bogged down in telling their whole life's history. Bluntly put, chronological writing is dull and will do nothing for your chances at admission.

Applicants also often decide to write about the hardships they've experienced. This isn't necessarily a bad thing, as long as you're sure to remember not to make it all doom and gloom. You don't want to dwell on your hardships and bad luck. Admissions officers don't mind seeing that you've been able to overcome negative aspects of your life, but they don't want to read a sob story. They also don't want to see you exaggerate and make things worse than they really were.

On the outside chance that you don't know who you are—that is to say, that when you sit down and try to describe yourself you have a hard time coming up with character traits—ask your friends and family to list a few traits they think describe you. Then go back and ask them why they chose those traits and try to think of life experiences that exemplify those traits.

Here are some tips for dealing with the "Who are you?" question:

♦ **Tie yourself to the college.** Show why you are interested in attending and dive much deeper than "Harvard is the best fit for me because …." You can tie yourself to a college by showing that a strong interest of yours is a subject the college specializes in. It also helps to show that you know a bit about the school, both what it offers and what it looks like. Place yourself at the school and give enough detail to show the reader you've done your homework.

♦ **Sort through ideas and prioritize.** You cannot tell them everything, so be selective. For example, you don't want to go through your roles of being a son, brother, nephew, and cousin. If you've had to raise a sibling or be a support system for a parent more so than the typical high school student, then focus on that. Don't offer the reader a survey course of who you are. Take a specific characteristic and write about it.

♦ **Write about something you know and something only you could write.** No one else knows who you are or how you feel, so take advantage of that. It's important that you find something unique about your life to write about. The generic "How I felt on my first day of high school" won't do.

⊃ Real Life _____

"Realistically, there is no way that I should have gotten into Emory. I'm embarrassed to say that I think my admissions essay had a lot to do with it. My parents, guidance counselors, and every other person I asked insisted that I should write about the trials and tribulations of being born blind in one eye. I thought it was hogwash—being blind in one eye just isn't that bad. But I was 17, and I eventually gave in and wrote a heart-wrenching tale about the boy who endured pain and teasing as a child, then grew up to get a driver's license and be a starting linebacker on the football team. Today, I would never sign my name to such drivel, but it probably got me into Emory."

—Brandon Honig, Emory University Class of 1997

Why Us?

Another essay question often asked on college applications is "Why us?" For instance, Georgetown University in the past has asked students to "Please relate your interest in studying at Georgetown University to your future goals."

When faced with this question, start out by being positive. If you start your essay with "I am applying to your school because I won't be required to take physical education or a foreign language," chances are you'll be getting a very thin envelope back in response.

To be successful when dealing with this essay question, you first have to know what your goals for attending the university are. You want to go well beyond "Harvard will help me realize my potential" or "I am in the top of my class, and Princeton is one of the best schools in the country so we're a natural fit." Be specific in your goals and connect them to something at the school. If you know what you plan to major in and you know what that college offers in that department, you can write about the courses you're looking forward to taking and the professors you're looking forward to working with. Again, do your homework.

Being able to connect your goals to the school is where your school tours and college research come in. Hopefully, you followed my advice and took notes during your tours of the colleges. This should enable you to insert things into your "Why us?" essay that will let the reader know you're not applying based on name recognition alone. Further, if you've researched what the school offers academically—especially specific to your planned major—or better yet, sat in on a class in that major, you should mention what interests you in your department of choice.

Here are some tips for dealing with the "Why us?" question:

◆ **Be persuasive in showing the reader you are deserving of admission.** Remember your audience. Be careful not to gloat, but make sure you separate yourself from other applicants. Again, if the college has a strong chemistry program and that's your intended major, then point that out and write about how you've achieved and pushed yourself in the subject.

◆ **Consider the unique features of the institution.** Unique features could include the courses offered, the professors teaching them, research opportunities, or the ability to study abroad or with area companies. The more you know about a college, the easier it will be for you to pick a unique feature that fits within what you want to accomplish as a student.

◆ **Don't write a laundry list of why you love the school.** Instead, pick a few specific reasons why you think you're a good fit, such as your interest in a specific area of study that the school specializes in.

From Left Field

Some universities are a bit more creative with their essay questions. Here are examples of questions that go above and beyond "Who are you?" and "Why us?":

◆ Duke University has asked: "John Keats said, 'Even a proverb is no proverb to you till your life has illustrated it.' Please tell us about an experience in your own life which illustrated a proverb, maxim, or quote that has special meaning to you."

◆ UPenn has had a fun essay question that asks: "You have completed your 300-page autobiography. Please submit page 217."

◆ The University of Virginia in the past has asked students to write about their favorite word.

◆ The University of Chicago once asked students to write a proposal for a television pilot, incorporating some of these: a German opera, Enrico Fermi's personal trainer, van Gogh's severed ear, Bill Nye the Science Guy, and an evil clown.

◆ There's also the much more common: "Indicate a person who has had a significant influence on you, and describe that influence."

These types of questions obviously give you an opportunity to be a little more creative with your response. Still, you have to remember to streamline your thoughts to get a single point across. Ultimately, just as with every other essay question, you want to paint a picture of who you are and what you can contribute to the college.

For instance, with UPenn's question you have an opportunity to discuss where you hope your life will go. But don't forget to tie your future into what you still have to accomplish in four years of college. Don't go on and on about the great job you'll have and the great life you'll live. Essentially, you have to be able to show how your four years in college will help you accomplish your future goals. If you want to pursue medical

Beware

Be honest about your work. College admissions officers have a keen eye for picking up on plagiarized essays or essays that have been written by parents or hired advisers. You can ask people for help, but in general do your own work.

research, you need a strong lab background in college and must be able to understand and write grant applications. Remember that the schools want to see that you have big aspirations, but they also want to see that you're grounded enough to understand how much work you'll have to put in to achieve those goals.

Some people might balk at the question that queries applicants about their favorite word. But if it's good enough for James Lipton and *Inside the Actor's Studio*, then why shouldn't it be good enough for the University of Virginia? Writing about your favorite word can tell people as much if not more about who you are than 500 words about your summer vacation or how you overcame an ingrown toenail to win a 100-meter race.

As for the University of Chicago's question, I admit it's just weird. But as they say, when given a lemon, make lemonade. Parents of many applicants have criticized schools for asking essay questions that go above and beyond the watered down "Who are you?" and "Why us?" They worry that the acceptance process already is ambiguous enough without having to deal with a strange essay question. But you have to realize that with questions like the ones posed by University of Chicago, the school is looking for someone who can write, has a sense of humor, and doesn't take herself too seriously.

The common question about someone who had a significant influence on your life gives you an opportunity to pay tribute to someone important to you. But remember, the essay shouldn't be all about the significant person and her accomplishments. You're the one trying to get into college. You can go back and forth in the essay discussing the person who had an influence on you and how that influence shaped your life. An essay about someone who impacted your life does the reader no good if the actual impact isn't discussed.

> **Cheat Sheet**
>
> It sounds silly, but don't forget to answer the question. If the question asks who you are as a person, don't go on and on for 400 words about why you think Cornell's campus is so pretty and how you like the snow. Also, make sure you read all the instructions. If they ask for a 500-word essay, don't give them 501.

Time to Write

The most important part of writing your college essay may actually come before you ever put pen to paper. Deciding what you'll write about and how you'll structure your piece is about as important as it gets. Going in with a game plan instead of simply writing what comes to you will better your chances for success.

Planning includes brainstorming about a topic, reading sample essays, talking to friends and family, and outlining what you'll write about.

Think of the essay as a baseball game, with you as the starting pitcher. You wouldn't enter the game without throwing some warm-up pitches, would you? The same thing applies when you write your essay. Brainstorming your topic, writing an outline, and talking things out all are part of the warm-up process. The more you warm-up, the better your performance will be.

Brainstorm

Coming up with an essay topic can lead to several sleepless nights, but that's completely normal. Students need not freak out if they spend a day or two trying to come up with a topic and can't. The trick is to start early and give yourself plenty of time to go through the essay process. Start brainstorming as soon as you know what the essay question is.

There are a number of questions you can ask yourself that can help trigger the brainstorming process. Go to a comfortable, quiet place and jot down the questions; then write your answers without really thinking about your writing. Don't worry about grammar or spelling or where the thoughts are headed. Just worry about getting your thoughts on paper. Here are some tips:

- List your major accomplishments and why you consider them accomplishments. They don't have to be things for which you've received formal recognition; they just need to be important to you.

- Think about whether there's a skill or characteristic that distinguishes you as a person. How did you develop this trait or skill?

- List your favorite books, movies, and works of art, and consider why they're your favorites and how they've influenced you.

- Go back to the most difficult time in your life and think about how you dealt with things and how your perspective changed.

- What has been your greatest success? Why did you succeed?

- What has been your greatest failure? How did you respond to it?

- What any one thing would you do right now if you could? Where would you go? Who would you talk to?

- What was a time when your eyes were opened to some completely new thought or idea?

- What belief are you unwilling to waiver from?

- How would friends describe you? What would they write about you?

- What activities outside of the classroom are you most proud of?

- What do you need to accomplish in your life to consider it a success? What are your dreams for the next 40 years?

The Outline

Outlines aren't rocket science. They should ensure that your essay gets from point A to point B without making a whole bunch of detours. Outlines are useful in that they ensure you don't ramble. A good outline should include the points you want to get across in the essay and the order in which you want to present them. An outline also will help you decide if you're taking on too many subjects in the essay or if you're focusing too much time on any one given thing. If your outline starts to look like a chronology of your life or a laundry list of your accomplishments, take another stab at it.

Use your outline as a guide, not a rigid template of exactly what you have to do with the essay. Your essay will change numerous times right up until the point that you stick it in the envelope.

Sometimes in writing these essays, applicants are able to touch on a lot of good things—leadership, teamwork, ability, and so on—but still walk away with a flat, muddled essay. An outline will help you not only touch on the points, but also flesh them out.

For a good sample of what an outline should look like, go to: www.englishclub.com/writing/college-application-essays/lth_outline.html.

Pen and Paper

If you're not a writer, don't try to do something you're not capable of. Don't go out there wielding a pen you can't control, composing prose that makes no sense. Keep it simple and just write from the heart. If you do fancy yourself a writer, appreciate this opportunity because it's in your comfort zone. Just don't go overboard with a work that will befuddle and confuse the reader. Reign it in a little, and most importantly make sure that your *imagery* is appropriate and effective.

Here are some general rules to follow when you start writing your essay:

- **Don't go running for the thesaurus for every other word.** Bigger words don't necessarily mean better words. If you do use big words, make sure you're using them in the proper context. Instead of writing that you excogitated something, simply say you pondered or contemplated it. If you had a run-in with pirates as a youth, then say so; don't say you ran up against corsairs.

def•i•ni•tion

Imagery is a descriptive tool writers use to better describe scenes and paint pictures in the minds of readers. Types of imagery include metaphors, similes, and personification. It's an important aspect of essay writing.

- **Spend the lion's share of your time on the introduction.** Don't expect an admissions officer to spend an hour reading and rereading your essay. You need to be able to grab the reader's attention with the first sentence and hold onto it. Try to be active with your opening sentence and get the ball rolling with energy: "When I wake up to the ear-splitting sound of my alarm clock and blindly search for the snooze button, a sudden thought dawns: 'What am I doing?'"

- **Don't make your introduction a survey of what your essay will include.** Again, you want to catch their attention and keep it. If you start with "In this essay, I will show you why I am a great student and a great leader," think again.

- **Mystery isn't a bad thing.** You don't want to give away the punch line in the first paragraph. If you can raise questions that force the admissions officer to read on, you've done your job. If you've had some medical issues over the years, you can open the essay with an image of you lying in the hospital and lead the reader on a trip that eventually will unveil how you landed in that bed.

- **Don't ignore transitions.** Paragraphs must fit together. But don't be redundant by repeating the same transitional phrases such as *as a result*, *while*, *since*, and *in addition*.

- **End strong.** Your conclusion is your final opportunity to speak to the reader and convince him that you're a right fit for the school. Don't use the conclusion to remind the reader what you wrote about; your essay will be short enough that he won't need reminding. Also, avoid the phrases *in conclusion*, *in summary*, and *to conclude*. Instead, try to bring your essay full circle and give the reader a sense that he has just read a balanced piece, a short story.

Proof, Proof, Proof

Needless to say, a stray comma or a misspelled word could doom your application essay. You have to proof your essay over, and over, and over again. But after you've finished writing your essay, there's more you have to do than simply proof. In reality, the writing isn't done yet. You'll likely rewrite several sections.

This is a time when asking for help is a great idea. The more eyes that look at your essay, the better. You'll be amazed that although you've stared at your essay for weeks, the second you hand it over to someone else she'll find a glaring error within the first couple of minutes. This is because you've become too close to the process; you need to step away from it and let someone else take a look. But it's still important for your essay to sound like you and have your voice.

Cheat Sheet

Go through the essay and cut out every *very* and *many*. Words such as these are vague, and your writing is often stronger without them.

Not only will those outside eyes be able to find some errors you might not have caught, but they'll also give you an idea of how your ideas come across. Were your transitions effective? Was your narrative captivating? Most importantly, did they understand all of it?

When you think you've churned out what's an acceptable essay, hand it over to a friend or family member. In fact, don't look at the essay for a week or so and just think about your topic and whether you've included everything you would want to include.

After you take that time away, you can review any comments your family member or friend has about the essay and take your own thoughts into consideration after having given it a lot of thought.

When you hand the essay over to your editors, ask them to answer these questions:

- What is the essay about?
- Have I used active voice and verbs?
- Is my sentence structure varied?
- Do you detect any clichés?
- Do I use transitions appropriately?
- What's the best part of the essay?

- What about the essay is memorable?

- What's the worst part of the essay?

- What parts of the essay need elaboration or are unclear?

- What parts of the essay are immaterial to my case?

- Is every sentence crucial to the essay?

- What does the essay reveal about my personality?

- Could anyone else have written this essay?

Take the answers to these questions and use them to revise your essay. No author is above criticism and revision. At the least, there certainly will be a sentence that can be shortened or an idea that can be slimmed down or beefed up.

Editing takes time and can be a tedious process. But nothing is off limits when you go through edits of your essay. As part of the editing process, you should consider reordering your supporting details and deleting irrelevant sections. Allow your most important arguments to shine.

Additionally, always keep your audience in mind. You're not writing this for your friends, your parents—or yourself, for that matter. You're writing this for someone who knows very little about you and is using this essay to help make a decision about your future. The importance of taking your time and looking things over time and time again can't be overstated.

Cheat Sheet

Essays that include an active voice and verbs are easier and more interesting to read than passive essays. For example, you don't want to say you were bitten by a dog; rather say the dog bit you. Purdue University has a great instructional website on how to change passive phrases to active ones: owl.english.purdue.edu/handouts/grammar/g_actpass.html.

The Least You Need to Know

- Tell a story only you can tell.

- Be honest about who you are and what you've done.

- Stay within your abilities.

- Proof, revise, and proof again to make it perfect.

The Interview

In This Chapter

◆ When optional isn't really optional

◆ Common questions

◆ How to dress for success

◆ Getting over your nerves

Is there anything more stressful than a college interview? Generation after generation of high school students go into these pressure cookers thinking, "This is it, this interview will make or break me."

While I won't say that the interviews aren't important, they're certainly not as important as they used to be. Most top colleges don't require interviews anymore. In fact, none of the Ivy League schools require interviews, and if you do choose to interview, the school will try to find an alumnus who can interview you off campus.

A 2005 survey by the National Association for College Admission Counseling showed that nearly two-thirds of colleges said they give the interview little or no consideration, and 33 percent said an interview bears no importance at all, up from 30 percent the year before.

Schools used to make applicants go to the campus for their interviews, but that tradition faded away as schools became the focus of criticism for excluding potential applicants who couldn't afford to travel across the country for an interview. Schools also phased out the interview process because of the sheer number of students applying to college. The growing number made it increasingly more difficult for admissions officers to find the time to meet with each applicant.

Though optional at most colleges, interviews do have their benefits in some cases, all of which I get into in this chapter. But with that said, rest assured that the days of sitting in a sterile room with dozens of other applicants waiting for an admissions officer to interview you are long gone.

Types of Interviews and their Importance

There are basically three types of interviews: informational, on-campus, and alumni. I discussed the informational interview in Chapter 10. Informational interviews basically are for your benefit and enable you to find out information about the college. But, be sure that you realize that the person conducting that "informal" interview still might be taking notes, even if you don't see him writing anything down.

During an *on-campus interview*, an admissions officer or other representative of the college interviews you on campus, typically in the admissions office. You are given a chance to ask questions, but the main purpose of the meeting is for the interviewer to form an impression of you and make notes for the admissions committee. This is basically like a job interview.

def•i•ni•tion

On-campus interviews are just as they sound: interviews that take place on campus. Most colleges no longer require on-campus interviews because many applicants don't have the money to travel cross-country.

Alumni interviews typically occur somewhere close to where you live and are as likely to occur at a Starbucks as they are to be held in an office. Top colleges have regional alumni committees set up across the country, and someone from the alumni group in your area will contact you to set up the interview. Because the alumni interviews aren't conducted by admissions professionals, they tend to be a lot more conversational and relaxed and focus less on your academic qualifications. Like the on-campus interview, the alumni interviewers will forward their notes along to the admissions committee. However, some schools, such as UPenn, Harvard, and Yale, have recently tightened their interview process and given fairly strict guidelines to their alumni interviewers.

Optional Interviews

The overwhelming trend within the college interview world is a policy of optional interviews. On the website of nearly every top college you'll read that applicants have the opportunity to interview with an alumnus in their area if they choose, but they won't be penalized for turning down that interview. Some schools, like USC, Pomona, and Pitzer, can look negatively at kids from their area of the country who can't be bothered to drive the 1–2 hours for an interview.

"Don't be concerned if no interviews are available in your area," states Princeton's website. "We will give your application full consideration without an interview."

Dartmouth and nearly every other top college offer the same assessment. "Please do not worry if you are unable to interview," Dartmouth's website states. "The lack of an interview will not have an adverse impact on your admissions decision."

If they don't require you to interview, then why bother? Here comes your answer.

Deciding to Interview

Unless you anticipate flat out falling on your face in an interview, there's really no reason you shouldn't sit down for an interview if one is available to you.

The term *optional* can be sort of deceiving. Yale's website states that students are "urged" to take advantage of the opportunity to interview. The website then goes on to state that although it's not required, an interview is strongly encouraged. Get the hint?

What's important to understand is the difference between an interviewer not being available in your area and you turning down the opportunity to interview. While a school won't penalize you because it couldn't provide you with an interviewer, you might be penalized for saying "thanks but no thanks" to an interview.

Cheat Sheet

Most schools will tell you to wait for an alumnus to contact you to set up your interview, but it won't hurt to call the admissions office ahead of time to ask whether you can set up a time and date. Most schools will tell you no and won't let you speak to the admissions officer for your region, but being proactive never hurt.

On-Campus Interviews

For schools that offer on-campus interviews, they're also not required but can be beneficial to you in two important ways. First, the on-campus interview shows the college that you're serious about admission in that you're willing to travel to talk to someone at the school. It's just like a job interview. Even if you can interview over the phone, don't you think a prospective employer is going to think better of an applicant who took the initiative to interview in person?

Most officials from top colleges will tell you that on-campus interviews—if they offer them—and alumni interviews are given equal weight. However, there are intangible things that don't get written down in a college's official policy, and you might just impress someone and put your application over the top if you show that you were willing to travel from California to Columbia because that's how important attending that school is to you.

Second, an on-campus interview gives you another opportunity to form an opinion about the school that you can use down the road when you're deciding where you will attend. The back-and-forth between an admissions officer and a student could either solidify that this is the school for you or open your eyes to issues you might have missed before.

On-campus interviews are awarded on a first-come first-serve basis because of the huge number of students now applying to not only average colleges and universities, but also top schools. Most colleges offer online calendars that allow you to register for an on-campus interview and reserve a time slot. Be sure that if you can't make the interview you signed up for that you call to cancel or change the date as far in advance as you can. There might not be anything worse than simply not showing up for an interview.

If you do cancel your on-campus interview, ask if it's too late to set up an alumni interview where you live. If it's not too late, then set one up.

Prepare for a Conversation

There's really no standard formula for preparing for a college interview. Each interviewer and college measures success differently. And you can't prepare for an interview the same way you do for an exam, studying for weeks with flashcards and practice tests.

"So how do I prepare," you ask.

I get into what you can expect during an interview and how you can go in armed as best as possible later, but the best way to prepare is to realize that this should be as close to a conversation with a friend as possible. You, of course, should avoid saying things like *dude* and *booyah*, but the interview should be an informal exchange of ideas that gives the interviewer an opportunity to find out who you are above and beyond the piece of paper that is your application.

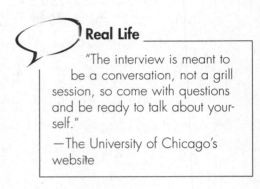

Real Life

"The interview is meant to be a conversation, not a grill session, so come with questions and be ready to talk about yourself."

—The University of Chicago's website

Be Yourself

It sounds cliché, but you should just be yourself during the college interview. Don't simply pretend to be who you think the interviewer wants you to be. There are several reasons it's important to be true to who you are.

First, there's no one who you're better at being than yourself. If you don't know anything about sports, don't pretend to. Don't ask if the interviewer watched the previous night's baseball game if you're going to end up calling a run a "goal." If you don't know anything about art, don't ask if the interviewer visited the most recent exhibit at the local museum if you're going to end up saying "dodoism" instead of "Dadaism."

Second, you don't want to fake interest in something and later find out that an overwhelming amount of people who attend that college have the same ideals and interests as the interviewer. Let's say, for instance, that the interviewer asks if you enjoy rowing and you say it's your favorite sport, when in reality you've never picked up an oar in your life.

What happens when you get to that school and rowing is next to breathing for a majority of the students? Will you continue to fake your interest? The interview isn't just an issue of impressing your interviewer; it's also about finding out whether you're a good fit for the school. The only way to do that is to be true to who you are.

Questions to Expect

The questions you'll field during an on-campus interview may be vastly different from what you're asked during an alumni interview. On-campus interviews tend to be more focused on who you are as a student and why you're interested in attending the college. You'll be asked to describe your strengths and weaknesses and outline why you think the school is the right one for you.

On the other hand, an alumni interview much more frequently can turn into a conversation that has nothing to do with college. This especially is the case with alumni interviews because you're sitting down with someone who lives in your general region and might have the same interests as you or your family.

You could end up talking about boating, football, or local theater for 25 minutes before you are asked the first question about why you want to attend the college. But don't for a second think that the "informal" conversation is any less important than how you answer the seemingly pertinent questions. If the interviewer feels comfortable with you as a person, he'll be more willing to send positive feedback to the admissions committee. The interviewer doesn't want to sit across from a robot who has practiced every answer in front of the mirror every night for weeks.

People who conduct alumni interviews often say they ask themselves during the session if they could picture the applicant in class or in the dorms with them back when they were at the college—and so much of that has nothing to do with whether you were president of the glee club.

> **Beware** _____
>
> Walk into your interview ready to show that you've done your homework on the school. Although you don't have to offer a 20-minute report on the history of the university, you should show that you're familiar with the campus, which programs are offered, and what it takes to succeed there, which is information you should gather during the application process and school tour. It is also helpful to Google the interviewer, if you know ahead of time who it will be. Often this gives you some information that can be used during the interview.

All that being said, some common questions are asked during interviews that you should prepare for. Remember that it doesn't mean preparing a speech and reciting it upon the interviewer's completion of the question. That is, unless you want to elicit a yawn out of your interviewer.

There's nothing wrong with preparing some thoughts before you head into an interview, but there's also nothing wrong with taking some time to think over a question before you give an answer. Don't be scared of a couple of seconds of silence. The silence shows that you're not someone who has come in with memorized answers, and you're also not someone who gives knee-jerk responses.

Here are some questions that might be asked during your interview:

- Why do you want to attend this college?
- What is your strongest/weakest characteristic?
- What have you done to prepare for college?
- What has been your greatest experience in high school?
- What do you want to do in the future?
- Tell me about yourself.
- Tell me about your interests.
- Tell me about your involvement in an extracurricular activity.
- Tell me about your family.
- What do you think about (a current event)?
- What is your favorite book?
- Which of your accomplishments are you the most proud of?
- If you could meet any important figure in the present or past, who would it be and what would you talk about?
- If you could be any animal, what would you be and why?
- What are your favorite subjects and why?
- Who do you admire most and why?
- What would you like to change about yourself?

There Are No Right Answers

There's no formula for how people judge interviews so there really are no right answers. Unless, of course, you don't know who your state's current governor is or you don't know who won last year's Super Bowl. Sounds silly, right? Why would someone not know who the governor is? Some people just don't keep tabs on current events, but to show that you're not just book smart, you should make sure that you're up on what's going on in the world before you walk into your interview. Not knowing what's going on in the news could result in some embarrassing moments during what should be a natural conversation.

But for virtually every other question that you'll be asked during an interview there really is no right or wrong answer, which means a lot goes into how you deliver the answer. A good rule of thumb is to avoid yes or no answers—basically avoid one-word answers altogether.

For example, "Do you think you'll be successful at Yale?" asks the interviewer. If you simply answer, "Yes," that doesn't give the interviewer anything to work with. Tell her why you think you'll be successful using the skills you put together over the years. And, don't be afraid to show some vulnerability by saying you feel you'll be successful in a number of aspects of college life but realize that you'll have to work on a couple of issues, such as living with a roommate. Don't make academics and studying one of the issues that you feel you'll have to work on, though.

I've also mentioned how you shouldn't memorize your answers. You don't want your interviewer to feel like you're simply pushing the play button in your head and answering everything just like you wrote it out at home a month ago. There has to be some spontaneity.

Here are a couple of other tips for how to answer questions that might seem like no-brainers. Not abiding by them could quickly lead to a bad interview experience:

- **Don't be arrogant.** That doesn't mean you shouldn't be confident, but there's a difference between confidence and arrogance. For instance, don't answer the "Do you think you'll succeed at this college?" question with, "Of course I'll succeed. Failure is not in my vocabulary. In fact, I don't understand people who let themselves fail. It just reeks of weakness to me." You definitely want to tone that down a lot.

- **Don't lie.** It might be later in the interview or a week or a month down the road, but a lie will come back to haunt you, especially if you say you've accomplished something you haven't.

- **Don't tell the interviewer that the school is your safety.** That's definitely not a wise way to answer the "Why do you want to attend this college?" question.

Questions You Can Ask

Don't forget that the interview is as much about you getting a feel for the school as it is the school getting a feel for you. Often an interview will end with the interviewer asking, "Do you have any questions for me?"

Come prepared with questions. It shows that you have interest in the school and you're not afraid of turning the tables to get some information out of the person who's getting information out of you. If you don't ask questions, the interviewer could think you're not interested or that you're not taking advantage of the opportunity to pick the brain of someone who is close to the college and truly knows what it takes to succeed there.

Don't ask questions you could easily find the answers for in a catalog or on the school's website. If you ask whether the college offers a business program or an arts major, you'll simply be seen as someone who didn't do her homework. Instead, ask questions that dig deeper into student life and what it takes to be a student there. If you're interviewing with alumni, ask about how he transitioned from high school into college. If you have an on-campus interview, ask if the admissions officer or a student could show you some places where students meet and get to know each other.

Real Life

"When April comes and they're sitting with five decisions in front of them, five schools in front of them, now the roles are reversed. We want them to think back to their Penn interview as a great experience."

—Maria Ho, a UPenn alumnus who coordinates alumni interviews in New Jersey

Here are some other sample questions you can ask during an interview:

- ◆ What do you think draws students here?

- ◆ What kind of orientation program does the college offer?

- ◆ How can I find out more about part-time job opportunities or internships on campus?

- ◆ Is there anything else I can tell you about myself to help you make a fair and informed decision about my application?

Put Your Best Foot Forward

You'd think you wouldn't have to tell people not to chew gum or blow bubbles during their college interviews, but alas some people will do that unless they're told not to. Some people also won't shave, won't wear a tie, won't button all the buttons on their blouse, and won't leave the Birkenstocks at home.

The best way to determine what to wear and how to act at an interview is this: if you have to think about it, then you shouldn't do it. You also should consider whether you'd wear that same outfit to a court deposition or funeral. Would you wear ripped jeans to your sister's wedding? Chances are that you wouldn't, so don't wear them to your college interview.

Men going to college interviews should wear a suit or a collared shirt with a tie, slacks, and sports jacket. Women going to college interviews should wear a pantsuit or a skirt suit. The same basic rules apply for men and women. Their outfits should be conservative, and they should be well groomed. Avoid anything that's too tight or too loose. Basically, you want to be comfortable in your chair and you don't want to fidget around, which might end up happening if you don't wear something that fits correctly. Taking the time to clean up and dress up for an interview shows the interviewer that you respect the process and you're serious about wanting to attend that college.

Cheat Sheet

It's a good idea to send your interviewer a thank-you note after you've talked with her. It's best to write the note the same day and get it in the mail as soon as possible so that she might receive it before she submits her notes on you.

There are, of course, people who are self-described rebels and maintain that they won't live in the box that society is trying to place them in. But the truth is that this is the world that you're trying to succeed in. If you want to get into a top college, you have to realize that someone interviewing you might not be as liberal when it comes to piercings as you are.

Here are some other things to keep in mind:

♦ **Don't be late.** The only thing worse than not showing up for an interview might be showing up late. I only say this because by showing up late you not only annoy your interviewer, but you actually have to sit across from that person and be embarrassed by how you annoyed him. If you're going to be late, have a good excuse.

♦ **Don't wear a lot of cologne or perfume.** Talk about coming on too strong. You never know if someone you're dealing with has allergies, so don't go in smelling like you just walked through the sample line at Macy's. You want your words to linger after you've left the room, not your smell.

♦ **Don't swear or use slang.** I don't think this one needs much of an explanation. It goes without saying that you shouldn't walk into an interview and start dropping a lot of curses. And using slang doesn't show that you're with the times; it shows that you're sort of clueless.

♦ **Don't be rude to a receptionist or anyone else you meet.** People talk, and although you may have had a great interview, if your interviewer finds out you were rude to someone in his office, all bets are off and your good report might be headed out the window.

♦ **Don't bring your parent into the interview.** This isn't the first day of kindergarten. Make mom and dad wait in the car.

Nerves of Steel

After reading all this, hopefully you're not still nervous about your college interview. So many things go into whether you'll be accepted into a top college that it makes no sense to get worked up over the interview.

However, if you still find yourself anxious about the interview, here are a few techniques you can practice to calm yourself:

♦ **Visualization.** It's no different from how many athletes prepare for a big game. If you visualize success, then you'll be successful. In the days leading up to the interview, take 10 to 15 minutes a day to close your eyes and imagine how the interview will go. Imagine yourself being very comfortable, and think about how you will answer the questions. If you repeatedly play this scene in your head, you will feel more comfortable when it's time to do the real thing.

♦ **Breathing.** It's always important to control your breathing whether you're taking a test or being interviewed. In the days leading up to the interview, take time to monitor your breathing and focus on taking 10 seconds for every inhale and then another 10 seconds for every exhale. This is a yoga technique that will calm you and can be used right before you head into the interview.

♦ **Prepare.** Be sure you've done your homework on the school and take the time to sit down with a friend or family member to go through a mock interview. Have the person playing the interviewer ask some of the questions that were included in this chapter, and answer them just as you would if it were the real thing. You even can have the pretend interviewer ask you a question that's not on the list so you can prove to yourself you're able to think on your feet.

The Least You Need to Know

◆ Don't turn down a college interview if given the option.

◆ Alumni interviews tend to be much more conversational than on-campus interviews.

◆ Dress for an interview like you would a wedding or funeral. An interview isn't the time to make a fashion statement.

◆ Don't let your nerves get the better of you. The interview won't make or break your application.

Part 5

Letters Start Rolling In

Waiting for a college application response could be one of the most stressful periods of a high school student's life. But your work doesn't end after that response does arrive. If you've been accepted to multiple schools, you have to decide which school you'll attend and then complete the process. If you've been rejected or wait-listed, a whole new process begins.

In Part 5, I discuss what essentially is the end of the race as far as the college application process goes. Although the process will be coming to a close, you don't want to limp across the finish line. There are many final steps you have to be sure you complete before you set foot on campus.

"Oh, boy. Must be college response season."

Chapter 18

So You've Been Accepted

In This Chapter

- Considering the cost of college
- Assessing various types of financial aid
- Figuring out your aid
- Making the final decision

There it is. Like an oasis in the desert, there sits in your mailbox a thick manila envelope with the name Harvard, Princeton, UCLA, Johns Hopkins, or University of Chicago stamped on it. Perhaps it's already made it to the dining room table where your mother and father have been sitting for the past four hours just waiting for you to come home so they can see the reaction on your face when you open the treasure map of your future. Or, maybe you've found out via the Internet in the form of an e-mail or college website.

Whichever way this scenario plays out for you, it all means the same thing: you've gotten into a top college and all the hard work you've put in over the years has paid off. That doesn't mean your work is over, though, as you're now faced with a whole new set of decisions and scenarios to work through. How will you pay for college? Is the financial aid package you've been offered going to cover enough? If you've been accepted to more than one college, how will you decide which one to attend?

Check, Please

Now that you've been accepted into the college of your choice, the number-one issue is how you're going to pay for it. Some costs you know, including tuition, and room and board. But some costs spring up on you unexpectedly—student fees, books, lab costs, and Saturday night pizzas. Chapter 11 covered the nuts and bolts of the financial aid process, but in this section I discuss in a bit more detail how to work through the process and the options you have.

You might feel like you're at the mercy of the college and the aid package it's offering you. But that's not necessarily the case. You can go in with a plan of attack and consider negotiating for a better aid package. There might even be things you can do—legally of course—within your family's finances that will increase your aid package.

Upon receiving your acceptance letter, you shouldn't simply sit back. You still need to be proactive to ensure that you can take advantage of your acceptance by working out an aid package that works for you and your family. Don't wait too long before making a decision, because whatever you do you don't want to miss a college's deadlines.

Hidden Costs

You can't simply consider the cost of tuition, and room and board when deciding whether you can afford the college of your choice. There are a host of other hidden costs that you have to consider, including lab and library fees, books, travel, school supplies, phone bills, laundry, club dues, and midnight Chinese food.

One expense that can be quite costly is the mandatory health insurance some schools require you to have but is not listed in total expenses. Another cost that varies and is really only an estimate in the total expenses is room and board. Sometimes different dorms are more expensive. Sometimes choosing a double room or a suite changes the cost, and meal plans vary in cost.

You will be allowed to pay for some of these hidden costs through federal and state aid along with assistance you receive from the college, while some colleges might simply waive certain fees because of your financial need. You shouldn't, however, expect to be able to pay for beer, pizza, clothes, and surfing trips with the aid money you receive. Any "extras" you might desire will have to come out of your pocket, whether it be from your family, a job (work-study or otherwise), or personal loans.

Hidden costs, of course, vary based on where you go to school. A pizza in Los Angeles while you're pulling an all-nighter at UCLA surely will cost a few bucks more than it will while cramming in New Haven at Yale. It's just like anything else in the world—the cost of living is higher in more densely populated areas.

College counselors suggest that you ask a financial aid officer at the college you're considering to estimate how much a student spends on miscellaneous costs every year.

Cheat Sheet _____

You should do your own research on how much college costs will go outside of the actual tuition, room, and board. Plenty of websites enable you to compare the cost of living of different areas. You can find one such calculator at www. bankrate.com/brm/movecalc. asp.

Assessing Your Future

When you try to put the pieces together, you need to determine how much money you'll be receiving from federal or state aid and how much money is coming from a merit-based scholarship. Considering those factors will help you get a grasp of your finances from your first day on campus to the last.

Financial aid experts agree that students who receive need-based scholarships, grants, and loans (including Pell Grants, Federal Supplemental Education Opportunity Grants, Stafford loans, and Perkins loans) typically will see their aid offers renewed for all four years of school. The aid also will increase in line with rises in inflation.

Understanding this gives you the peace of mind to realize that if you're dependent on those aid sources, you don't have worry about the rug being pulled out from under you in the middle of your college career.

> **Real Life**
>
> "If the family's financial situation stays approximately the same, if they're Pell-eligible the first year, then they're likely to be Pell-eligible the next years. That goes for all need-based aid. Need-based aid is awarded depending on the student's demonstrated financial need, and that need is going to increase as the cost goes up."
>
> —Cynthia B. Deffenbaugh, financial aid director at the University of Richmond

On the other hand, merit-based scholarships are based on just that—merit. Some scholarships might be fixed amounts that don't increase with inflation, and most are based on your academic performance. So you can't bank on having that money throughout your four years in college. If the scholarship is contingent on your grades, you have to deal with the added pressure of maintaining a certain level of excellence.

Deadlines

If you've applied early decision, you know that the deadline for returning your acceptance is earlier than it is for regular admission. You also know that your decision is binding, which means you won't get your deposit back and you run the risk of alienating other schools if they find out you backed out of your early acceptance, possibly risking your acceptance.

If you have applied early action or regular admission, you could be notified any time from before Christmas through early April. May 1 is the deadline by which you must submit your deposit and complete all the acceptance forms.

Be sure you check with each school that has accepted you to see when its deadlines are.

Forms to Fill Out

In addition to the federal forms discussed in Chapter 11, several schools have their own financial aid forms you have to fill out. Princeton, for instance, uses the Princeton Financial Aid Application to determine what it will award in terms of a *no-loan grant* or *scholarship*.

The Princeton Financial Aid Application is a six-page form that families have to fill out instead of the College Scholarship Service profile. The university prefers that you complete the form online but does allow for paper submissions if you don't have Internet access.

No-loan grant awards by Princeton range from 100 percent of tuition and room and

board to 47 percent of tuition. In addition, they can fluctuate based on the number of children in a home, the number of children in college at the same time, significant medical expenses, and significant or limited family assets.

No-Loan Grants for the Princeton Class of 2012

Family Income	Average Grant	What It Covers
$0–$75,000	$45,800	Tuition, room/board
$75,000–$100,000	$39,300	Tuition, 44 percent room/board
$100,000–$120,000	$35,750	Tuition, 13 percent room/board
$120,000–$140,000	$32,250	94 percent tuition
$140,000–$160,000	$28,850	84 percent tuition
$160,000–$180,000	$26,000	76 percent tuition
$180,000–$200,000	$22,250	65 percent tuition
$200,000+	$16,000	47 percent tuition

UCLA also has a unique financial aid system called Electronic Financial Aid Notification (EFAN). UCLA's program is entirely online and continually updates based on the status of a loan and payments made. It's essentially like an online bank for your college tuition.

Check with the college you're considering to find out what forms and programs are unique to its financial aid processes.

Considering Multiple Aid Packages

Considering multiple financial aid packages often ends up being as stressful as the actual college application part of the process.

Top students are frequently accepted by multiple schools, and the financial aid offered by each school becomes a critical part of the elimination process. When considering offers from different colleges, financial aid officials say you need to compare apples to apples. That means you should look at how your aid offer breaks down between loans you'll have to pay back, no-loan grants, and money received through work-study.

> **Real Life**
>
> "When folks open up their award letters, their eyes tend to go first to the bottom line, but it's important to understand each of the components. A $15,000 loan from one school actually may be better than a $2,000 scholarship from another school."
> —Marie Mons, Director of Student Financial Planning and Services for the Georgia Institute of Technology in Atlanta

Comparing apples to apples means coming up with a true understanding of what it will cost you to attend a school for four years, factoring in inflation and then subtracting the amount of no-loan aid offered over those four years. You are then left with the true cost of what you'll have to contribute toward your education. Sallie Mae's website offers a financial aid analyzer that enables you to compare your award offers at www.collegeanswer.com.

When comparing student aid, you also should ask colleges how a sudden drop in your family's ability to contribute toward your education or a sudden increase in your family's wealth could impact your aid status. Some schools do offer emergency financial aid, but what each school offers varies. Some schools could offer as little as a couple hundred dollars in an emergency, whereas others could give you several thousand. Again, this varies from school to school.

> **Cheat Sheet**
>
> Each school that sends you a financial aid package should include a sheet that outlines where the money is coming from and which awards are renewable. The sheet also should include any conditions you have to meet to retain scholarships. If you don't receive such a sheet or you have additional questions, you should immediately contact the financial aid office.

Negotiating for More

Colleges will tell you that under no circumstances will they negotiate financial aid packages. The standard line is that if one college is giving you a better deal than they are, maybe there is something you left off your worksheet with the school offering the lesser package.

Although they're not technically lying—they won't *negotiate*—many schools have certain processes in place, specifically a letter of appeal, that allow you to call on them to take another look at the aid you've been offered. Typically, a person appealing her financial aid award should be able to bring forth some extenuating circumstances that the FAFSA or CSS did not explain. Also, as a guidance counselor for 30 years, I often sent letters and made phone calls on behalf of students whose financial aid packages would have prohibited them from attending that particular school.

Most of the state schools are unable to act on these letters and calls, but many private schools will in fact consider these requests. I can recall numerous instances where a letter and/or phone call from the student, parent, or guidance counselor made a huge difference.

Several years ago, I had an extremely bright young lady who, in spite of insurmountable odds in her life, went to Tufts University for her undergraduate degree. The financial aid package Tufts originally offered her would have made it impossible for her to attend. Both she and I wrote letters and called, and the school increased her award by $8,000 in grant money.

When writing a letter of appeal, you should make it as personal and unique as possible. The only thing that's truly going to get a college to reconsider its aid package is if you explain that you've had some extenuating circumstance. These circumstances don't have to be of tragic proportions and simply could be an inability to come up with the money needed. Still, make your appeal as personalized as your admission essay.

A Different Decision

For some people, financial aid might not be an issue. For others, the financial aid packages they've been offered at multiple schools are basically equal. Under either of those scenarios, students face a different decision that could be just as tough. When the world is at your fingertips, how do you choose between Princeton, Harvard, UCLA, Stanford, and Georgetown?

Several years ago, I had an extremely bright and accomplished top student who was accepted to five out of her six choices. All merit aid was comparable (she did not qualify for financial aid), each of the schools was a comparable distance from home, and each of them had an extensive curriculum in her choice of major. All the schools were a great fit. She visited the schools either through school-organized events or visits over April vacation. She eventually made her choice based on the research opportunities that would be available to her as an undergrad.

Help with Choosing

Many colleges have what they call "accepted student events." These could be day programs, be overnight programs, and include events for parents.

Cornell uses its Cornell Days event, which runs for eight days, as an opportunity for prospective students to immerse themselves in what it would be like to be a student there. The event includes more than 30 organized activities, including tours of the libraries and dorms. Prospective students also are given an opportunity to sit in on classes. Cornell's is probably one of the most extensive prospective student events, but other schools have similar programs that provide more extensive tours and student interaction than you might be privy to when you're just an applicant.

Earlier in this book I discussed *yield*, which is the percentage of accepted students who actually attend the school. That rate, or yield, is a competition among the top schools, so after you've been accepted, most schools will do all they can to show you around campus and get you comfortable with the idea of attending their institution.

Most schools also have some sort of ambassador program that pairs you with an enrolled student and allows him to give you a tour of the school. You also might have an opportunity to stay overnight in that person's dorm or in a guest dorm. Spending a night on campus is a great way to get an idea of what a college is like, and spending more than just a couple of hours with a student gives you more time to hear the truth about a school and not just the typical presentation. Don't expect to party during your night on campus, though, as most schools have stringent rules that don't allow prospective students to visit fraternities or sororities.

Rank the Schools

Call it what you will: soul searching, ranking, or assessing. What you really need to do is figure out what's important to you and then what's *most* important to you. My parents always used to tell me to make a pro and a con list to help me through a tough decision, and this isn't much different. There are several items you should consider when making your final decision; then you should assign each of those items a positive or negative ranking or a number from 1 to 5.

It doesn't really matter how you go about ranking the schools and the individual aspects of each school. What's important is that you get all your thoughts down on paper or bounce them off a friend or family member. This way, you won't come back later with regrets about not considering the kind of community a college is in or its climate.

Beware _____

Don't rush your decision. You have until the spring to decide where you'll end up at college, so use all the time you have. Resist the urge to make a quick decision just so you have some closure. Closure will come soon enough; now is the time to make sure you get it right.

Here are some factors you should rank and consider when making your final decision:

♦ **Location.** Is the school near a large city or in a small town? How far is it from your home? Do you want to be near a large city? Do you want to be near home?

♦ **Size.** How big is the school? How many students are in an average class?

♦ **Academics.** Does the college offer classes that interest you? Obviously, top colleges offer top classes, but does it offer classes in your specific areas of interest?

♦ **Extracurriculars.** Does the school offer extracurricular activities that interest you? Is there an opportunity to organize activities you're interested in?

After you've jotted down notes and grades for each of these items, you can bring them to a friend, a family member, or your guidance counselor and bounce your ideas and thoughts off of that person. It's always good to get some outside input, but don't forget to be honest with yourself.

Your Decision's Made

Now that you've made your decision, your work isn't quite done. You have to sign all your paperwork and turn in your deposit. Make sure you follow all the college's specific instructions when it comes to filling out the information it needs from you. An oversight on a form or a missed deadline could result in you not living in the dorm you were hoping for and other inconveniences.

You also should send notes to the colleges you won't be attending. The sooner you're able to let them know that you don't plan on attending, the sooner they'll be able to offer your spot to someone on the waiting list. A simple and polite thanks but no thanks letter is just a nice thing to do and will earn you some good karma.

Deferring Enrollment

Most schools give you the opportunity to defer your enrollment for up to two years to explore *gap year* opportunities.

def•i•ni•tion

A **gap year** is a year you take off between your senior year of high school and your freshman year of college. Several gap year options are available, ranging from simply taking a year off to participating in any number of organized programs.

Be sure that you research each school's deferral policies before you make a decision. Most schools allow you to use the gap year to travel, work, perform military service, or study abroad. However, many schools have policies that forbid you from using your deferred enrollment to enroll in courses at another college or university. "Taking such a step would cause you to forfeit your admission to MIT," the school's website states.

Still other schools, including Harvard, go beyond simply offering you a year off. Harvard actually promotes taking a year off as a way to avoid the burnout that is common for college students. About 70 students who are admitted to Harvard defer enrollment every year.

"Regardless of why they took the year off or what they did, students are effusive in their praise. Many speak of their year away as a 'life-altering' experience or a 'turning point,' and most feel that its full value can never be measured and will pay dividends the rest of their lives," Harvard's website states. "Many come to college with new visions of their academic plans, their extracurricular pursuits, the intangibles they hoped to gain in college, and the career possibilities they observed in their year away. Virtually all would do it again."

A more detailed look at gap year programs is included in Chapter 19.

The Least You Need to Know

◆ Be sure you calculate all college costs, including personal expenses and hidden fees.

◆ Understand where every last dollar is coming from in your aid package and what requirements are attached to each loan, grant, or scholarship.

◆ Colleges won't "negotiate" aid packages, but you can write a letter explaining why you feel your circumstance requires that you receive a little more help.

◆ Be honest with yourself when deciding which school to attend, and make sure you know what you hope to get out of the college experience.

Chapter 19

So You've Been Rejected

In This Chapter

- ◆ Hoping for a mistake
- ◆ Filing an appeal
- ◆ Taking part in a gap year program
- ◆ Considering your second choice

Some things don't change over the years with the college application process. You rush home after school every day to see what mail has come for you, and if you see a small envelope from your top choice you immediately know what it means: You've been rejected.

Initially the reality of it all will knock you in the stomach like a punch to the gut. But rest assured, your life is not over, and this rejection isn't an indication of who you are as a person or even a student. The key is to remember that while top colleges are accepting individual students, they're doing so with an eye toward forming a class that represents several different cultures, skills, and personalities. And although you might be the most accomplished student at your school, there could be dozens, if not hundreds, of students who fit your profile who also applied to that college.

Still, you have to deal with the reality of a rejection and decide whether you're going to attend your second- or third-choice school, take a year off, or even appeal the rejection. It's a whole new process, and the sooner you start reacting to your rejection, the sooner you'll know where this new path takes you.

Holding Out Hope

Short of a formal letter of *appeal*, the only hope you have of seeing your rejection overturned is to find out that the college lost a piece of your application paperwork.

def•i•ni•tion

A formal **appeal** of a college rejection means you think the college has misjudged your application or lost a portion of it. To appeal a rejection, you must send a formal letter to the school asking that your application be reconsidered.

It's possible that you were rejected because some of your admission information was missing. You should have submitted all your paperwork via the Internet or certified mail to ensure that it arrived. So, if you didn't receive confirmation that all the portions of your application were received by the school, you should send a letter or call to inquire. Even with the Internet, things can still get lost.

If the error is on your side of the ledger—even if the post office is the one that lost something—then the missing information likely won't be legitimate grounds for an appeal. You should have done everything you could to ensure that the information arrived in time.

However, sometimes the admissions office loses paperwork. If that was the case, then it's likely your application will be given a second look. The only way to find out whether everything was received is to ask. Again, you really shouldn't wait until after you've been rejected to submit that inquiry.

Real Life

"Of course (students) should check. If we're in the business of 'don't bother me,' we're in the wrong business. Mistakes happen—we're all human, and humans can correct mistakes."

—Mara O'Laughlin, Admissions Director of Hobart and William Smith Colleges

Fighting the System

If you're not ready to give up your dream of a Harvard education quite yet, you can submit a formal appeal of your rejection. You do, however, need to realize that although numbers are hard to come by, most guidance counselors agree that a private college is overwhelmingly less likely to reconsider and ultimately admit a rejected student than is a public school. And the public school numbers aren't that strong to begin with.

Different colleges have different policies for reconsidering rejected applications. Some colleges will under no circumstances reconsider an application; others do have protocols set in place to deal with students who want their paperwork given another look. Ultimately this is a long shot and you'll likely end up being disappointed, so don't put all your eggs in this basket.

Different Policies

As I said, some schools allow you to appeal your rejection and have a formal process established, while others simply do not consider appeals.

"If your application to Columbia is denied, that decision is final," the university's website states. "There is no appeal process for admission decisions, and applicants are not reconsidered for admission."

Other schools are open to appeals, although they make it clear that your appeal has to have significant merit and include information that previously wasn't disclosed.

"For an appeal to have merit, it must bring to light new academic and personal information as well as information pertaining to extenuating circumstances that was not present in the application—information that clearly shows the student to be stronger than had been earlier evidenced," says UCLA's website.

You should also make note of when a college will issue its decision on an appeal. UCLA's website states that the university can't guarantee a response on an appeal by June 1, which is a couple of weeks beyond when most colleges want students to submit their responses about whether they're attending. Don't convince yourself that your appeal is going to work out when it's likely not going to, and in turn forget to send your response to another school.

Rates of Appeal

Finding definitive figures on the number of rejections that are appealed and then overturned is difficult, and colleges typically don't report them.

A 2001 survey by the Associated Press found that the University of California reversed its decision on 1,400 of the 5,000 appeals it received in 2001. Numbers at other public colleges showed that appeals were successful about 10 percent of the time. The University of California system also reported its 2003 numbers for successful appeals.

That year, UC Berkeley received about 1,000 appeals and granted admission to about 125 of those students. UCLA received about 1,300 appeals and granted admission to about 75 of those students.

> **Beware** _____
>
> Disregard consulting services that say they'll all but guarantee that your appeal will be successful. Numbers show that appeals are typically successful no more than 10 percent of the time, and you truly having an extenuating circumstance will determine your success. An appeal won't be successful if you contract with a consultant and sit down to determine which portion of the rejection you're going to appeal.

When to Appeal

Before you appeal an admissions decision, ask yourself why you're appealing. If the reason simply is because you really, really want to attend that school, you're appealing for the wrong reason.

There really are only a select number of reasons that could lead to a successful appeal. Here are some legitimate reasons for submitting an appeal:

- ◆ **Something has changed.** Maybe you've just won a major award or have received an SAT or ACT score that is heads and tails better than the scores you submitted. Those are things that could sway an admissions office, although more times than not it will lead to them telling you to reapply the following year.

- ◆ **There has been a clerical mix-up.** There's always the possibility that a portion of your application was lost or misplaced, or maybe your standardized test scores were misreported.

- ◆ **Health issues have arisen.** Maybe you were running a 104° fever the day you took the SAT or ACT and you couldn't see straight. Before you receive an admissions decision is a better time to let the admissions office know about this kind of issue, but it also could be the basis of an appeal.

So now that you know when you can appeal, how about when you shouldn't? On many occasions your application will be rejected with the option of reapplying in a year. Appealing just for the sake of appealing could sour the admissions office on you and jeopardize any hopes you have of being admitted in the future. Here are some examples of when it's not a good idea to appeal:

- Just so the admissions office will take another look at your application.

- Someone you know who had similar grades and test scores was admitted.

- You thought you met all the school's standards.

- You really want to attend that school.

- You got into a "better" school.

- You found out a long-lost relative is a graduate of that school.

What the Appeal Looks Like

Your appeal is basically just a letter stating why you think your application should be considered. The letter should be succinct and to the point; this isn't your admissions essay or a letter of recommendation.

The only way most schools will reconsider your application is if you present some new information in your appeal. Place the new information that you hope will sway the admissions office at the top of your letter. You also should include any supporting material, such as a copy of the award you received, a changed transcript, or new test scores.

> **Real Life**
>
> "You don't want to call up the admissions office and whine and accuse them of treating you unfairly. Your best approach is a mature phone call or letter to the admissions office that respects the original rejection, but then explains the new information that you hope will make the admissions staff change their mind."
>
> —Allen Grove, About.com's guide to college admissions

Again, there's no hard-and-fast rule to what an appeal looks like. It basically just needs to be a clean, formal letter outlining why you believe your rejection should be reconsidered. Present the new information that you believe will sway the admissions office and then pray for the best.

Overcoming the Shock

I've already said that you need to realize that a rejection letter isn't personal and doesn't mean you're a terrible student. Remember that top schools are rejecting valedictorians and students with near-perfect SAT scores left and right.

Still, if you need a little help overcoming the rejection before you're able to move on with your life, here are some tips that can help get you out of bed:

♦ **Again, don't take it personally.** Your rejection simply could have been because there were many students who fit your profile.

♦ **You're not going it alone.** The rejection rates among top schools are staggering in recent years because of the number of qualified students applying. Although you might feel all alone, you're really not.

♦ **Don't focus on name recognition.** If you wanted to go to Harvard simply so you could say you went to Harvard, you need to adjust your thinking. A lot more goes into the education process and life than a school's name, and if you've been accepted by another top school, then be happy about that.

♦ **Don't stand around and ask why.** The time you spend questioning why you were rejected could be better used coming up with a strategy for the future.

♦ **See it as a blessing and not as a curse.** Guess what, you're going to be disappointed at some point during your life. It's how you deal with that disappointment that truly defines you as a person. Take this disappointment and turn it into a positive.

What's Next?

If you've been rejected by your top choice—and accept that you've been rejected—you have many options moving forward:

♦ Accept admission to your next choice and plan on four years there.

♦ Accept admission to another school and attempt to transfer to your top choice.

♦ Take a gap year between high school and college and reapply to your top choice during your gap year.

The decision on how to move forward after you've been rejected is a very personal one. Several people excel in gap year programs and need that time to recharge their batteries. Others need the structure of school and decide to move on to their second- or third-choice schools. Still others see the rejection as a challenge and try to use their gap year or their first year at another school as an opportunity to eventually transfer to the school that rejected them. The choice is yours.

The Gap Year

The decision to take a year off is an individual one. If your intent is to use the gap year to better your chances at getting into a college that rejected you, then you need to sign up with a reputable gap year program.

Even after a year off, your application to the school that rejected you still will be based primarily on your high school grades and test scores, which is why you need to make sure your gap year decision is a wise one. It's difficult for a gap year program alone to put you over the top with an admissions office. Therefore, if you hope to get any value out of your gap year decision, you have to be sure you choose the best of the best.

What a gap year program should provide is leadership and work experience that will prove to an admissions officer that you spent your year bettering yourself and the community around you. A year simply backpacking through Europe won't accomplish that. For a list of reputable gap year programs see Appendix I.

A program like AmeriCorps is worth looking into if you feel that you are not ready to commit to your second-choice college, or ready in general to continue with your education.

Several years ago, I had an excellent student who was accepted to the Naval Academy. He did not last more than five weeks there, and then he enrolled in AmeriCorps, where he taught in literacy programs in Mississippi. While he was there, he applied to a number of schools and ended up at Emory the next fall.

Your Second Choice

Your second- or third-choice school always is an option after you've been rejected. Whether you plan on attempting to transfer to your top choice—which I'll discuss in a bit—or you intend on committing yourself to that college, there's nothing wrong with your second choice.

Being rejected from your top choice actually might be a blessing and not a curse. More often than not, students wind up at their second-choice school, love it, and wonder how they ever could have considered going anywhere else. And if you're a top student applying to top schools, chances are your second or third choice still is one of the top schools in the nation and the difference is marginal.

Real Life

Several years ago, I had a student who was wait-listed from her first-choice school and then was eventually denied. She was inconsolable. She reluctantly went to her second-choice school, and the summer following her freshman year I bumped into her in the grocery store. She threw her arms around me and said, "I am so glad that I didn't get into my first choice. I am so happy and could not see myself any other place."

What you do have to be careful of is going to a school that you really can't see yourself at with the intention of eventually transferring. Many students have every intention of transferring but never do. Then, you end up at a school that you didn't want to be at in the first place.

If you do go to a second or third choice, make sure it's a school you can truly see yourself at and not one you think will be easy to transfer out of. Transferring into a top school is very difficult, so don't set yourself up with an unrealistic goal.

Transferring

If you've been rejected by your top choice and your first reaction is, "No problem, I'll just go to another school and transfer after three semesters," think again. Students who plan on transferring to a top college often face one of two scenarios.

The first scenario, as I discussed earlier, is that a student goes to his second choice, all set to transfer after two years. Then, he finds himself very happy where his is and stays put.

The other scenario is that the student has every intention of transferring and then later realizes just how difficult it is to transfer into a top college.

Yale, for example, admits about 30 transfer students every year out of a pool of about 800 applicants. That's an acceptance rate of about 4 percent, and the rate of acceptance for transfers at other top colleges isn't any better. UPenn accepts about 175 transfer applicants every year out of a pool of about 2,000, and very few of those transfers are accepted to the Wharton School of Business.

In 2007, Harvard decided it would significantly reduce the number of transfer applicants it accepted. Harvard then later decided it would not enroll any transfer applicants in 2008–09 or 2009–10. The future of the Harvard transfer program hasn't been determined.

Although it's not easy or likely, transferring isn't impossible and there are a couple of things you can do to help yourself.

First, be sure that you make the most of your first three semesters at the college you land at. If you want a fighting chance of being able to transfer into a top college, straight As isn't too much to expect of yourself.

Second, just like you did when you applied out of high school, pay special attention to your admissions essay—only this time admissions officers likely will have more time to read it. Because you're competing among a much smaller pool of applicants, the admissions office will be able to spend more time on each application and read every word of your essay. Additionally, if given the opportunity, be sure you carefully craft your message of why you want to attend that school. More than ever, the school you're applying to will be looking for that special student who will round out the student body and who somehow was overlooked the first time around.

All the rules that you're to live by when applying straight out of high school also apply when you're a transfer applicant. You need to paint a picture of how you've grown and how you've bettered yourself during your time at another college.

Cornell breaks all the rules when it comes to transferring into a top college with the Pathway to Success Community College Partnership program. Unlike most top schools that significantly limit their number of transfer students, Cornell admits about 500 transfer students annually, and about a third of those students come from community colleges.

Cheat Sheet

Although you're likely limited by a first-year schedule of prerequisites at the school you're trying to transfer out of, challenge yourself if given the opportunity. Schools weighing transfer applicants don't want to see students who took easy classes to guarantee As.

"One goal of the Pathway to Success Partnership is to encourage low- and moderate-income community college students at Borough of Manhattan, Monroe, Morrisville, Nassau, and Suffolk to pursue a bachelor's degree at Cornell," the school's website states. "Another goal is to develop potential partnerships between other community colleges and selective four-year institutions, using this program as a model."

Similarly, the University of California system offers several programs that make it easier for community college students to transfer to one of the university campuses. Students wishing to attend UCLA, for instance, can take part in the Transfer Alliance Program. Through that program students at participating community colleges can work with counselors to map out a rigorous course load that will better position them for admission to UCLA as a transfer. Completion of the program doesn't guarantee them admission, but the student is given priority consideration.

The Least You Need to Know

◆ If rejected, you should check to make sure all your application information was received by the college.

◆ A formal appeal of a rejection rarely results in a reversal of an admissions decision.

◆ Being rejected by your top choice could be a blessing in disguise. Often, someone ends up loving his second choice more than he ever would have liked his first.

◆ Most top colleges offer very few seats to transfer students. Yale admits only about 4 percent of the transfer applications it receives.

Chapter 20

The Wait List

In This Chapter

- ◆ Changes in wait list policies
- ◆ The limbo of being on a wait list
- ◆ Accepting your predicament
- ◆ Ways to get yourself off the list

Is there a bigger "ugh" than finding out that you've landed on a school's wait list? For students who face that predicament, it becomes the perfect storm of uncertainty, disappointment, and anxiety:

Should I move on to my next choice?

Should I spend time trying to get myself off the wait list?

Do I even have a fighting chance of getting off the wait list?

Why did I get placed on the wait list to begin with?

All these questions will go through a student's mind as she considers her future. Suddenly, what a student thought would be a yes or no answer to the college admission question has become a maybe. So, what now?

Times Are Changing

The rate at which top colleges are going to their wait lists for students has dramatically changed over recent years. It used to be that landing on the wait list was another way to say you've been rejected. The top schools would go years without dipping into their pools of wait-listed students.

If a student found himself on the wait list just five years ago, he would be advised to forget about that school and send a deposit to his second or third choice. But times have changed.

Harvard accepted 50 students off the wait list for the Class of 2011, and that number quadrupled for the Class of 2012 with the university accepting 200 students off the wait list.

And not only are more students being accepted off the wait list, but more students are being added to it than ever before. So, why the huge difference?

More Applicants

Changes in the application and financial aid processes have completely changed the way top colleges are putting together their freshman classes.

As I mentioned earlier in the book, several universities recently have made sweeping changes to their admissions policies. The elimination of binding early admission programs at several top colleges means students are taking longer to decide where they'll end up and are applying to more colleges than in the past. In turn, the *yield* (which is the percentage of students who actually accept the admission offered to them) at top universities is decreasing, even though those same universities are turning away a record number of students.

Harvard originally expected the yield for the Class of 2012 to be 78 percent, but it ended up being 76 percent, which sent the admissions office reaching for the wait list. The yield was lower than expected because students who didn't have to abide by early admissions rules that had determined where each student would land in the past now were able to weigh offers from several schools and take their time in doing so.

The same scenario played out at top schools across the board. Penn offered admission to 90 students from its wait list of 1,352 for the Class of 2012, and Swarthmore College offered admission to 20 of the 350 students it had on its list. Penn took 65 students off its wait list for the Class of 2011, and Swarthmore offered admission to 15 students from its list.

Easier Financing

In addition to the elimination of the early application process at several top schools, the expansion of financial aid options also has led to an exponential growth in the number of applicants and acceptances.

The change in financial aid programs, specifically the increase in no-loan grants, has enabled more students to realistically consider admission to more top colleges. Although the intended goal of expanding their financial aid policies was giving more students the opportunity to attend a top college, an unintended consequence was the expansion and fluidity of the wait list program.

> **Real Life**
>
> "If students are less worried about financial aid, they can choose more where they'd like to go to school rather than where the best deal is."
>
> —Eric Kaplan, Admissions Director at UPenn

Stuck in Limbo

All it takes is one student turning down an acceptance at a top college to set off a chain of students being taken off the wait list, turning down other schools, and then forcing those schools to go to their wait lists.

Let's say that Sally turns down Harvard because she can afford to go to Princeton due to its new no-loan grant program. Now, Harvard has to replace Sally and offers a seat to Billy. Billy had already sent his deposit to Yale but then decides he will attend Harvard. So Yale has to replace Billy and offers a seat to Sue. Sue was planning on going to Cornell, but now she'll attend Yale and tell Cornell "thanks, but no."

And so the spiral continues many times over. "Harvard may take someone from Brown, Brown may take someone from Swarthmore," said Jim Bock, Dean of Admissions at Swarthmore. This scenario didn't happen as frequently in the past because students had to commit to the schools that they applied early to.

Not only does the change mean that more students are being accepted from the wait list, but it also means more students are being placed on the wait list, leaving them in limbo with that school. The increase is due to schools having to guard against not having enough students to admit if other top schools pilfer their applicant pools. "Around May 1 many of us found we had fewer students in class than we like to have," said Kaplan at UPenn.

UPenn placed 2,300 students on its wait list for the Class of 2012, up more than 500 students from last year. MIT wait-listed 739 applicants for the Class of 2012, up nearly 50 percent from the year before. Northeastern University wait-listed 1,400, a 17 percent increase, and Dartmouth wait-listed 1,500, up 15 percent.

"Students are applying to more colleges and colleges are wait-listing more because they are worried about how many will come," Brad MacGowan, a longtime college counselor, told *The Boston Globe*. "They feed off each other."

Changing the Timeline

All these changes have completely altered the application and acceptance timeline for colleges and those students who find themselves on any wait list, even if they've already accepted a seat at another school. Schools typically have their freshman classes set by early May, but with the fluidity of the process as it stands, changes and decisions now could come as late as June.

> **Real Life**
>
> "It's a tough time. I really hope they accept me. I told them I will definitely go if they do."
>
> —Cheng Ji, a Boston-area high school senior told *The Boston Globe*. Li was accepted by the University of Massachusetts but was hoping to be accepted off of Northeastern's wait list.

Unable to accurately predict the admissions trend, Georgetown kept an extended wait list for the Class of 2012 until the end of June. "It's a guessing game," Charles Deacon, Dean of Admissions at Georgetown, told the school newspaper. "But it's as good as we could have hoped for."

It's more than a guessing game. For students, it's their future. For admissions officers tasked with gathering the best admissions classes possible, it's their professional careers that are on the line. "It's nerve-racking trying to determine how many students will take you up on the offer," said Kristin Tichenor, Vice President for Enrollment Management at Worcester Polytechnic Institute. "My counterparts and I are on pins and needles, so there's something of a hedging of the bets."

Dealing with the Wait List

The rules of dealing with being placed on the wait list have changed now that the number of people being accepted from and added to those lists has increased.

As I said, in the past you could basically interpret a spot on the wait list as a rejection, but that's no longer the case. And, with some schools extending their wait lists into the summer before you're expecting to attend your first year of college, how do you play the waiting game? There are some tried-and-true methods for giving yourself the best opportunity to get off the wait list and into your top school.

There's also the issue of deciding to attend your top choice after it initially placed you on the wait list. Do you really want to be the second choice of a school that at first didn't want you?

As many guidance counselors have expressed, it's difficult for students to ride the emotional rollercoaster of being turned down by their dream school, courted by another school, and then told that their dream school actually does want them.

"It would have been nice if these decisions had been made by the colleges initially," said Anne Hall, Director of College Guidance at Episcopal Academy in Merion, Pennsylvania, said of the fluidity of the college acceptance process.

Playing the Waiting Game

The college wait list is just like a game of poker, and everyone is hedging their bets. If you land on the wait list at your top choice and are accepted by another school, you have to decide whether you're going to submit your deposit (if the school requires one) to the school that accepted you or take your chances on the wait list.

Colleges usually require that you let them know by May 1 if you're going to attend. But the wait list process, as I said, now extends well into the summer for many schools. You can call the admissions office of the school that wait-listed you all you want. However, officials there won't be able to give you an idea of what the school's yield looks like, and in turn how many students will be taken off the wait list, until after May 1. So, what are you to do?

Most college counselors will tell you that if you want to attend college right after high school, you need to send your deposit to at least one school by the May 1 deadline. If your dream school accepts you after you've sent that deposit, then you have the option of forfeiting your deposit and deciding to attend your top choice.

"You have to proceed as if you're not going to be taken off the wait list," said college counselor Brad MacGowan. "You can't rely on it, psychologically or practically."

Others will tell you that being placed on the wait list at your top choice is a blessing and will force you to consider gap year options. If wait-listed, you can decide to defer enrollment at your second choice and pursue a gap year program. If, before you enter that gap year program, your top choice comes through with an acceptance, then everything worked out.

def•i•ni•tion

The **courtesy wait list** is, as it sounds, a courtesy for students with special connections. Colleges have no intention of accepting students on the courtesy list, and applicants likely won't even know they're on this quasi-wait list.

The options really are limitless. The true question is whether you have the nerves to wait out a wait list and the money to lose if you pay a deposit to another school.

You also have to consider that you might have been placed on the *courtesy wait list*. While not readily acknowledged by top colleges, professionals agree that there is such a thing as a courtesy wait list that students who have special connections or situations land on with the understanding that they'll never be accepted off the wait list.

Emotional Highs and Lows

The ups and downs that come with trying to navigate the college wait list are not for the faint of heart. Rejection could turn into a new opportunity, but what if the rejecter later wants you back?

In 2008, Jim Bock, Dean of Admissions at Swarthmore, offered a spot to a wait-listed student who in April had written him a letter "expressing her sheer and genuine love for Swarthmore," according to the *Philadelphia Inquirer*. She turned him down. "She said, 'Why didn't you just take me in April?'" Bock said.

Colleges say they understand the emotions that accompany the process and don't take what a student goes through lightly. "I do feel for them," Eric Kaplan of UPenn, said of wait-listed applicants.

So how do you deal with being wait-listed (which you'll interpret as rejection), deciding you're going to attend somewhere else, and then seeing your rejection overturned? You have to be grounded and decide what you really want out of college and life. Is a school's rank more important than your happiness? Just as I mentioned when dealing with rejection, you have to consider that being placed on the wait list is actually a blessing in disguise. You might end up very happy at a school you otherwise wouldn't have really considered.

Cheat Sheet

Most schools will ask you to send them a correspondence acknowledging that you want to remain on the wait list. Students often automatically send that note without considering whether they'd be better off at their second choice, thus avoiding the emotional limbo. Take some time to consider the wait list before you agree to be on it.

Kavya Rao, a member of the University of California at San Diego's Medical Scholars Program for the Class of 2012 was placed on the wait list at Harvard but ultimately decided to attend UCSD. "I would have loved to go to Harvard," she told *Time* magazine. "Now I don't want to leave UCSD and all the people here who can help me become a doctor."

It might sound cliché, but everyone from your parents to your friends and guidance counselors will give you the same message when it comes to this subject: College is what you make of it.

Fighting Your Way Off the List

If Princeton was expecting its yield to be 78 percent and it actually was 76 percent, the school simply goes to the wait list and picks the applicants with the best grades and test scores, right? Not so much.

As Dick Nesbitt, Director of Admissions at Williams College, put it, the wait list is "a great way to shape the class and meet our institutional priorities. Maybe we could use a few more artists or a few more math or science researchers." Admissions officers essentially have to search the wait list for students who will complement the students who already have agreed to attend.

So, how do you make yourself stand out during the wait list process?

Although professionals across the board agree that you shouldn't send roses, chocolate, or any other gifts, you can do some things that will slightly better your chances of being accepted off the wait list. That being said, I will preface the following advice by saying that of everything I've done in the field of college counseling, the wait list remains the most ambiguous and unclear to me.

Some schools say they don't rank students from the wait list, which always baffles me. If they are not ranking, how will they know whom to pick if they do in fact go to the wait list? On many occasions, I have called colleges where my students were wait-listed and asked whether there was anything we could do or send. Most of the schools, however, told me they had everything they needed.

As ambiguous as it might be, there are things you could and should do because every other wait-listed student is probably doing it. So, if you don't follow through, you'll likely fall through the cracks. Here are some tips:

- **Don't be afraid to ask what system a school uses to accept students off the wait list.** Some schools will acknowledge that they do employ some sort of ranking system. Others will tell you they replace students based on the intended major or skill of the student who turned down the initial acceptance.

- **Do send the school your third-quarter grades.** But make sure they are out-standing! Guidance counselors agree that this is the least you need to do if you find yourself on the wait list.

- **Do send a cheesy letter telling the admissions office how badly you want to attend that school.** It's a necessary evil. Also, don't forget to include some-thing in the letter asking if there's anything else you can send the school that might aid in its decision.

Beware _____

If you wind up on the wait list, don't send the school any information without first checking with the admissions office. Some schools do not want you to send them new information, and ignoring that mandate could doom your application.

- **Do stay in frequent contact with the admissions office.** Let the office know about any new achievement or award you might have received.

- **Don't let persistence turn into stalking.** There's nothing wrong with fre-quently checking in with a college's admissions office, but a daily call is a little much. If you have to ask yourself if you're calling too much, you probably are.

- **Do stay active in school.** It's important that you show the school that has wait-listed you that you've remained active in sports, clubs, and other extracurriculars.

- **Do request an interview at the school if you never had one.** If you did have an interview, then request a second one. You might not get it, but it's worth a shot.

Gimmicks

Tread lightly when considering employing a gimmick to gain acceptance off a college's wait list. Although some people might find the gimmick cute and funny, others might be turned off by it and toss your application in the trash. This is another time when you're gambling when deciding what will be effective.

One college counseling service suggests that if a student's application lists a special tal-ent in music or art, he should consider composing a piece of music or creating a piece of art that's specific to the school.

There's nothing wrong with being creative. But you don't want to seem scary or desperate. Jean Jordan, Dean of Admissions at Emory, said she admitted a student who rewrote the words of the school song to explain why she should be accepted. But Jordan also said she's sick of receiving shoes from students who "want to get their foot in the door."

The Least You Need to Know

♦ Changes in admissions and financial aid policies are leading to more students being accepted off of wait lists.

♦ More acceptances from wait lists also are resulting in more students being placed on wait lists.

♦ Although more students are getting into schools off of the wait list, you still need to accept the reality that your dream of attending a certain school might end with the wait list.

♦ Be sure you follow a college's rules when sending information that you hope will help your chances of being accepted off of the wait list.

Chapter 21

Wrapping It Up

In This Chapter

- What's in the big envelope?
- Finishing the financial aid process
- Making dorm and meal decisions
- What you'll need to buy

You're to the point when all the hard work pays off.

You've decided where you're going to attend college, and all that's left is to submit your deposit, your housing information, and your financial aid and loan package, and to do a little shopping.

This is not the time to get forgetful and overlook anything that could ultimately leave you on the outside looking in. Be sure you pay close attention to the details and read every last word the college has sent you. You'll absolutely hate yourself if a missed or ignored deadline means you've done a whole lot of hard work for naught.

What You'll Receive

After you decide which school you're going to attend, you'll be inundated by paper-work. Everything from housing and health-care options to meal plans and suggested freshman shopping lists will find their way to your doorstep.

There's a reason the acceptance envelopes are fat and the rejection envelopes are skinny. Each piece of paper, no matter how seemingly mundane, is important; otherwise, the college wouldn't have sent it. In fact, most of what is sent to you requires a decision and signature before it's sent back. If you don't stay on top of things, you could miss out on a good dorm slot or jeopardize your class selection.

To keep things straight, it's helpful to make a worksheet that outlines everything you have to send in along with due dates. Each time you complete a step, cross it off the worksheet.

The Deposit

Turning in your deposit late or failing to send it in altogether could result in your acceptance being retracted.

As you know, most schools require your decision and deposit by May 1. But don't for-get that some schools have revolving, fluid admissions and acceptance dates.

Not all schools require that you submit a deposit, but for those that do, don't play around with that step in the process. The deposit is your way of telling the school you're accepting its offer of admission. It's the answer to the most important question in your life to date, so don't delay in sending back the answer.

Cheat Sheet _____

Many schools now offer online services for paying your deposit. Paying online is efficient and provides you with immediate confirmation that the deposit has been received. You should utilize the online payment option when possible.

Finalizing Your Aid Package

The hard work that comes with dealing with financial aid, at least initially, was com-pleted when you found and worked out an aid package that was able to meet your needs. Hopefully that aid package was a contributing factor when deciding which school you would attend, and you'll be able to spend four years at that college without having to stress too much about money.

Now you simply have to review and sign your award letter, which outlines the amount and sources of all your aid, scholarships, grants, and loans.

However, if something has significantly changed in terms of your or your family's financial status between the time you first received your award letter upon being accepted and when you turn it in, then you have to inform the financial aid office. That includes any sort of savings or inheritance that might be turned over to you when you turn 18. Or, maybe someone in your family has won the lottery. You can't hide from changes that could affect the amount of aid you'll receive, and you need to deal with any issues before you've set foot on campus. The worst thing in the world is to be bogged down during your first couple of days on campus having to deal with financial issues.

You'll also have to fill out your loan paperwork before you begin your first semester. Most lenders require you to take part in some sort of loan counseling or interview before your money is released. Some loan counseling sessions are even offered online.

Review Chapters 12 and 18 if you still have questions about the financial aid process associated with attending a top college.

Housing Options

A bit more fun than financial aid, loans, and deposits is deciding where you'll live. Some schools mandate where you live as a freshman, but others give you the ability to choose between a dormlike environment, theme houses, an apartment or a condo, and a *residential college*.

def•i•ni•tion

Residential colleges are utilized by several top schools, including Princeton, Yale, University of California at San Diego, and Rice. These combine a residential community with academic and cultural development. At Princeton, each residential college has a faculty master, dean, director of studies, and director of student life. Academic advising for freshmen and sophomores is centered at the colleges, and juniors and seniors also are encouraged to confer with their college advisers for nondepartmental academic advising throughout their undergraduate careers.

Some schools require that you participate in the residential college system and see it as a way for students to grow together in an environment that can't be duplicated anywhere else.

"The experience of college residence is indispensable to conveying the rich flavor of academic life at Rice, allowing students to combine their usual studies with an array of social events, intramural sports, student plays, lecture series, innovative college-designed courses, and an active role in student government," states Rice University's website.

Northwestern, for instance, offers houses, halls, residential colleges, and fraternities and sororities as housing options for students, although fraternities and sororities aren't available to freshman. Northwestern, like most other top schools, guarantees on-campus housing if you request it on your admission application.

When given a host of housing options, it's important to do as much research as you can on each setup. If you can tour the campus after you've been admitted with an eye toward where you'd like to live, you should. Otherwise, try to rely on any notes you gathered if you took a tour before admission or use any number of websites that offer virtual college tours. You need to seriously consider, if available, the options of singles versus doubles versus suite living; they all have pros and cons. At Northwestern, the humanities, journalism, and theater students generally live on the south campus, closer to those departments, while science and math students tend to live on the north campus, which is closer to those departments. Your experience can be greatly impacted if you have to trudge miles through snow to get to class.

Beware

Submit your housing decision as soon as you can. Although some schools guarantee freshman housing, not all do. Housing typically is distributed on a first-come, first-serve basis.

You've hopefully also established contacts at the school you're planning on attending so you can ask them about housing and what they believe are the best options.

Meal Plans

Meal plans at some schools can be harder to decipher than the periodic table of elements. Take Georgetown, for instance. There, you can choose from six meal plans. Meal plans at each school basically vary based on the number of times you can eat in the cafeteria each week. Most schools also have some sort of "flex point" system that basically works as a debit card at restaurants and other stores around campus.

When dealing with a meal plan, you have to be realistic about how much you think you're going to eat. If you're not a breakfast person and don't each much more than a cereal bar in the morning, you don't need a plan that offers three square meals a day.

Most schools require that freshmen pick up some sort of meal plan, and schools have a default plan for freshmen if you don't make a choice. The default plan might be the most expensive plan, so be sure you choose what you want. After all, you're paying for it.

Visit the Doctor

Health care is another issue you'll have to take care of ahead of arriving at college.

Schools require that you arrive on campus with some sort of health-care provider. If you don't have health care, you can sign up for a school plan. If you do have health care that meets the school's standards, the school might let you waive its plan. However, some schools require you to sign up—and pay for—their plan regardless of whether you have your own insurance.

In addition to selecting or waiving a health-care plan, you also have to pay your doctor a visit before you enter college. Most colleges require incoming students to submit the results of a recent physical exam, along with a vaccination history.

Tying Up Loose Ends

In addition to everything already mentioned, you also have to make time during the summer before your freshman year to attend an orientation, prepare for placement tests, and make sure your final high school transcript is sent to the college in time. In reality, the process of getting into college really doesn't end until you sit down in your first class.

Here's more on those final items you'll have to take care of:

◆ **Orientation.** Find out whether you're required to attend an orientation event the summer before your freshman year. Many schools hold these events several times over the summer as a way to help students get to know each other before the real work begins. Some summer orientation programs include outdoor trips or community service projects.

◆ **Placement tests.** Many schools require that you take a placement test for certain subjects, especially if you plan on studying a foreign language. Do what you can to keep your brain sharp over the summer to ensure that you arrive on campus in good standing.

More than Forms

Not all of preparing for college is boring forms and tough questions about how many meals you're going to eat a week. There's also shopping, buying a new computer, and meeting your roommate.

Spending all that money might not be much fun, and there's always the anxiety that comes with living with a new person, but it's all necessary. College is a series of events that will help you grow as a person, and these are just the first of those events.

Shopping

Outside of what probably will be your largest purchase—a computer—there are several things you'll need to bring to college with you.

I'll get to the computer in a bit, but the rest of your shopping list will include everything from a laundry bag to a desk lamp, drying rack, and toolkit. A number of websites are available that can provide you with a basic shopping list for your freshman year of college. Some of the colleges themselves even provide a list of what they think you'll need.

Cheat Sheet

The College Board website (www.collegeboard.com/parents/apply/college-applications/21381.html) provides an extensive list of items you'll need for college. That list even includes how many pairs of underwear you'll need.

Understand that you don't have to buy everything on this list—they're only suggestions. You, of course, will need clothes, blankets, and pillows, but did you consider that you'll also need a surge protector, hangers, and a bottle opener?

The key is to be able to assess what you'll actually use. I'll never forget that my mother sent me to school with a cup, plate, knife, fork, and vegetable peeler. Why in the world would I need a vegetable peeler in college, I wondered. Did I use the vegetable peeler during my freshman year? Nope. But I still have it and it's a great memory that we laugh about.

Most schools also are either near stores or have stores on campus where you can buy anything you've forgotten or didn't think you'd need. On campus, though, you can be pretty certain you'll be buying it at a markup.

Your Computer

You're going to need a computer in college, there's no way around it. Everything from writing papers to retrieving assignments online will require the use of a computer.

This will be one of your priciest expenses heading into college. Most students opt for a laptop instead of a desktop due to the laptop's portability. It's up to the professor, but many classes allow you to bring your laptop with you to take notes and work on assignments.

Real Life

"These tools are more powerful than we've ever had in the course of human history. They deserve respect and, when used properly, they're entirely empowering."
—Michael Bugeja, Director of the Greenlee School of Journalism at Iowa State University, on the importance of laptops in the classroom

Before buying a computer, you should check with the school you're going to attend for two reasons. First, the school might offer some student deals. Second, the school might prefer Macs or PCs. That's not to say if your school prefers Macs you can't bring the PC you bought in high school, but if you're starting fresh you should consider buying what's most compatible with the school.

In addition to the computer itself, which could range from $700 to more than $2,000, you'll also have to buy all the peripheral items, including memory sticks, CDs, and DVDs. You also should consider some sort of security system to protect your computer, whether it's a software program that allows only you to access the computer or an actual physical lock for your laptop that will attach it to your desk.

Contact Your Roommate

Contacting your future roommate is one of the most exciting and nerve-racking things you'll do before you set foot onto a college campus.

Contacting your roommate before you get to campus is a good way to get to know the person you're going to be living with. Ask what his intended major is and what he does for fun. Which extracurricular activities does he hope to get involved in?

Also, you'll want to ask what your roommate is going to be bringing to campus. There's no reason for both of you to bring a television, refrigerator, and microwave.

Contacting your roommate also could be a good way to have someone you're account-able to as your senior year winds down. As you know, your final grades do matter to your new school, so you can't slack. But if you make contact with your roommate, you can check in with each other to find out how your classes are coming. It could be easy to see the finish line and limp across it as you complete high school, but talking with your future roommate can help solidify for you that the race actually begins when you set foot in college.

The Least You Need to Know

- Submitting your deposit late could result in forfeiture of your acceptance.

- Housing typically is distributed on a first-come, first-serve basis, so don't delay in turning in your request.

- A computer is a must at college.

- Contacting your roommate could be a good way to have someone hold you accountable for your senior grades.

Glossary

Academic Index   Developed in the mid-1980s as a way to establish minimum academic standards for Ivy League athletes. It's a way high schoolers can get a quick glimpse of where they are in terms of competing for an Ivy League seat, but it's typically not used by admissions officers unless you're an athlete. Also, many schools aren't keen on sharing up-to-date academic indices.

Academic Subject Requirements   Also known as a-g requirements, they are the minimum academic standards high schoolers must meet in order to gain acceptance into several California colleges and universities.

ACT   The American College Testing Program was started in 1959 to compete with the SAT. It's a standardized test accepted by all top colleges.

admission rates   The percentage of students accepted by a school.

advanced placement   Types of courses overseen by the College Board as a way to give high school students an opportunity to take college-level classes.

alumni committees   Set up regionally, these usually are responsible for organizing off-campus interviews for prospective students.

appeal   A process used when a student feels he has been wrongly denied admission to a college.

billable costs   Costs that refer to tuition, room and board, health fees, and student fees; they don't include books and travel.

class rank A student's position within a high school class based on GPA. Some schools do not rank their students. Very few California high schools rank.

Common Application Used by dozens of schools across the country to enable students to fill out one application that can be sent to different schools. Most top schools have supplemental applications that students have to fill out along with this.

composite score The average of the scores a student receives on the ACT's four sections.

courtesy wait list A wait list that students with special connections are placed on with the general understanding that they won't be accepted off the wait list.

CPS The Central Processing System is a federal program that processes FAFSA data.

CSS Profile A profile distributed by the College Board and filled out by the parents; it's used as a tool for colleges to get a better idea of a student's financial situation. It assesses family assets.

curriculum What's taught during a student's high school career.

deferred enrollment The ability to delay attendance at a school for a year in order to pursue other activities.

dual enrollment When a student is registered for classes that will give her both high school and college credits.

early action A school with this type of application policy allows prospective students to apply early to as many schools as they want. Acceptance to an early action school isn't binding.

early decision A school with this type of application policy allows a prospective student to apply to the school early but doesn't allow the student to apply to other schools until the regular admission process. Acceptance from an early decision school typically is binding.

EFC The Expected Family Contribution is a formula worked out to help determine how much financial aid a student needs.

electives Optional courses students can take in high school.

extracurriculars Activities outside of the classroom that can be school or community related, including athletics, clubs, and community service.

FAFSA   The Free Application for Federal Student Aid is a form all college students must fill out. The form enables the federal government to decide how much federal aid should be made available to each student. Many schools use this to calculate their own financial aid packages.

fast app   An application sent by a school with an offer to waive the essay requirement and application fee.

financial aid   The combination of grants, scholarships, loans, and part-time employment from federal, state, institutional, and private sources that help a student pay for college.

gap year   A year that a student takes off between high school and college. Students often use their gap years for traveling or working.

GPA   Grade point average.

guidance counselor   A high school employee tasked with advising students and helping them through the college application process.

home school   A system that allows students to learn out of their homes. The curriculum for home-schooled students can be either developed by the teacher/parent or provided by a home-school agency.

honors classes   Upper-level courses offered by high schools.

International Baccalaureate (IB)   A worldwide program designed to challenge students with an international education and rigorous assessment, with a particular focus on exposing students to different cultures. IB programs are considered to be on the same level as advanced placement.

Ivy League   A group of schools comprised of Brown, Columbia, Cornell, Dartmouth, Harvard, Princeton, UPenn, and Yale. Also, know as the *Ancient Eight* and *the Ivies*. The group of schools got its *Ivy* name because of its age and the ivy that grows on the schools' walls.

legacy   Someone who has at least one parent who attended the school to which she is applying. Some schools extend legacies out to grandparents.

meal plans   Options given to students that allow them to decide how many meals they want to pay for a week.

no-loan grant   Financial aid that's awarded by a college that doesn't have to be paid back. The amount of aid awarded under these programs typically is determined by a student's financial need.

nonbillable costs The cost of books along with personal and travel expenses; these don't include tuition, room, and board.

Pell Grant A federal, low-income loan program based on several factors, including income, the number of people in the household, and the state where the student lives.

preparatory school A private school that prepares students to move on to college.

prerequisites The courses students need to take before they're eligible to register for certain upper-level courses.

PSAT The Preliminary Scholastic Aptitude Test is taken in October of a student's junior year in high school as a way to help prepare for the SAT 1 and to qualify the student for the National Merit Scholarship Corporation's scholarship programs.

recommendation Required by all colleges and written by teachers and guidance counselors to provide schools with an idea of what a student is like.

residential colleges On-campus communities set up by colleges that incorporate residential life, community service, and academics.

restrictive early action Under restrictive early action, the university typically provides an admissions decision by December 15 but the admitted student has until May 1 to decide whether they will accept the admission.

SAT 1 The Scholastic Assessment Test 1, also called the reasoning test, is widely regarded as the most popular admissions exam used by colleges and universities.

SAT 2 The SAT 2 is an SAT subject test administered by the College Board.

scholarships Financial aid that's awarded by a college that doesn't have to be paid back. The amount of aid awarded under these programs typically is determined by a student's financial need.

self-assessment A form filled out by a student and given to people writing referrals; it's intended to give the referral writer background information about a student.

single-choice early action Under single-choice early action, the university provides an admissions decision by December 15 but the admitted student has until May 1 to decide whether they will accept the admission.

transfer When a student leaves one school to attend another.

Universal College Application An application that students can use to apply to several schools. This is used by fewer schools than the Common Application.

virtual tours   Provided by several websites to give students an idea of what the campus is like without having to set foot on it.

wait list   Wait-listed students are ones who aren't accepted but could be offered acceptance after the college determines its yield.

weighted GPA   A grade point system that takes into account the difficulty of courses; tougher courses carry more weight than easier courses.

work-study program   Places students in full- or part-time jobs, with the money earned either going directly to tuition or to the student to be used on college-related expenses.

yield   The percentage of students who accept a school's admission offer. If 100 students are offered admission and 78 accept, the school's yield is 78 percent.

B

Further Resources

The Internet is a great resource for finding all kinds of material about colleges and the college application process. Just make sure that you don't take what you find online as the gospel.

Often, information can be inaccurate or out-of-date—so make sure you call each school to confirm what you've found. Here's a list of helpful websites you can use.

Websites

ACT: www.act.org

American School Counselor Association: www.schoolcounselor.org

Better Business Bureau: www.bbb.com

Brown University: www.brown.edu

California Institute of Technology: www.caltech.edu

California State Schools: www.CSUmentor.edu

College Board Articles: www.collegeboard.com/article/0,,2-7-0-33,00.html?orig=sec

College Board Online: www.collegeboard.org

College Confidential: www.collegeconfidential.com/

College Confidential College Rankings: www.collegeconfidential.com/college_rankings

College Data: www.collegedata.com/

College Is Possible: www.collegeispossible.org

CollegeApps.com: www.collegeapps.com

CollegeBound News: www.collegeboundnews.com

Collegiate Choice Walking Tours Videos: www.collegiatechoice.com

Columbia University: www.columbia.edu

Cornell University: www.cornell.edu

Dartmouth College: www.dartmouth.edu

Duke University: www.duke.edu

eCampusTours.com: eCampusTours.com

Educational Testing Service: www.ets.org

Emory University: www.emory.edu

EssayInfo.com: www.essayinfo.com

Free Application for Federal Student Aid (FAFSA): www.fafsa.ed.gov

FairTest: The National Center for Fair and Open Testing: www.fairtest.org

FinAid: www.finaid.org

Financial Aid Resource Publications from the U.S. Department of Education: studentaid.ed.gov/students/publications/student_guide/index.html

Harvard University: www.harvard.edu

Independent Educational Consultants Association: www.educationalconsulting.org

Johns Hopkins University: www.jhu.edu

Kaplan: www.kaplan.com

Massachusetts Institute of Technology: web.mit.edu

National Association for College Admission Counseling: www.nacacnet.org/MemberPortal/

Northwestern University: www.northwestern.edu

Number2.com Free SAT/ACT Prep: www.number2.com

Peterson's: www.petersons.com

Peterson's financial aid website: www.petersons.com/finaid

Peterson's StudentEdge: www.studentedge.com

Princeton Review: www.princetonreview.com

Princeton University: www.princeton.edu

Rice University: www.rice.edu

Scholarships.com: www.scholarships.com

Stanford University: www.stanford.edu

Student Scholarship Search: www.studentscholarshipsearch.com

U.S. Department of Education's Online Educational Resources: www.ed.gov/about/organizations.jsp

U.S. News & World Report Rankings: www.usnews.com/usnews/edu/eduhome.htm

Unigo: www.unigo.com

University of California schools: www.universityofcalifornia.edu

University of Chicago: www.uchicago.edu

University of Notre Dame: www.nd.edu

University of Pennsylvania: www.upenn.edu

Washington University in St. Louis: www.wustl.edu

Yale University: www.yale.edu

Admission Rates

Overall Admission

Overall admission is the total number of students accepted through both early application programs and general admission. The following tables show the overall admission figures for some of the nation's top schools.

Class of 2012

School	Number Admitted	Number Applied	Percent Admitted
Brown	2,742	20,630	13.29
Columbia	2,269	22,569	10.05
Cornell	6,735	33,011	20.4
Dartmouth	2,190	16,536	13.24
Harvard	1,948	27,462	7.09
UPenn	3,769	22,922	16.44
Princeton	1,976	21,369	9.25
Yale	1,892	22,813	8.29
Total Ivies	23,521	187,312	12.56
Chicago	3,461	12,418	27.87
Duke	3,814	20,337	18.75
Emory	4,500	17,448	25.79
Johns Hopkins	3,578	16,606	21.55
MIT	1,554	13,396	11.6
Northwestern	6,327	25,027	25.28
Notre Dame	3,548	14,506	24.46
Stanford	2,400	25,298	9.49
Vanderbilt	4,000	16,875	23.7
Williams	1,229	7,538	16.3

Class of 2011

School	Number Admitted	Number Applied	Percent Admitted
Brown	2,693	19,097	14.05
Columbia	2,255	21,343	10.57
Cornell	6,503	30,383	21.4
Dartmouth	2,166	14,176	15.28
Harvard	2,058	22,955	8.97

School	Number Admitted	Number Applied	Percent Admitted
UPenn	3,637	22,646	16.06
Princeton	1,791	18,942	9.46
Yale	1,860	19,323	9.63
Total Ivies	22,953	168,865	13.59
Chicago	3,628	10,408	34.86
Duke	4,053	19,207	21.1
Emory	4,200	15,374	27.32
Johns Hopkins	3,588	14,848	24.16
MIT	1,553	12,445	12.48
Northwestern	4,852	20,649	23.5
Notre Dame	3,548	14,506	24.46
Stanford	2,464	23,958	10.28
Vanderbilt	4,238	12,911	32.82
Williams	1,190	6,448	18.46

Class of 2010

School	Number Admitted	Number Applied	Percent Admitted
Brown	2,531	18,316	13.82
Columbia	2,296	19,851	11.57
Cornell	6,935	28,098	24.68
Dartmouth	2,186	13,938	15.68
Harvard	2,124	22,754	9.33
UPenn	3,617	20,483	17.66
Princeton	1,790	17,564	10.19
Yale	1,878	21,101	8.9
Total Ivies	23,357	162,105	14.41
Chicago	3,673	9,542	38.49
Duke	4,101	19,386	21.15

continues

Class of 2010   (continued)

School	Number Admitted	Number Applied	Percent Admitted
Emory	4,535	14,232	31.86
Johns Hopkins	3,726	13,900	26.81
MIT	1,513	11,369	13.31
Northwestern	5,434	18,385	29.56
Notre Dame	3,492	12,796	27.79
Stanford	2,444	22,333	10.94
Vanderbilt	4,128	12,189	33.87
Williams	1,146	5,999	19.1

Class of 2009

School	Number Admitted	Number Applied	Percent Admitted
Brown	2,257	16,911	15.12
Columbia	2,312	18,125	12.76
Cornell	6,621	24,452	27.08
Dartmouth	2,171	12,756	17.02
Harvard	2,102	22,796	9.22
UPenn	3,916	18,824	20.8
Princeton	1,807	16,510	10.94
Yale	1,880	19,451	9.67
Total Ivies	23,366	149,825	15.6
Chicago	3,628	9,039	40.14
Duke	3,996	18,089	22.09
Emory	4,395	12,011	36.59
Johns Hopkins	3,910	11,278	34.67
MIT	1,494	10,440	14.31

School	Number Admitted	Number Applied	Percent Admitted
Northwestern	4,819	16,221	29.71
Notre Dame	3,582	11,317	31.65
Stanford	2,426	20,195	12.01
Vanderbilt	4,115	11,663	35.28
Williams	1,095	5,822	18.81

Early Admission

The following figures show admission figures through early application programs. Not every school has the same early application policies in terms of a student being contractually obligated to attend if he's accepted under an early application process.

Class of 2012

School	Number Admitted	Number Applied	Percent Admitted
Brown	555	2,461	22.55
Columbia	597	2,582	23.12
Cornell	1,142	3,095	36.9
Dartmouth	400	1,429	27.99
Harvard*	0	0	0
UPenn	1,147	3,929	29.19
Princeton	0	0	0
Yale*	885	4,888	18.11
Total Ivies	4,726	18,384	25.71
Chicago	1,191	2,432	49.21
Duke	472	1,247	37.85
Emory	481	1,577	30.50
Johns Hopkins	457	1,055	43.31
MIT	522	3,928	13.29

continues

Class of 2012   (continued)

School	Number Admitted	Number Applied	Percent Admitted
Northwestern	561	1,516	37
Notre Dame	1,150	4,288	26.81
Stanford	738	4,551	16.22
Vanderbilt	531	1,468	36.17
Wiiliams	233	600	38.83

Harvard and Princeton no longer offered early admission for the Class of 2012.

Class of 2011

School	Number Admitted	Number Applied	Percent Admitted
Brown	525	2,316	22.67
Columbia	594	2,429	24.45
Cornell	1,101	3,015	36.52
Dartmouth	380	1,285	29.57
Harvard	859	4,008	21.43
UPenn	1,178	4,001	29.44
Princeton	597	2,276	26.23
Yale	709	3,541	20.02
Total Ivies	5,943	22,871	25.98
MIT	390	3,494	11.17
Stanford	750	4,644	16.15

Class of 2010

School	Number Admitted	Number Applied	Percent Admitted
Brown	543	2,379	22.82
Columbia	583	2,236	26.07
Cornell	1,110	2,849	38.96
Dartmouth	398	1,321	30.13
Harvard	813	3,869	21.01
UPenn	1,181	4,120	28.67
Princeton	599	2,236	26.79
Yale	724	4,984	17.73
Total Ivies	5,591	23,094	25.77
MIT	377	3,091	12.2
Stanford	853	4,503	18.94

Class of 2009

School	Number Admitted	Number Applied	Percent Admitted
Brown	571	2,046	27.91
Columbia	578	2,157	26.8
Cornell	1,072	2,572	41.68
Dartmouth	397	1,171	33.9
Harvard	885	4,213	21.01
UPenn	1,169	3,420	34.18
Princeton	593	2,039	29.08
Yale	704	3,933	17.9
Total Ivies	5,969	21,551	27.7
MIT	390	2,796	13.95
Stanford	867	4,644	18.67

Sample Resumé

Resumés are an important part of the college application process and give admissions officers an opportunity to see who you are outside of the classroom. Included in this appendix is a comprehensive resumé from a top high school student.

Leadership Positions

New York State Board of Regents

Education Summit (2008)
Selected as one of four student delegates from Shaker High School to participate in discussions relating to language, income, disability, race, and ethnicity issues with leaders from education, business, and community organizations.

Shaker High School

Student Government Pep Rally Co-Chairperson (2008)
Worked closely with student government supervisor and co-chair to organize pep rally attended by the entire student body.

8th Grade Parent Night (2006, 2007, 2008)
Selected to speak to incoming freshmen and their parents about my experiences—academics, clubs, sports, time management—at Shaker High School.

Congregation Beth Emeth Youth Group (CBEYG)

Vice President of Fundraising and Treasury (2008–2009)
Elected by peers to the CBEYG executive board. Manage and oversee all programs and projects involving CBEYG funds. Responsible for planning and implementing one social program a month for entire group. Write articles for monthly newsletter. Propose, encourage, and carry out monthly fundraisers. Raise several thousand dollars annually.

Executive Board Treasurer (2007–2008)
Elected by peers to manage all youth group funds and serve on executive board. Coordinated all aspects of fundraisers and delivered monthly financial reports. Managed checking account.

Youth Group Retreat Co-Chairperson (2006)
Selected to plan and lead all programs at URJ Camp Eisner weekend retreat for over 50 youth group members.

North Colonie School District

North Colonie School District Leadership Training (2005)
Selected as one of 12 students to participate in two-day leadership development workshops. Learned new concepts and enhanced leadership skills.

Recognitions and Academic Achievements

National Honor Society (2007–2009)
Selected in junior year to be a member of the Shaker High School National Honor Society based on academic achievements, extracurricular activities, and leadership.

Tri-M Music Honor Society (2008–2009)
Selected in junior year to join the Shaker High School Tri-M Music Honor Society based on academic achievement and participation in music and the arts.

Shaker High School Chorus (2008)
Student of the Month—Selected by chorus teacher as February student of the month based on achievement in the classroom.

Congregation Beth Emeth Confirmation Class (2007)
Rabbi Roth Best Essay Award—Selected by a panel of rabbis and teachers as confirmation class award recipient based on a written essay.

Colonie Youth Court (2006)
NYS Youth Court Conference Scholarship Winner—Selected to attend annual Youth Court conference in Upstate New York. Participated in workshops and lectures learning court procedures and policies regarding the judicial system.

Honor Roll and Merit Roll (2005–2009)
Recognized for academic achievement, citizenship, and good conduct in all marking periods at Shaker High School.

Community Service

Regional Food Bank (2005–2009)
Work in warehouse sorting and transporting food and nonperishable goods. Supervise developmentally disabled individuals sorting food and other goods. Help in office with clerical work.

Habitat for Humanity (Summers 2006 and 2008)
Cleaned backyard of an inner-city home. Removed glass and pieces of metal and helped build a fence in the yard. Also helped build a home in North Albany that was sponsored by Congregation Beth Emeth.

Shaker Crew (2006–2008)
Annual Row-a-Thon—Rowed 6 to 10 miles on ergometer in Crossgates Mall to raise money for Shaker Crew Team and various other local charities.

St. Peter's Hospital (2006–2007)
100 hours of volunteer work—Worked throughout the hospital performing different tasks. Worked in the flower delivery room, receiving flowers from florists and delivering them to patients in all departments of the hospital. Helped with clerical tasks in the human resources and volunteer offices. Also managed information desk to assist patients and visitors.

Sidney Albert Albany Jewish Community Center (Summer 2006)
Camp Olam—Volunteered as a camp counselor for young children at waterfront day camp. Helped coordinate daily schedule and activities. Worked as a team with older counselors.

Additional Educational Experiences

Shaker High School Career Exploration Internship Program (2008–2009)
Selected to intern fall semester at Ed Lewi Associates, a public relations firm. Learn all aspects of marketing, promoting, and coordinating special events.

Cornell University Government Intern Program (2007–2008)
Selected as a junior to study Albany County government. Awarded academic credit/independent study for this school-year–long internship. Met twice a month and attended day-long workshops at various locations throughout the county.

Exploration Program at Yale University (Summer 2007)
Participated and lived at Yale University for three weeks and took courses in theater and mock trial. Attended seminars on important national issues including sweatshops and business tactics.

Cornell University Career Exploration 4-H Program (Summer 2006)
Lived on the Cornell University campus and participated in entrepreneurship basics workshops.

Extracurricular Activities and Clubs

Shaker Theater (2005–2009)
Held principal roles in every fall play and spring musical throughout high school. Selected as a junior, with seven seniors, for an eight-member cast. During rehearsal and production periods, rehearsed almost every day after school for 2 to 5 hours a day.

Congregation Beth Emeth Youth Group (CBEYG) (2005–2009)
As a member, meet every Wednesday, participating in social action and educational programs. As a board member and chairperson, work several hours per week preparing weekly programs and events. Participate in regional executive board trainings and retreats. Meet with other board members, adult advisors, and rabbi regularly.

North American Federation of Temple Youth (NFTY) (2005–2009)
CBEYG is a member of NFTY Northeast. As a member of this organization, participate in institutes, conclavettes, and social events to discuss topics of interest to youth. Active participant in week-long NFTY National Convention in Los Angeles in February 2008, attending seminars and discussions with over 2,000 Jewish youth from America and Canada.

Colonie Youth Court (2005–2009)
Initially participated in a 30-hour training program to become familiar and learn all aspects of criminal law. Since the training, serve on cases one to two times a month in the role of judge, clerk, jury foreperson, defender, or prosecutor.

Shaker High School Student Government (2007–2009)
Meet weekly to discuss important affairs at Shaker High School. Served on multiple subcommittees, including Homecoming Dance, Pep Rally, and Equinox Thanksgiving preparation.

Shaker High School Yearbook Committee (2008–2009)
Work closely with yearbook supervisor and editors to put together Shaker High School Yearbook. Attend weekly meetings and work after school to organize yearbook pages.

Athletic Experience

Shaker Crew Team (2004–2008)
Rowed as member of the Shaker High School crew team for four years, two years on novice and JV team and two years on varsity team. Won several medals at local, regional, state, and national levels. In addition to rowing on water during the fall and spring, participated in winter training program between seasons.

Shaker Ski Club (2005–2006)
Skied weekly with school club, enhancing my skiing ability.

Work Experience

Cold Stone Creamery (2007–2008)
Work 25 hours/week during the summer of 2007 and approximately 12 hours/week during the school year. Make ice cream creations and serve customers. Also sing songs and entertain customers while mixing ice cream.

Park Playhouse (Summer 2008)
Worked approximately 40 hours/week at six-week theater-in-the-park program. Prepared and served food to customers at the concession stand. Managed food operations and collected and counted monies.

Presidential Estates (Summer 2008 and Summer 2009)
Worked approximately 30 hours/week lifeguarding at townhouse complex. Watched patrons at the pool. Also responsible for daily cleaning and maintaining chlorine and pH levels of pool.

Abercrombie & Fitch (Winter 2008–Spring 2009)
Worked approximately 10–15 hours/week as sales representative and cashier in store.

Outback Steakhouse (Spring 2009–Summer 2009)
Worked approximately 20–25 hours/week bussing tables at restaurant.

Certifications

American Red Cross CPR recertification (Summer 2009)

American Red Cross CPR certification (Spring 2008)

American Red Cross lifeguarding certification (Spring 2008)

NYS Driver's Education Course (Summer 2008)

Sample Essays

Included in this appendix are two essays that were accepted by Harvard and Stanford. The essays were written about two very different topics. The essay accepted by Harvard asks the writer to pick a character from film or literature that he would want to emulate. The Stanford essay, on the other hand, asks the writer to take an inventory of himself and write about how he has grown up over the years.

Accepted by Harvard

Of all the characters that I've "met" through books and movies, two stand out as people that I most want to emulate. They are Atticus Finch from *To Kill a Mockingbird* and Dr. Archibald "Moonlight" Graham from *Field of Dreams*. They appeal to me because they embody what I strive to be. They are influential people in small towns who have a direct positive effect on those around them. I, too, plan to live in a small town after graduating from college, and that positive effect is something I must give in order to be satisfied with my life.

Both Mr. Finch and Dr. Graham are strong supporting characters in wonderful stories. They symbolize good, honesty, and wisdom. When the story of my town is written, I want to symbolize those things. The base has been formed for me to live a productive, helpful life. As an Eagle Scout, I represent those things that Mr. Finch and Dr. Graham represent. In the child/adolescent world, I am Mr. Finch and Dr. Graham, but soon I'll be entering the adult world, a world in which I'm not yet prepared to lead.

I'm quite sure that as teenagers Atticus Finch and Moonlight Graham often wondered what they could do to help others. They probably emulated someone who they had seen live a successful life. They saw someone like my grandfather, 40-year president of our hometown bank, enjoy a lifetime of leading, sharing, and giving. I have seen him spend his Christmas Eves taking gifts of food and joy to indigent families. Often when his bank could not justify a loan to someone in need, my grandfather made the loan from his own pocket. He is a real-life Moonlight Graham, a man who has shown me that characters like Dr. Graham and Mr. Finch do much much more than elicit tears and smiles from readers and movie watchers. Through him and others in my family, I feel I have acquired the values and the burning desire to benefit others that will form the foundation for a great life. I also feel that that foundation is not enough. I do not yet have the sophistication, knowledge, and wisdom necessary to succeed as I want to in the adult world. I feel that Harvard, above all others, can guide me toward the life of greatness that will make me the Atticus Finch of my town.

ADMISSIONS COMMITTEE COMMENTS:

This essay is a great example of how to answer this question well. This applicant chose characters who demonstrated specific traits that reflect on his own personality. We believe that he is sincere about his choices because his reasons are personal (being from a small town and so forth). He managed to tell us a good deal about himself, his values, and his goals while maintaining a strong focus throughout.

Accepted by Stanford

When I look at this picture of myself, I realize how much I've grown and changed, not only physically, but also mentally as a person in the last couple of years. Less than one month after this photograph was taken, I arrived at the Gressville Academy in Pennsylvania without any idea of what to expect. I entered my second year of high school as an innocent thirteen-year-old who was about a thousand miles from home and was a new member of not the sophomore, but "lower-middle" class. Around me in this picture are the things which were most important in my life at the time: studying different types of cars and planes, following Kobe Bryant's latest move, and seeing the latest blockbuster movie like "The Matrix." On my t-shirt is the rest of my life—tennis. Midway through my senior year at Gressville, the focuses in my life have changed dramatically.

If there is one common occurrence which takes place for every single person in the diverse student body at Gressville, it is that we all grow up much faster for having lived there. I do not know whether this speeding up of the maturing process is generally good or bad, but I definitely have benefited.

The classroom has become a whole different realm for me. Before, the teachers and students alike preached the importance of learning, but it was implicitly obvious that the most important concern was grades. At Gressville, teachers genuinely believe that learning is the most important objective and deeply encourage us to collaborate with each other and make use of all resources that we may find. In fact, in a certain class this year, my teacher assigned us to prepare every day of the week to discuss a certain book; there were only two requirements in this preparation—we had to maximize our sources, gleaning from everything and everyone in the school, but we were not allowed to actually look at the book. As a result, I know more about that book than any other that I have actually read. It is teaching methods such as this which ensure that we will learn more. Indeed, this matter of "thinking" has been one of the most important aspects of my experience. Whether in physics or English, I'm required to approach every problem and idea independently and creatively rather than just regurgitate the teacher's words. In discussion with fellow students both inside and outside of class, the complex thoughts flowing through everyone's brains is evident.

However, I believe that the most important concepts that I have espoused in being independent of my parents for half of each year deal with being a cosmopolitan person. The school's faculty and students are conscious about keeping all of the kids' attention from being based on the school. Every single issue of global concern is brought forth by one group or another whether it be a faculty member, publication, ethnic society, or individual student. Along with being aware of issues of importance, after attending Gressville my personality has evolved. First, my mannerisms have grown: the school stresses giving respect to everyone and everything. Our former headmaster often said, "Character can be measured not by one's interaction with people who are better off than him or herself, but by one's interactions with those who are worse off." The other prime goal of the school's community is to convert every single timid lower-classman into a loud, rambunctious senior. Basically, if you have an opinion about something, it is wrong not to voice that opinion. Of course, being obnoxious is not the idea. The key is to become a master of communication with teachers, fellow students, all of whom are a part of the community, and most importantly, those who are outside of the community.

I do not want to make Gressville sound as if it produces the perfect students, because it doesn't. But the school deserves a lot of credit for its efforts. Often, some part of the mold does remain. As the college experience approaches, I am still the same person, only modified to better maximize my talents. Although I still have some time to play tennis and see movies, perhaps one of the few similarities between this photograph and me now is my smile.

ADMISSIONS COMMITTEE COMMENTS:

This essay is fairly well written. The essayist makes boarding school his focus, using it to explain and describe how and why he has changed over the years. A lot of students write about what wonderful people they have become, but they fail to do a good job of understanding and explaining the forces that prevailed to make them change. This writer focuses on the strengths of the school itself. He demonstrates the sort of values it tries to instill in its students such as, "Encouraging us to collaborate with each other and make use of all resources that we may find," and "Giving respect to everyone and everything." Because the writer does so, the reader never doubts that the applicant possesses all the qualities that he credits to the school. Using this method has two advantages. First, the positive, upbeat attitude he has toward his institution is rare. Second, Stanford, for one, recognized that this would reflect well on his ability to adapt to and be a positive force at their school.

Appendix **F**

Summer Programs

What you get done during your high school summers is a critical aspect of molding yourself into a student whom top colleges will take a strong look at.

Here are a number of reputable summer programs that would look great on your resumé. This list includes many of the nation's top programs, but it's only a sample of what's out there.

Boston University Summer Term

www.bu.edu/summer/program_high_school_students/

Boston University offers two programs:

The six-week undergraduate summer academic program is for students who will be seniors in high school. "Students can either enroll in two Boston University summer classes and earn up to eight college credits or pursue scientific research under the guidance of a faculty mentor," according to the program's website.

There's also a two-week summer program for students who will be entering their sophomore, junior, or senior years.

Brown's Environmental Leadership in Hawaii

www.brown.edu/scs/pre-college/overview.php

A week-long science and culture program for high-school students on Hawaii's Big Island.

Brown Focus Courses

www.brown.edu/scs/pre-college/overview.php

This is Brown's most popular offering, according to the university's website. "Students in grades 9–12 explore subjects in a noncredit environment," the site states.

Brown's Intensive English Language

www.brown.edu/scs/pre-college/overview.php

This program is designed for high-achieving, university-bound students who do not speak English as their native language.

Brown Leadership Institute

www.brown.edu/scs/pre-college/overview.php

This program lets students learn leadership skills as they apply to environmental, trade, health, security, human rights, conflict, and diversity issues.

Brown Scholar-Athlete Program

www.brown.edu/scs/pre-college/overview.php

Students who are interested in sports and want to attend a top university should consider the Brown Summer Scholar-Athlete Program.

Brown Science for Middle School Students

www.brown.edu/scs/pre-college/overview.php

This program is for seventh and eighth grade students who show an interest in science. The courses "are designed to expose the intellectual concepts of familiar topics that are part of the student's world," according to the university's website.

Brown's Seven-Week Credit Courses

www.brown.edu/scs/pre-college/overview.php

Rising or graduated high school seniors earn college credit in a seven-week course, studying side-by-side with Brown undergraduates.

Brown Theatre Bridge

www.brown.edu/scs/pre-college/overview.php

This highly selective six-week program provides students who want to pursue acting an opportunity to use their imaginations and skills.

Carnegie Mellon

www.cmu.edu/enrollment/pre-college/

Carnegie Mellon's pre-college program offers classes in several courses of study: architecture, art, design, drama, music, or the National High School Game Academy. Students also can take two challenging college courses to gain advanced placement in college.

Center for Talented Youth

cty.jhu.edu/summer/

"Johns Hopkins' summer programs offer eligible students from all over the country and around the world the opportunity to engage in challenging academic work in the company of peers who share their exceptional abilities and love of learning," according to the program's website. The programs focus on both academics and the social experience.

Columbia University

www.ce.columbia.edu/hs/

Columbia University offers summer programs for high schoolers. The programs are offered in New York City and Barcelona for students in grades 9–12. The program allows students to experience college life, meet other highly motivated high school students from all over the world, and earn an official Columbia University Statement of Attendance.

Cornell Summer College

www.sce.cornell.edu/sc/

Cornell University Summer College offers a variety of programs. Sophomores, juniors, and seniors in high school can attend Cornell for one, three, four, or six weeks and earn an average of three to six credits.

COSMOS

www.ucop.edu/cosmos

The California State Summer School for Mathematics and Science (COSMOS) "aims to create a community of students who participate in and contribute to an intensive academic experience delivered by distinguished educators and scholars," according to the program's website.

The program gives students an opportunity to learn advanced mathematics and science and to prepare for careers in these areas.

Emory University

www.college.emory.edu/program/precollege/

The Emory Pre-College Program exposes college-bound high school students to academic and residential life at the university. Students have the opportunity to attend a small summer program tailored to their academic interests while living the college life and exploring Atlanta.

Exploration Summer Programs

www.explo.org

Exploration Summer Programs feature ungraded courses, activities, athletics, and trips.

A broad array of academic options are offered in subjects such as forensic science, West African dance, and broadcast journalism.

Experiment in International Living

www.worldlearning.org/225.htm

Through this program each "experimenter" lives with a local family and explores themes from the arts to ecology. This experience serves as an opportunity to learn about another way of life. The international summer high school programs include opportunities in Europe, the Americas, Africa, Oceania, and Asia. "Through home-stays, adventure travel, experiential learning, and language immersion, students build leadership and communication skills, gain essential international experience, increase their self-confidence, and enhance their global awareness," according to the program's website.

Harvard Secondary Summer School

www.summer.harvard.edu/2009/programs/ssp/

More than 1,000 high schoolers are accepted into Harvard's summer program every year and have the opportunity to earn college credit in college-level courses. Students work with university faculty, use the labs, and study in the largest university library system in the world.

High School Summer Scholars

ucollege.wustl.edu/programs/highschool/overview

The High School Summer Scholars Program at Washington University in St. Louis lasts five weeks. High School Summer Scholars are part of a small group of high school sophomores and juniors exploring college life. Students earn up to seven units of college credit that will transfer to most accredited colleges and universities.

Interlochen Summer Arts Camp

www.interlochen.org/

Each summer more than 2,500 students go to Interlochen to live, learn, and perform with peers and educators.

Founded in 1928, Interlochen offers visual and performing arts programs for student artists in grades 3–12.

Math Camp

www.mathcamp.org/

Canada/USA Mathcamp is a five-week summer program for high school students interested in mathematics.

According to its website, the program's goals are:

> "To inspire and motivate these students by introducing them to the beauty and variety of advanced mathematics

> To impart valuable knowledge and skills for the pursuit of mathematics in high school, university, and beyond

> To provide a supportive and fun environment for interaction among students who love mathematics."

MIT Minority Introduction to Engineering and Science Program

www.mitadmissions.org/topics/before/summer_programs/

A six-week residential academic enrichment program for about 80 high school juniors who intend to pursue careers in science, engineering, and entrepreneurship. The program is focused on minority groups and those from other underrepresented segments of the population.

MIT Research Science Institute

www.mitadmissions.org/topics/before/summer_programs/

The institute brings together about 70 high school students each summer for six weeks at MIT. This program stresses advanced theory and research in mathematics, the sciences, and engineering. Participants attend college-level classes and complete hands-on research. High school juniors are eligible for the program.

MIT Women's Technology Program

www.mitadmissions.org/topics/before/summer_programs/

A four-week summer academic and residential experience where 60 female high school students explore engineering through hands-on classes that are taught by female MIT graduate students. This program is available to students during the summer after their junior year.

Nicaragua Summer Exchange

www.nicaraguastudyabroad.org/

This high school exchange program is hosted in Central America's oldest colonial high school.

Northwestern's National High School Institute

www.northwestern.edu/nhsi/

The National High School Institute, established in 1931, is the nation's oldest and largest university-based summer program for outstanding high school students.

Approximately 850 of the nation's best students enroll each summer in the Institute's six divisions: Coon-Hardy Debate, Speech, Journalism, Music, Film & Video Production, and Theatre Arts.

Notre Dame Summer Scholars

summerscholars.nd.edu/about-summer-scholars

ND Summer Scholars gives academically outstanding high school students the chance to explore 1 of 13 academic fields of study. "In the classroom, some of Notre Dame's finest faculty members engage their students in academic study and fieldwork. Simultaneously, students experience the social and spiritual connections that are integral components of residential life at Notre Dame," according to the program's website.

Penn Pre-College Program

www.sas.upenn.edu/lps/highschool/summer

In the six-week Penn Pre-College Program, students choose one of two challenging curricula: One college-credit course and one rigorous noncredit course, or two college-credit courses.

In both curricula, academic tutoring and advising are provided. The noncredit academic enhancement courses include public speaking, critical reading and academic writing, academic writing for international students, online research techniques, and SAT/ACT preparation.

Penn Summer Biomedical Research Academy

www.sas.upenn.edu/lps/highschool/summer

Students are exposed to some of the most cutting-edge areas of biomedical research, including cardiovascular disease, oncology, immunology, and neuroscience, during this four-week program.

Penn Summer Forensic Science Academy

www.sas.upenn.edu/lps/highschool/summer

UPenn's forensic program covers everything from fingerprints and DNA matching to ballistics and blood-spatter analysis. Students in this four-week, noncredit program also hone their skills in critical thinking and data analysis as they learn about crime-solving.

Penn Summer Physics Academy

www.sas.upenn.edu/lps/highschool/summer

The physics academy is taught by members of Penn's Department of Physics and Astronomy and other regional physics teachers. It includes in-depth lectures and discussions on mechanics, electromagnetism, quantum dynamics, and astrophysics.

Penn Summer Theatre Workshop

www.sas.upenn.edu/lps/highschool/summer

The workshop is led by the director of Penn's undergraduate Theatre Arts Program and offers intensive study of theater performance. The curriculum is taught by Penn faculty, alumni holding advanced degrees or certificates, and theater professionals, according to the program's website.

Princeton

www.princeton.edu/main/news/archive/S11/99/00E41/

Princeton students, faculty, and staff lead an array of on-campus programs for students and teachers in an attempt to expose them to cutting-edge research and build other skills. In addition to exposing students and teachers to the country's premier academic opportunities, the program also gives students knowledge about preparing for college.

PROMYS

www.promys.org

PROMYS is a six-week summer program at Boston University designed to encourage high school students to explore mathematics in a community of peers, counselors, research mathematicians, and visiting scientists.

Research Science Institute

www.cee.org/rsi

The institute is sponsored by the Center for Excellence in Education in collaboration with the Massachusetts Institute of Technology. CalTech also runs the RSI program.

Approximately 75 high school students gather for six weeks. The students participate in a program that emphasizes advanced theory and research in mathematics, the sciences, and engineering. Students attend college-level classes taught by nationally recognized teachers.

Rice University

gscs.rice.edu/scs/Rice_for_High_School_Students.asp

High school students can choose from more than 20 courses offered in a variety of subjects including math, science, and English. Each summer course offers three to four credit hours, which entails four to six hours of classroom time per week and approximately one to three hours of homework per class meeting.

Summer at Georgetown University

www12.georgetown.edu/scs/sphs/index.cfm

Summer at Georgetown University in Washington, D.C., is a challenging learning environment. During the summer, students receive an exclusive introduction to the academic community of Georgetown University.

Summer at Stanford

summer.stanford.edu

High school juniors and seniors are eligible to apply to Stanford's High School Summer College program; applications from top sophomores are also considered. Summer College students take eight-week undergraduate courses and earn Stanford University credit. Participants explore the sciences, humanities, arts, business, and languages. Credit earned may be eligible for transfer to another college or university.

Talent Identification Program

www.tip.duke.edu/summer_programs/

Duke TIP Summer Studies Programs offer students in grades 7–10 the opportunity to learn highly challenging material. Students enroll in a single Duke TIP-designed course for three weeks and attend nearly 40 hours of class each week. Programs are offered on a variety of college campuses. Classes have approximately 16–18 students and are taught by Instructor-Teaching Assistant teams.

University of California Berkeley

summer.berkeley.edu/mainsite/type_highschool.html

During the summer, up to 300 high school students spend their summers in the San Francisco Bay Area while earning college credit and a UC Berkeley transcript of completed coursework. Students can receive a personal commendation letter from the Director of UC Berkeley Summer Sessions upon passing their courses.

University of California Los Angeles

www.summer.ucla.edu/FAQ/faq.htm

Summertime at UCLA is when highly motivated high school students can take advantage of all that UCLA has to offer. A wide range of courses are offered, though a high school student can't take more than two courses during a single summer session.

University of Virginia Summer Session

www.alumni.virginia.edu/about/summerprograms.aspx

Each summer the University of Virginia offers courses to more than 4,000 students through its Summer Session. Many of these courses are not available during the academic year.

University of Virginia Summer Language Institute

www.alumni.virginia.edu/about/summerprograms.aspx

Enrollment at the Summer Language Institute is open to advanced high school students. "The Summer Language Institute provides the opportunity to fulfill language requirements, prepare for study abroad or travel, expand job opportunities, and expand intercultural skills," according to the program's website.

Languages include French, German, Italian, Latin, Russian, Spanish, Tibetan, and English (ESL).

University of Virginia Summer Enrichment Program

www.alumni.virginia.edu/about/summerprograms.aspx

Offered to rising fifth through eleventh graders, the Summer Enrichment Program is a program for gifted and/or high-ability students. Activities in the program are designed to: "expose students to new interest areas; provide interaction with students with similar interests and abilities; enhance interest in learning by providing stimulating and challenging activities; encourage creative/productive thinking and expression; and foster skills for independent learning," according to the program's website.

University of Virginia Young Writers

www.alumni.virginia.edu/about/summerprograms.aspx

Offered to rising ninth graders through rising college freshmen, the Young Writers Workshop of the University of Virginia brings students together in a noncompetitive atmosphere to allow them to explore their creativity. The writing program lasts for two weeks.

Vanderbilt Summer Academy

pty.vanderbilt.edu/vsa.html

At Vanderbilt Summer Academy, gifted students can learn at a rapid pace. Vanderbilt Summer Academy offers courses in math, science, and the humanities. The program integrates resources from the university's many research programs directly into the classroom experience.

Yale Summer Session

www.yale.edu/summer/index.html

Yale annually welcomes hundreds of high school students from all over the world to the university. Instructors cover the same amount of material in 4 weeks as they do in a 13-week term during the academic year. Most of the foreign language courses cover a year's worth of material in just 8 or 10 weeks.

Appendix G

Talent Searches and the States They Serve

Four major talent search programs serve the United States. The talent search in which a student participates depends on where he lives. Here are the four talent searches and the states they serve.

Duke University Talent Identification Program

www.tip.duke.edu/

Alabama

Arkansas

Florida

Georgia

Iowa

Kansas

Kentucky

Louisiana

Mississippi

Missouri

Nebraska

North Carolina

Oklahoma

South Carolina

Tennessee

Texas

Johns Hopkins University Center for Talented Youth

cty.jhu.edu/

Alaska

Arizona

California

Connecticut

Delaware

District of Columbia

Hawaii

Maine

Maryland

Massachusetts

New Hampshire

New Jersey

New York

Oregon

Pennsylvania

Rhode Island

Vermont

Virginia

Washington

West Virginia

Northwestern University Center for Talent Development

www.ctd.northwestern.edu/

Illinois

Indiana

Michigan

Minnesota

North Dakota

Ohio

South Dakota

Wisconsin

Rocky Mountain Talent Search

www.du.edu/city/

Colorado

Idaho

Montana

Nevada

New Mexico

Utah

Wyoming

Math and Science Contests

Math and science contests are a great way for high school students to bolster their resumés and earn money for college.

Here's an overview of the country's top contests.

American Mathematics Competition

www.unl.edu/amc/

The American Mathematics Competitions (AMC) has been dedicated to the goal of strengthening the mathematical capabilities of the nation's youth for more than 50 years. The AMC identifies, recognizes, and rewards excellence in mathematics through a series of national contests.

The AMC contests are intended for everyone from the average student at a typical school who enjoys mathematics to the very best student at the most special school. To ensure this mission is served, each year the AMC solicits enrollment by mailing an Invitation Brochure to all schools in the United States teaching grades 6–12.

American Regions Mathematics League

www.arml.com/index.php

The American Regions Mathematics League's (ARML's) annual competition brings together the nation's finest students. They meet, compete against, and socialize with one another, forming friendships and sharpening their mathematical skills. Since its inception in 1976, ARML has mushroomed into a national program, involving almost 2,000 students and teachers from almost every state. Simply put, ARML is the World Series of mathematics competitions. The contest is written for high school students, although some exceptional junior high students attend each year. The competition consists of several events, which include a team round, a power question (in which a team solves proof-oriented questions), an individual round, two relay rounds (in which a contestant solves a problem and passes his answer to another team member who uses this answer to solve another problem), and a super relay. In all, about 120+ teams participate. A team consists of 15 students, high school age or lower. The competition takes place the weekend immediately following Memorial Day. Most teams arrive on campus Friday afternoon, stay in university dorms, and leave the day after the competition. The competition begins early Saturday morning at Penn State, the University of Georgia, and the University of Iowa, and in the early evening on Friday at UNLV.

Davidson Fellows Scholarship

www.davidsongifted.org/

The Davidson Fellows Scholarship awards $50,000; $25,000; and $10,000 scholarships to extraordinary young people under the age of 18 who have completed a significant piece of work.

Application categories are Mathematics, Science, Literature, Music, Technology, Philosophy, and Outside the Box.

FIRST Robotics Competition

www.usfirst.org

The FIRST Robotics Competition challenges teams of young people and their mentors to solve a common problem in a six-week timeframe using a standard "kit of parts" and a common set of rules.

Intel Science Talent Search

www.intel.com/education/sts/index.htm

The country's premiere precollege science competition, the Intel Science Talent Search (Intel STS), a program of Society for Science & the Public, brings together the 40 best and brightest young scientific minds in America to compete for $1.25 million in awards and scholarships.

Every year, some 1,600 American high school seniors enter Intel STS with original projects from a wide range of mathematics and science disciplines. The field of 1,600 is narrowed to 300 semifinalists and then to 40 finalists.

Junior Science and Humanities Symposium

www.jshs.org

The Junior Science and Humanities Symposium (JSHS) Program promotes original research and experimentation in the sciences, engineering, and mathematics at the high school level and publicly recognizes students for outstanding achievement. By connecting talented students, their teachers, and research professionals at affiliated symposia and by rewarding research excellence, JSHS aims to widen the pool of trained talent prepared to conduct research and development vital to the nation.

MATHCOUNTS

mathcounts.org/Page.aspx?pid=195

The mission of MATHCOUNTS is to increase enthusiasm for and enhance achievement in middle school mathematics throughout the United States. MATHCOUNTS is a national enrichment, coaching, and competition program that promotes middle school mathematics achievement through grassroots involvement in every U.S. state and territory.

Math Olympiads

www.moems.org/

Created in 1977 by Dr. George Lenchner, an internationally known math educator, the Math Olympiads went public in 1979. More than 150,000 students from 5,000 teams worldwide participate in the Olympiads every year. All 50 states and 25 other countries are represented.

National Science Bowl

www.scied.science.doe.gov/nsb/default.htm

The National Science Bowl is a highly visible educational event and academic competition among teams of high school students who attend science seminars and compete in a verbal forum to solve technical problems and answer questions in all branches of science and math. The regional and national events encourage student involvement in math and science activities, improve awareness of career options in science and technology, and provide an avenue of enrichment and reward for academic science achievement.

sanofi-aventis International BioGENEius Challenge

www.biotechinstitute.org/programs/biogeneius_challenge.html

Under the Biotechnology Institute's direction, the sanofi-aventis International BioGENEius Challenge is an annual competition for high school students that recognizes outstanding research in biotechnology.

Science Olympiad

soinc.org

For the past 25 years, Science Olympiad has led a revolution in science education. What began as a grassroots assembly of science teachers is now one of the premiere science competitions in the nation, providing rigorous, standards-based challenges to more than 5,300 teams in 48 states. Science Olympiad's ever-changing event lineup—ranging from Disease Detectives to Electric Vehicle to Bio-Process Lab—provides a buffet of career choices and exposure to practicing scientists and mentors.

Siemens Competition

www.siemens-foundation.org/en/competition.htm

The Siemens Competition in Math, Science & Technology recognizes remarkable talent early on, fostering individual growth for high school students who are willing to challenge themselves through science research. Through this competition, students have an opportunity to achieve national recognition for science research projects that they complete in high school.

Team America Rocketry Challenge

www.rocketcontest.org/

The Team America Rocketry Challenge (TARC) is the world's largest rocket contest, sponsored by the Aerospace Industries Association (AIA) and the National Association of Rocketry (NAR). It was created in the fall of 2002 as a one-time celebration of the Centennial of Flight, but enthusiasm for the event was so great that AIA and NAR were asked to hold the contest annually.

Approximately 7,000 students from across the nation compete in TARC each year. Teams design, build, and fly a model rocket that reaches a specific altitude and duration determined by a set of rules developed each year. The current goal is to design, build, and fly a one-stage model rocket to an altitude of 750 feet; keep it aloft for 45 seconds; and return two raw eggs unbroken. The contest is designed to encourage students to study math and science and pursue careers in aerospace.

USA Computing Olympiad

www.uwp.edu/sws/usaco/

The USA Computing Olympiad (USACO) holds six Internet Contests during the academic year and in the late spring conducts the US Open, a proctored exam. Based on the results of these contests, 16 students are invited to an all-expense-paid training camp in the early summer, where 4 students are selected to be on the US Team at the International Olympiad in Informatics (IOI).

Gap Year Programs

Several students choose to take a year off between college and high school, sometimes called a gap year. Here is a list of just some of the gap year programs out there.

The Center for Interim Programs
The agency works with groups worldwide to create unique gap year programs for each student.
www.interimprograms.com

The AmeriCorps
AmeriCorps places people in communities throughout the country and gives them opportunities to lead and better an area.
www.americorps.org

City Year
City Year places students across the country and gives them full-time jobs in 18 U.S. locations and Johannesburg, South Africa, and positions them to be mentors and role models.
www.cityyear.org/home.aspx

Dragons
Dragons programs feature extended itineraries. The programs encourage deep immersion into different physical and cultural landscapes, and combine the best in experiential education, travel, service learning, and physically and intellectually challenging experiences.
www.wheretherebedragons.com

LEAPNOW
LEAPNOW combines traveling across the globe with internships and career training programs.
www.leapnow.org

National Outdoor Leadership School
NOLS teaches outdoor skills and leadership at locations across the world.
www.nols.edu

Semester at Sea
Semester at Sea combines studying abroad with sailing the world and gives students an opportunity to learn and explore new places.
www.semesteratsea.org

Taking Off
Taking Off works closely with the student to develop and implement a well thought-out plan that maximizes the individual's time and experience and ensures that "stopping out" doesn't become "dropping out."
www.takingoff.net

Index

Internet posts, 114-115
legacies, 108-109
race, 109-112
talent, 113
interviews, 187-188
    alumni interviews, 188
    answering questions,
        193-194
    asking questions,
        194-195
    calming techniques, 197
    common questions,
        191-193
    informational interviews,
        188
    on-campus interviews,
        188-190
    optional interviews, 189
    preparation, 190-197
    thank you notes, 196
rates, 6-8
recommendations, 165
    assisting, 173-174
    benefits, 166-167
    guidance counselor rec-
        ommendations,
        169-170
    requirements, 167-168
    self-assessments, 171
    soliciting, 170-173
    teacher recommenda-
        tions, 167-170
spring admissions, 149-150
yield, 222
Advanced Placement (AP)
    classes, 26
African American students, Ivy
    League schools, 110
AI (academic index), admis-
    sions standards, 29-30
alumni interviews, 188
    answering questions,
        193-194
    asking questions, 194-195
    calming techniques, 197

common questions,
    191-193
preparation, 190-197
thank you notes, 196
American College Testing
Program (ACT). *See* ACT
(American College Testing
Program)
Amherst, admission rate, 8
AP (Advanced Placement)
classes, 26, 69-72
    IB (International
        Baccalaureate) classes,
        compared, 74-75
appeals, rejections, 212-215
    policies, 213
    rates, 213-214
    reasons, 214-215
applications, 151-152
    assisting, 173-174
    business programs, 16-21
    checklist, 152-154
    Common Applications,
        157-158
    deadlines, 159-161
    e-mail addresses, 115
    early applications, 139-140,
        145
        amendments, 144-145
        benefits, 141-142
        binding agreements,
            143-144
        detriments, 141-142
        early action, 140-147
        ED (early decision),
            140-145
        requirements, 142-143
        rolling admissions,
            148-149
        rounds, 148
        single-choice early
            action, 140, 146
    essays, 175
        active voice, 185
        brainstorming, 181-182

honesty, 179
imagery, 182-183
outlines, 182
proofreading, 184-185
subjects, 176-180
writing, 180-183
fast applications, 157
guidance counselor recom-
    mendations, 169-170
mailing, 159
missing information, 162
online applications,
    152-157
recommendations, 167-168
requirements, 155
self-assessments, 171
soliciting, 170-173
teacher recommendations,
    169-170
tracking, 161-162
appointments, guidance coun-
    selors, scheduling, 37-38
athletics, participation, 84-85
average salaries, business pro-
    grams, 15-16

B

Banks, Katherine Rose, 51
Bauld, Harry, 176
Best 109 Internships, The, 88
billable costs, 128-130
    payments, 130-135
binding early actions, 143-144
Bock, Jim, 223, 226
Bowdoin College, admission
    rate, 8
Brenzel, Jeff, 10, 35, 110
Brigham Young, business
    program, 14
Brown University, admission
    rate, 6-7
Bugeja, Michael, 237
Bush, George W., 109

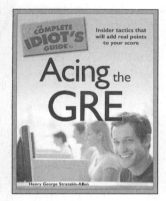

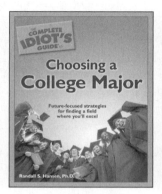
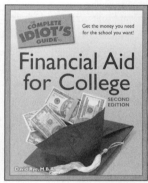

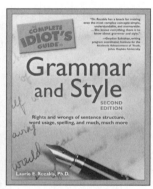